Photos

over

Online Artwork

In order to access the mystery-theater artwork and forms in this book (.pdf format), with blanks you can fill in with your own information and then print out, go to Scarecrow's website at www.scarecrowpress.com and then do the following: At the top right of the screen, click on the arrow next to "keyword" and select "author." Type "siwak" into the box below and hit Enter. Scroll down on the book's web page and click on "Supplementals" (next to "Book Flyer").

VOYA Guides
Series Editor: RoseMary Honnold

Designed for library professionals who work with teens, the VOYA Guides book series expresses the mission of the magazine *Voice of Youth Advocates* (*VOYA*) to promote youth participation, advocacy, and access to information.

These lively, practical VOYA Guide handbooks:

- Showcase innovative approaches to the youth services field
- Cover varied topics, from networking to programming to teen self-expression
- Share project ideas that really work with teens
- Reflect the real world of the library, classroom, or other spaces where teens gather
- Focus on adult mentoring and advocacy of teens
- Feature teen voices and input
- Target librarians, educators, and other professionals who work with teens

1. *Teen Volunteer Services in Libraries*, by Kellie M. Gillespie, 2004.
2. *Library Teen Advisory Groups*, by Diane P. Tuccillo, 2005.
3. *Library Programs for Teens: Mystery Theater*, by Karen J. Siwak, 2010.

Library Programs for Teens
Mystery Theater

Karen J. Siwak

VOYA Guides, No. 3

The Scarecrow Press, Inc.
Lanham • Toronto • Plymouth, UK
2010

Published by Scarecrow Press, Inc.
A wholly owned subsidiary of The Rowman & Littlefield Publishing Group, Inc.
4501 Forbes Boulevard, Suite 200, Lanham, Maryland 20706
http://www.scarecrowpress.com

Estover Road, Plymouth PL6 7PY, United Kingdom

British Library Cataloguing in Publication Information Available

Library of Congress Cataloging-in-Publication Data

Siwak, Karen J., 1967–
   Library programs for teens : mystery theater / Karen J. Siwak.
      p. cm. — (VOYA guides ; no. 3)
   Includes bibliographical references and index.
   ISBN 978-0-8108-4992-1 (pbk. : alk. paper)—ISBN 978-0-8108-7284-4 (eBook)
   1. Young adults' libraries—Activity programs. 2. Libraries and teenagers.
3. Mystery games. I. Title.
   Z718.5.S59 2010
   027.62'6—dc22   009040483

♾™ The paper used in this publication meets the minimum requirements of
American National Standard for Information Sciences—Permanence of
Paper for Printed Library Materials, ANSI/NISO Z39.48-1992.

Printed in the United States of America

CONTENTS

Contents

ACKNOWLEDGMENTS

I am so grateful to have worked with all of the great folks at the Tinley Park Public Library. The staff is composed of incredibly creative, talented, and brave people who always jumped on board to help with our mystery theater programs, even when they were not exactly sure what they were getting into! Thank you, in particular, to Laura McFarland (especially for all of your pre-editing assistance), Amanda Ghobrial, Rich Wolff, Julie Kanjo, Mary Lou Seery, Pamela Deiters, Vicki Lamm, Kim Borgia, and Jennifer Lowe. Over the years, you have allowed me to bounce ideas for characterization and motivation off you. Many of you helped to take our group to the next level, to become the performing group The Whodunits. I would also like to acknowledge the following people who have made this book a reality:

- Cathi Dunn Macrae for taking a chance on me with this book, and RoseMary Honnold for taking it the last mile.
- My family and friends—thanks for letting me pick your brains relentlessly.
- The teens of Tinley Park who have participated in mystery theater—you are the best!
- Dear Youth Advisory Council members (and your parents, who were so supportive)—your ideas and enthusiasm for all things theatrical are pure magic!

CREDITS FOR TEXT AND ARTWORK

Clip art is courtesy of ArtToday at clipart.com and Gifart.com. E-mail excerpt reprinted with permission of Val Thomson, Augusta County Library, 2002. "Mystery Planning Tips" reprinted with permission of Janet Dickey, 1998. Photographs of Rudy Boesch reprinted with permission of Rudy Boesch, 2002. "Who Will Survive Teen Mystery Night?" reprinted with permission of Heather Blicher, Virginia Beach Public Library, 2002.

INTRODUCTION

"Did you poison Gabriella, the traveling bard?"

"Isn't it true that in your fury, you dognapped the library administrator's dog, Zoe?"

"Did you eat Helen Smith's prize-winning blueberry pie?"

"Out of love for Madeleina, did you steal the treasure map from the pirate ship?"

"Is this archaeological site under an ancient curse, or is it merely a matter of sabotage?"

> It is the dim haze of mystery that adds enchantment to pursuit.
>
> *Antoine Rivarol*

Watch out, or you may find yourself bombarded with questions like these during a mystery theater program in your library! Mystery theater is fun, exciting, interactive, and a great tie-in to the popular mystery genre. According to Mary Anne Nichols, author of *Merchandising Library Materials to Young Adults*, mystery stories are the top pick for many teenagers. Librarians can capitalize on teens' enjoyment of the mystery genre to make any subject come alive through mystery theater.

One of the benefits of mystery theater is that it provides an excellent opportunity for teens to practice cooperation in a social setting. It is also a fantastic way for teens to interact with adults in an enjoyable, relaxed manner. In addition to providing a unique and unusual type of program that attracts traditional nonusers to the library, mystery theater promotes communication between library staff members who are apprehensive about dealing with "those unruly teenagers" and older, responsible teens who are recruited to volunteer as suspects. Both adults and teens will benefit from the exposure to each other.

In a school setting, mystery theater is an alternative way to provide instruction. Students will learn in a manner completely different from the traditional lecture format, creating an optimal learning environment for higher-level thinking. The school library media specialist can work with teachers to formulate a specialized mystery script in a topic area of their choosing. For example, the focus could be on biographical figures from a specific historical incident or time period. Your personalized script could also zero in on art, music, classic literature, or the latest popular book. As teens think critically to figure out the mystery, they will easily internalize the new information you have incorporated into the program.

Below is an excerpt from an e-mail I received from Val Thomson of the Augusta County Library, which shows teenagers' responses when Val used the *medieval murder mystery* theater script (chapter 7) in her library:

> The Teen Advisory Board played all the roles, including Sister Beatrice (Brother Bertram). They were wonderful and had a ball. They wore a variety of costumes and really entered into the spirit of the evening. We served summer sausage, grapes, and chunks of bread with honey, cheese, and apple juice for refreshments. We also served pretzels—my teens said we had to have the pretzels. We gave the winning teams chocolate bars as prizes. The Teen Advisory Board was very pleased with the Medieval Murder. They loved the idea of costumes and a script set in history. Everyone who attended raved about the unusual evening and was very enthusiastic.

Even with the obvious benefits of this type of program, you may still wonder if it is worth the effort to write and put on a mystery theater program. It *is* a lot of work for a brief time period. Perhaps you feel that mystery theater wouldn't work in your library. Your administration isn't supportive. You don't have enough help. You certainly don't have the time. Despite these obstacles, you can still create an awesome mystery theater program! Try one of the complete mystery scripts in Part 2 of this book before you try writing your own.

As *Library Programs for Teens: Mystery Theater* progresses, you will find information about the basic elements necessary to write a script and detailed instructions on how to produce a mystery theater program in your own library. Creating a script and putting on a mystery theater program will take some time, but you will see that your investment of time and energy will be well rewarded in benefits for your teen patrons.

Although I will present primarily one type of mystery program style in this book, there are other formats. I have included Heather Blicher's "Who Will Survive Teen Mystery Night?" as an alternative approach to making the mystery genre come alive for teens. There are other options available for mystery theater programming, including Janet Dickey's "Anyone's Guess" mystery kits and individual mystery programs written by public librarians available on the Plano Library's website. This book's appendix lists mystery theater games and kits available for purchase, and the bibliography details other resources.

Working with young adults at the Tinley Park Public Library in Evergreen Park, Illinois, has given me the opportunity to create and produce many mystery theater programs for teens, many of which are included in this book. Months and even years after a mystery theater program is performed, teens who attended will come up and say, "I know you. You're that lady who played _____" or "You were that person who always _____."

In addition, teens who help put on mystery programs get a different view of libraries. Older teens from the library's Youth Advisory Council (YAC) have often played the role of suspects. These teens become our associates for the program's duration, and as a result they are more invested in the library. No matter what these teens go on to do in their adult lives, these experiences will help them consider the library a vital, positive, and necessary place, a place worth spending their time. These same teens are willing to come back to the library and spend countless hours volunteering for different projects. Mystery theater programs are just one segment of the bigger picture of a library environment filled with meaningful and thoughtful activities that make the public library the jewel of the community and the library media center the heart of the school.

REFERENCE

Nichols, Mary Anne. *Merchandising Library Materials to Young Adults.* Greenwood Village: Libraries Unlimited, 2002.

CREATING YOUR OWN MYSTERY SCRIPT

The Basic Formula

This chapter will guide you in how to write your own mystery script tailored to your library's or school's needs. The main purposes are to enable you to start thinking outside the box, to open up your imagination, and to create a customized script. You will be taking your ideas and plugging them into each step of the basic formula. You will learn how to pick an appropriate crime and create compelling characters. Details such as developing optional clues and props and handling costumes, food, and decorations are also included.

> I have found power in the mysteries of thought.
> *Euripides*

You do not need to be a professional writer to write a mystery script. The end result should be creative, organized, and logical from the first to the last details, but it does not have to be a beautifully written and eloquent Shakespeare-worthy script. If you truly feel that you don't have any writing ability, you may wish to team up with someone who can take your ideas and fit them into the basic formula. Everyone should try it, however, because it is definitely within the average writer's grasp.

Follow the basic formula in this chapter as you go through the process. Don't expect to fill in details in chronological order. Jot down any ideas you think might work that occur to you. Allow yourself plenty of time to develop your mystery; each person in your cast will need to review the completed script before the date of the program. Don't be discouraged if you can't fill in all of the spaces in one sitting. Sometimes you need to leave your script for several days and then come back to it. Details that have arranged themselves in your subconscious mind will flow from your pen onto the page. The important thing is to begin writing down your ideas. Keep a pen and notepad handy to jot down inspirations. Ask who, what, where, when, and why for each suspect.

Here are job descriptions for the characters involved in the mystery programs:

- **Chief inspector.** The cast member who is in charge of welcoming assistant detectives and organizing them into teams, explaining the rules, collecting completed forms from assistant detectives, and conducting the final interrogation of suspects
- **Suspects.** The cast members who have a motive for committing a crime
- **Non-suspects.** The cast members who do not have a motive for committing a crime, but are necessary for the flow of the program
- **Assistant detectives.** Participants who form teams to solve the mystery

I will go through each element of the basic formula so that you will have a better idea of what to do for each section. This process will help you to create a complete and detailed script for you and your cast to use when you perform the program.

SCRIPT COVER

The script cover includes these details:

- Name of mystery
- Date of program
- Time of program
- Location of program
- Names of suspects (and actors playing the parts)
- Others on the scene but not suspects, including the chief inspector and (optional) victim

PURPOSE

Before you start to fill in the blanks, it is important to identify the reasons for putting on your mystery theater program. If the mystery is intended to be educational rather than entertaining, consider what you would like your students to learn. You might relate the script to the curriculum or library instruction. Here are a few examples:

- The history of North America, specifically the impact of the fur trade on settlement, the voyageurs, and the big trading companies.
- Societal concerns during the Revolutionary period in the development of the United States, with historical characters George Washington, Betsy Ross, and Benjamin Franklin.
- Current events focusing on a group of international spies, one of whom is guilty of providing the enemy (the current country of concern) with state secrets such as weapons locations and military strengths.
- For geography, use the United Nations General Assembly as your backdrop and have delegates from several conflicting countries be suspects to tie these countries together. Assistant detectives could be delegates from uninvolved countries.
- Travel through space and time to a land far away and introduce the science fiction or fantasy genre to teens. The space-time continuum could be disrupted with authors, scientists, inventors, and other famous individuals brought from one time period or from several different time periods. Participants would need to determine who disrupted the space-time continuum and why they did it.

Once you decide upon your focus, you will find yourself more easily discarding or including ideas as they come to you.

SETTING

It is important to choose the setting early in the script-writing process. Decide whether the crime occurs in a foreign country or your own. Will the mystery take place in a specific location or in multiple places? At what hour of the day will the crime occur?

CRIME

What crime has been committed? Traditionally, mystery programs revolve around a murder; unfortunately, real-world crime abounds in many different forms, so you may opt to choose a different type of crime such as kidnapping, theft, or arson. Consider your audience and what your community would deem appropriate. The audience will be aware that you are putting on a theatrical performance and that the suspects in question are acting. To be on the safe side, though, have the actors return to the room at the end of the performance to reassure the audience of everyone's well-being.

TIMELINE

In order to avoid confusion among your cast members, write a general timeline of events. You will want to include the approximate time the crime occurred and the

---

THE CRIME DETAILS

Different crimes call for different types of script details. Here are just a few examples of the types of crimes and the details you can focus on for each type. Refer to this list in the Suspect Biographies section when you are completing the motivation category.

- For a murder mystery, the victim is a truly nasty villain whom every other suspect despises or fears enough to have the necessary motivation to kill. Other suspects will probably benefit from the victim's death in some way, even if they don't particularly fear or dislike the victim.
- With a theft, decide what object was stolen and then ask how each suspect would benefit if he or she had stolen the item. Has anyone's life changed dramatically in a positive way or will anyone's life improve because of the theft? Has anyone's life simply changed in some manner?
- In a kidnapping case, you need to ask what the reasons are for different suspects to want to kidnap (or dognap in the *Library Dognapping* script) the victim. Did the suspect like or dislike the kidnapped person? Would the suspect benefit in some way if the kidnapped person never returned?
- In the case of arson, depending upon what was destroyed, what possible benefit would each suspect have?
- You could also create a scenario in which an innocent person has been framed and is in jail. A lawyer might gather all of the other possible suspects to prove his or her client's innocence. What reasons would each suspect have for wanting to frame the prisoner? What is each suspect trying to hide?

Once you decide on the type of crime, write a brief paragraph that describes the crime and the time the crime occurred. For whatever crime you choose, you will need to create a credible motivation for each suspect to benefit from the crime.

criminal's description. The descriptions can be very detailed here, or you can provide more details in each individual suspect's biography.

SUSPECT BIOGRAPHIES

The setting and the type of crime committed will drive the suspects you create. If you take an idea from a book in popular culture to write your mystery, it would obviously be necessary to use the characters from that book. Most of the characters will end up being suspects, but you will also need a chief inspector (or someone in charge of organizing the mystery) and non-suspect characters involved (such as a victim, if you do a murder mystery). For many of the mysteries you need an odd number of characters to be suspects, when the determining factor of guilt is based on not having an alibi from another suspect. The guilty party does not have an alibi. There are other ways of determining guilt, and we will address these possibilities in the Alibi/Weapon section below.

The number of suspects will determine the length of the program. The more suspects you include, the longer the investigation will take. The scripts in this book are written for 7 to 11 suspects because this number is appropriate for a 75-minute time period. If you choose a shorter or longer time span, you can adjust the number of suspects.

Name and Description of Character

How do you decide what each character's personality traits will be? If you are creating your suspects from scratch and not from historical or popular culture figures, start by assigning occupational roles for each suspect. Sometimes a person's job will lead to character development. The roles may change as your ideas become more focused.

When describing characters, look at each person's social standing, quirks, liabilities, habits, likes, and dislikes. Pick one or two personality traits to magnify to larger-than-life proportions. Suspects in mystery theater are one-dimensional and tend to be obsessed with one important subject or ideology in their lives. For example, Mike loves his new MINI Cooper. He names it Simone and buys accessories for it all the time. He spends $500 on a custom leather steering wheel cover. If someone were to damage his car—even just scratch it—the result might be an insane reaction. Here is Lyle as another example: Lyle loves to write and recite poetry. In regular conversations, he insists on using iambic pentameter. To the disgust of his friends, Lyle uses limericks when he is trying to be funny. If someone were to mock him because of his poetry, Lyle might be driven to performing a violent act. By focusing on one, often ridiculous, personality trait or set of interests, you will set the stage for humor and the provision of necessary clues.

Motivation

In a murder mystery, the victim should be detested or feared by every suspect for one reason or another. In other types of crimes, characters will demonstrate emotional responses and rationales, depending upon what the crime is and how it has affected them. It is important to know your audience. Certain sensitive crimes, motivations, and character descriptions may not be appropriate in every situation. Mystery theater performed in a public setting should be kept light and playful. Even if the crime is what brings everyone together, it is the process of solving the crime that is the focus of the program.

Alibi/Weapon

As we stated earlier, the simplest formula for writing mystery theater scripts and the easiest ones to solve are the mysteries where every suspect but the criminal has an alibi. You will pair up all of the suspects except for the criminal. The suspects will acknowledge their counterparts to be their alibis. Assistant detectives will be able to deduce that the criminal is the suspect without an alibi.

If you perform several mystery programs with the same group of teens, you will need to adjust the formula because the teens will catch on after a few programs. One alternative is for several or all of the suspects to not have alibis. Then it would not matter if you had an even or odd number of suspects, because planted clues point to the true criminal. Perhaps the criminal possesses a talent or a piece of knowledge that allowed only him or her to perform the crime. In *Shivermetimbers! A Pirate Mystery* (chapter 9), assistant detectives need to figure out that only the captain has the key to getting the treasure map and only Madeleina knows how to read it—therefore they are both the guilty criminals. Evidence may prove guilt; for example, specks of fake blood on a shovel or a tear in someone's clothing. This type of mystery would work well with older and/or more sophisticated teens.

Suspect to Be Discredited

To make the mystery lively and to create suspicion and doubt, each suspect is assigned at least one other suspect to talk about to each team of assistant detectives. Suspects can express dislike, distrust, or concern. It is essential that each suspect disclose some information and generally malign the assigned suspect to shift attention away from himself or herself. The suspect he or she discredits should not be the suspect who is his or her alibi. Have at least two of the suspects discredit the real criminal, to ensure that each team has heard suspicions about the criminal. You may also assign two suspects to be discredited, but this is optional and sometimes becomes complicated for the cast, especially one with teen volunteers.

Others on the Scene, Including the Chief Inspector and the Victim

These characters are necessary to include for the organizational flow of the program. They do not participate as suspects.

- **Chief inspector.** It is essential to have a master or mistress of ceremonies—your chief inspector. The chief inspector's role is to make the program flow smoothly and set the general tone. He or she does not have to be called "chief inspector."

You could invent a personality for him or her as well. Sometimes you might want to have guards or deputy sheriffs.

- **Victim.** Do you need to have a person play the victim in your mystery? This depends on the crime. In murder mysteries, your victim is usually already dead, or you could kill off that character dramatically at the beginning of the program. In other types of mysteries, the victim may or may not be present, depending on what makes sense.

PROGRAM SCHEDULE

Each of the mystery theater scripts in this book is divided into three parts. The suggested program length is 75 minutes. When performing the mystery, you may adjust the time portions presented in this book to suit your needs. Parts I and III will take place in the same room (usually a meeting room or one area of the main library) and Part II will take place in another area of the library, possibly in the stacks if you have only one main program room. The program should be scheduled after hours or at a time when your library is not too busy, because the program can become chaotic and noisy.

PART I (15 MINUTES): INFORMATION FOR THE CHIEF INSPECTOR AND THE SUSPECTS

Participants are introduced to the suspects and given guidelines for the program. A group of participants who are approximately the same age will be at approximately the same intellectual playing level, but you can open the program to a wider age range. Ideally, you will have between 20 and 60 teens participating. With fewer teens, the competition won't be as exciting, but participants will still enjoy themselves. If you have more than 60 teens, be prepared for working chaos, but more than 80 is too many.

If the program is in a public library, sort the participants into teams as they arrive. You may assign participants to a team prior to the program, but that is unnecessary and consumes a lot of time. It is easier to set chairs for the number of teens you want on each team in rows or groups, and let the teens sit where they would like. The chief inspector should tell teens to sit with others they would like to be on a team with. Allow friends to be on the same team to maximize enjoyment of the program. In a school, you can strategically determine the teams beforehand. Team sizes will depend upon the number of teens who attend. You should not create more teams than there are suspects, since only one team at a time may question a suspect. Also, limit the number of teens on a team to the number of prizes you have purchased for members of the winning team. (In any case, it's always a good idea to purchase extra prizes.)

To create a dramatic mystery program from the start, you may choose to have the crime occur when the assistant detectives are already present. The crime occurs right before their eyes or is discovered in front of them. Alternatively, the chief inspector could make a simple statement that a crime has occurred and describe what happened. The mystery would progress from there. If this is your choice, the chief inspector will read the prepared paragraph you write in the Crime section describing the crime that has occurred. Include some background information, such as, "A crime has been committed. Someone has stolen a rare volume from Sir Oliver's study. It occurred this afternoon at 3:30 p.m. You have been called here today to solve this crime."

The chief inspector's basic duties include reading the paragraph about the crime, introducing the suspects, giving the assistant detectives their worksheets, and explaining how to fill them out. Listed on the worksheet are questions that assistant detectives may ask the suspects to start their investigation, such as:

- "Where were you when the crime was committed?"
- "Can anyone confirm your whereabouts?"
- "What did you talk about?"
- "Did you have any reason to dislike the victim?"
- "Do you think any of the other suspects had a reason to benefit from the crime? Why?"

There is other general information that assistant detectives need to begin the investigation. The chief inspector will enlighten assistant detectives as to their role throughout the investigation. The rules and guidelines for each script are similar and include the following:

- Each suspect will wear a name tag.
- Only one team is allowed to ask questions of a suspect at a time.
- Assistant detectives should not necessarily believe any of the suspects right away when they are told something. The suspect may be lying. Verify statements with another suspect.
- Assistant detectives have a maximum of 45 minutes to solve the mystery, but the first team to turn in the correct answer wins. The chief inspector will mark down the time that each team finishes.
- After a team has turned in the form to the chief inspector, they may return to the meeting room.

The chief inspector can introduce suspects to the participants in a variety of ways, depending upon the desired effect. In some mysteries, suspects may be sitting in the audience and they will act surprised, aghast, and indignant when the chief inspector introduces them as suspects. Alternately, the suspects might wait in another room and the chief inspector introduces them all at one time as the suspects that the participants are to interrogate. If you have a curtain in your library, another option is to introduce the suspects after the curtain is raised. Regardless of the way suspects are introduced, the scriptwriter should provide details of the placement of the characters, standing or sitting, when the chief inspector explains the details of the mystery to the assistant detectives.

Each cast member will take the description of his or her character and personalize it to make it come alive for the participants during the program. Cast members should internalize details written about their characters and then "become" that person. They will stay in character from the time teens enter the room, even if it is before the actual start of the program. In most scripts, suspects do not have to memorize lines unless their character is known for some particular phrase or saying. Other than staying in their respective roles, the suspects don't say much during Part I. Assistant detectives may start to deduce things about the suspects' characters from facial expressions or overheard conversations, but they will not have a lot of information before they begin their own investigations in Part II.

After the chief inspector introduces the suspects, the suspects will be told to go to another room to be questioned by the assistant detectives (in Part II). The chief inspector will then explain to each team how to fill out the worksheets.

Part II (45 minutes): Information for the Chief Inspector and the Suspects

In this portion of the program, assistant detectives in their respective teams will go to each of the suspects and ask questions. Assistant detectives must attempt to determine the identity of the criminal through questioning and deductive reasoning. Once a team believes it has identified the criminal, it will turn in the "Who Did It?" worksheet to the chief inspector. The first team to turn in a correct "Who Did It?" worksheet to the chief inspector wins the game.

In Part II, the suspects have the opportunity to shine. Their chief responsibility during this portion is to answer the questions on the assistant detectives' worksheet. The suspects will act surprised that they are being accused and will be very quick to incriminate others, even if it goes against their code of honor. They are out to save their own skin at all costs. It is absolutely critical that suspects discuss or discredit the assigned suspect(s). Suspects are trying to deflect attention away from themselves and onto someone else. Suspects should be positioned closest to their antagonists and those they are discrediting because the suspects have a chance to play off each other with insults and derogatory remarks so the liveliness and fun of the program increases. As in Part I, the scriptwriter tells the suspects where they will be placed.

If assistant detectives haven't paid attention in Part I, they may not realize that there are questions on their worksheets with which to start the investigation. Suspects may need to guide them in the right direction. For example, if a group of assistant detectives fails to ask a suspect if he or she knows anything suspicious about another suspect, the suspect being questioned needs to stop the group and say, "Wait, I have to tell you something important! It's about that other suspect over there."

The chief inspector drifts about in Part II, generally keeping an eye on things. When the chief inspector receives the "Who Did It?" worksheet from each team, he or she will record the time and the order that each team has finished. Teams that have turned in the form to the chief inspector may return to the meeting room. If you'd like some feedback on your program, give participants a review form to fill out at this time. You could also serve food or beverages at this time. Have a volunteer or staff member supervise this room until the adults return.

Assistant detectives are allowed to return to any suspect as many times as they like as long as no other team is questioning the suspect. Some teams may get quite silly by the end of the questioning period, but other teams will be ruthless, so be prepared for both ends of the spectrum. After the last group of assistant detectives turns in the worksheet and returns to the meeting room, suspects should return together to their original places.

Part III (15 minutes): Information for the Chief Inspector and the Suspects

The suspects have now returned to the original room and are in their respective places and awaiting their final interrogation questions from the chief inspector before the criminal is revealed. As the scriptwriter, you formulate the chief inspector's questions and suggest answers for each suspect. This may seem like a contradiction to what was stated earlier (that there are no lines to memorize); however, it may prove helpful for some of your more anxious suspects to have a sample answer for the final interrogation. After the first time your players participate as a character in a mystery program, they will realize that if they possess a good knowledge of their character, the answers will be obvious and come easily. For a dramatic conclusion to your program, it is essential that the chief inspector ask a series of questions that will eventually incriminate the criminal. The chief inspector may choose to memorize the questions or just read them unobtrusively off the sheet.

When composing the questions, review the descriptive paragraph(s) you created in the Suspect Biographies section. The chief inspector should ask questions in a logical sequence that will leave no one in doubt that each suspect had a real motivation to commit the crime. The order in which suspects are questioned is up to the scriptwriter. Place the characters so that they are linked in some way, although this is not strictly necessary. As each suspect is addressed, he or she should stand to answer the questions. During the questioning, encourage your actors to ad-lib and make snide comments. Suspects should try to ham it up. Often the criminal is questioned last because this makes for a dramatic conclusion to the program. You could also question the criminal in the midst of the other suspects and then tie him or her to the crime at the very end. The truth might come out by accident. Perhaps the criminal is defiant. The criminal may try to run away and have to be apprehended by guards or police (non-suspects). Whichever way the truth comes out, try to be as dramatic as possible.

After the criminal is revealed, the chief inspector thanks all of the teams for their assistance. He or she reads the names of the winning team and presents each member with a prize.

OPTIONAL CLUES AND PROPS

You have the option of creating or collecting additional clues and props. Various items such as a newspaper clipping, a train ticket, a pair of shoes, a glass with fingerprints, a piece of jewelry, or a handkerchief left at the scene of the crime can help assistant detectives in their investigations. Some of the clues may point to the real criminal, but some of the clues and props may turn assistant detectives in the wrong direction. Use your creativity and you will be able to introduce some interesting and imaginative clues.

The various characteristics of each suspect will determine if additional props are needed. For instance, in *Mysterious Mona* (chapter 5), Della Bert has a pet mouse. You could provide the actress with a mouse puppet to use as a prop, which will provide a clue about the nature of Della Bert's character. When weapons are used to point evidence to the criminal, you must write a possible weapon into every suspect's description. Each suspect must be sure to bring that weapon to the interrogation, even if it's as simple as a necklace in a case of strangulation. To make it simpler for yourself as the program planner, ask that the cast be responsible for obtaining their own props as much as possible. If it is a paper clue or prop, the scriptwriter will be responsible for this item.

COSTUMES

Costumes may or may not be necessary in your mystery theater performance. Once you decide upon the time period, setting, and characters, you will have a good idea as to what types of special costumes, if any, are necessary for the program. Because of time constraints, I always try to make costumes the responsibility of the players. Include in your recruitment form that players are responsible for their costumes, but that you are available to help if needed. If you use older teenagers for your suspects, expect to be more proactive in getting their costumes ready than for your adult co-workers. If I have teens acting, I assume responsibility for their costumes. I also involve the teens' parents, especially those who would probably view acquiring a warrior princess costume as some kind of weird challenge. In my experience, most of the people we've recruited for mystery theater go beyond the call of duty with their costumes.

If you are a perfectionist and like everything a particular way, you might opt against doing a historical or fantasy/science fiction script, and choose a modern script instead so everyday clothes can be used for costumes. In modern scripts, players should try to wear something that represents their character. A stodgy professor might wear a bowtie and glasses. A hip young librarian would wear the latest trendy clothing.

When you have a historical script, look at books and go online to determine what clothing from a particular time period looked like. Draw some representations and try to work from the simple lines of your drawing. Fabric stores also carry many historical, science fiction, and fantasy costume patterns. Use your imagination for the science fiction and fantasy genre scripts. Elaborate costumes are unnecessary.

If you need to adapt clothing or start from scratch, it might be a good idea to find a seamstress or tailor willing to help you or to learn the art yourself. It's not as hard as you might think, especially for some costumes that require only a few seams. No one will ever know if the costumes aren't "perfect." Look at your library's collection of books on sewing for one like Susan Purdy's *Costumes for You to Make*. This old classic gives plenty of great techniques for simple costumes. If you have tried to sew and find it an impossible task, capitalize on your contacts. Call in some favors. Ask your sewing friends and acquaintances to help you. Bribe them with homemade cookies!

If you don't sew and can't find anyone who will help you, start by looking at clothing in books and on the Web for pictures and ideas. You don't need to go out and purchase new clothing—take a trip to your local resale store. If you purchase costume pieces cheaply, it won't be the end of the world if you've cut them incorrectly or have to start over again. You can often find adaptable elements of the clothing pieces you need. Fabric glue and notions go a long way for non-sewers. Think creatively. With a little imagination and persistence, you can put together a costume that will be perfect for your purposes. An exact duplication is not necessary, especially considering the amount of time that the costume will be worn.

A wonderful book to look at is Barb Rogers's *Instant Period Costumes: How to Make Classic Costumes from Cast-Off Clothing*. This excellent resource demonstrates exactly what types of pieces to buy from resale stores and how to cut and glue these pieces to create the look you want. Practically speaking, you probably don't have the time or money for elaborate and expensive costumes. Your teenage audience will likely not know or care. Finally, if—and that's a big "if"—you have the budget, you can always purchase costumes or rent them.

DECORATING FOR THE EVENT

My tendency toward library programs is to make them a big production because I feel that library patrons recognize and appreciate our personal touches. The personal touch keeps them coming back for more. To this end, I always try to decorate the area where the program will be held according to the script's theme. A few elements here and there will make all the difference. If the script is in a library setting, decorations are unnecessary.

FOOD

What would a library program for teens be without food? Feed them and they will come! When a script covers a general topic, I keep it simple, serving soft drinks and cookies or chips. If you have a thematic script, you could serve food and beverages that tie in with the time period or with specific details of the script. For instance, in *The Case of the Looney Librarian* (chapter 6), I served jelly doughnuts, since a doughnut was the means of incapacitating the librarian-victim. Keep in mind that some teens may have food allergies.

GRAPHICS AND PUBLICITY

RECRUITMENT FORM

Potential players will need to step into a certain character, learn minimally about one or two other suspects, and come prepared to ham it up and discuss these facts with the assistant detectives who will quiz them. Look first within your organization. Send out a recruitment letter to fellow staff members. Some may be somewhat reluctant to commit to playing a suspect, fearing that they will say the wrong thing. Others may be "closet" actors, however, who just need a little push to get the ball rolling. Reassure them that they don't have to memorize lines and that everyone simply ad-libs from general information you provide. Do whatever is necessary to persuade them. Play upon their sympathies if necessary. Remind them that professional acting experience is unnecessary. If your gentle persuasion doesn't work, you may need to ask your administrator or principal to use his or her influence. On the other hand, some people will not be at all comfortable with having to ad-lib, and you shouldn't force the issue. Not everyone is cut out for mystery theater.

If you have an established teen group of any kind, such as a Youth Advisory Council or Teen Advisory Board, this is a prime spot to look for players. Selected high school students make excellent suspects. Make sure, however, that you know the teens and that they demonstrate maturity and the ability to improvise. Anyone who agrees to be a suspect must review his or her script ahead of time, become very familiar with his or her suspect's character, and discuss or discredit the appropriate persons. I have used teens in my mystery programs for many years and have had much success. One loyal teen has played the role of chief inspector in at least six performances. Other Youth Advisory Council members fight for the opportunity to play a suspect and even feel slighted if they're overlooked. It is important to have some adults in the mystery on most occasions. A balanced combination of adults and teens helps maintain decorum and your own sanity.

You could also call on board members, parents, school volunteers, Friends of the Library, and personal friends (provided your administrator or principal approves) to help out. It truly is amazing to see that different groups of people can work so well together. Everyone begins to see a different side of one another that they didn't know existed. Staff members who don't have much opportunity to talk during the workday may find themselves bonding over the excitement, drama, and sometimes sheer silliness of putting on a mystery program. In addition, most teens don't realize how much fun library staff can be when they are in a more casual setting.

Depending upon who volunteers for your cast, you may choose to have a rehearsal prior to the program, especially if it is the first time you are doing mystery theater as a group or if your group is on the younger side. This meeting is not a traditional rehearsal in which cast members review lines. The purpose of this meeting is to spend time quizzing each other and getting into character. Don't be afraid to make mistakes. Take turns asking each other the two sets of questions—the questions on the assistant detectives' worksheet and the final interrogation questions. By the third quizzing, everyone will feel quite comfortable answering the questions. Characters should also review these questions with one another right before the program begins. To reiter-

"I have never performed in any type of play and was nervous at first. But after acting in my first Mystery Theater, I was hooked. It is such fun dressing up, becoming a character, and playing make-believe with teens."—Kim Borgia, librarian

"'Starring' in one of the mystery plays is always fun, especially if you and fellow participants get a chance to shake off the usual personality stereotypes. Your conservative librarian as a kitchen wench, for example."—Vicki Lamm, librarian

"Being involved in a Mystery Theater performance was awesome! I loved being able to pretend I was someone else, and trying to trick other people was pretty cool. Having a Mystery Theater production is probably one of the greatest ideas ever!"—Elizabeth Keating, age 16

"The best part of being involved in Mystery Theater is the fact that my family has been able to participate alongside me. From hobbits to droids to the king and queen of the realm, my family and I have enjoyed the thrill of taking on new personas and losing ourselves in the roles. It's a blast!"—Rich Wolff, public library administrator

(Rich's wife and two children have acted or assisted with many programs over the years)

"The interactive Mystery Theater is unlike any other theater experience. You never put on the same show twice, and what makes it work is the audience participation. If you go to see Shakespeare, chances are it will be the same as every other production of the show, and the actors can continue without any audience, but without an audience for Mystery Theater, there is no show. I think it gives the kids a real appreciation for mysteries and logical thinking. It's fun and educational for all."—MaryBeth Rodgers, age 17

ate, line memorization is unnecessary. When you read about your character's ideology and personal issues and then start answering the questions, you will be surprised at how easily you slip into that character's personality. See the sidebar for some comments from adults and teens about their experiences with mystery theater.

Publicity Posters
Put these up around the library and send them to local community organizations.

Publicity Bookmarks
In a public library setting, bookmarks sent to every student in local schools should provide you with plenty of interested teens. If you are in a school library, you could promote an after-school program by giving bookmarks to all students checking out books. Make the bookmarks peppy and fun sounding. Be sure to mention that you are serving refreshments and that prizes will be awarded to the winning team. If the program is held during class time, you already have a captive audience.

Assistant Detective Worksheets
Two worksheets, "Who Did It?" and "Information, Characters, Guidelines, Sample Questions," are given to assistant detectives to assist in their investigation. Basic information and suggested questions are included, as well as the rules that each team must follow.

Name Tags

Use a publishing program to make name tags for suspects and non-suspects, or simply write each suspect's name on a plain sticker. Name tags are necessary for assistant detectives to identify the persons they are to question.

Short News Release

If you are advertising for a public library, write a short news release about your program to send to the local newspaper, cable television station, and community organizations. Include the information on your library's website and in its newsletter and on your organization's marquee if you have one. In a school, advertise during announcements.

To-Do List

1. **Recruit chief inspector, suspects, and other non-suspects.**
2. **Assign places to stand or sit during Parts I–III.** Place your suspects according to their alliances and/or adversarial relationships as you see fit in Parts I and III. During Part II, station suspects who discredit each other close to one another.
3. **Purchase refreshments.** Refreshments may be favorite teen foods, or follow the theme of your mystery script.
4. **Purchase prizes.** Prizes can be as cheap or as expensive as your budget allows. Paperback copies of mystery novels or bookstore gift certificates for each member of the winning team have proved satisfactory. Don't hesitate to ask local businesses for donations, and be sure to give them credit for those donations. The number of prizes that you purchase for the winning team will depend upon how many spaces you open up and what your budget can accommodate. If you have the means, a smaller gift like candy or a bookmark is nice to give to all of the participants or the runner-up team.
5. **Take pictures, if desired.** Make sure the camera battery is charged.
6. **Write thank-you notes and/or buy small gifts.** It's always a good idea to acknowledge those who volunteer their time and assistance to help as suspects and other characters in the program. Gifts do not have to be expensive, merely thoughtful. If your budget simply does not allow for gifts, personal notes are always appreciated.

Book Tie-Ins

Because one of our primary functions is to promote reading and literary pursuits, it's always appropriate to set up a display with mystery fiction and nonfiction titles. The focus could also be on specific subject matter titles, depending on the mystery theater script being used. An annotated list with some or all of the selected titles is a nice giveaway. When assistant detectives finish their investigations in Part II, they can return to the original room and browse through the titles you have pulled.

PRODUCTION NOTES

This portion is for adding any additional instructions for the cast not covered elsewhere in the script.

REFERENCES

Purdy, Susan. *Costumes for You to Make.* Philadelphia: Lippincott, 1971.

Rogers, Barb. *Instant Period Costumes: How to Make Classic Costumes from Cast-Off Clothing.* Colorado Springs, Colo.: Meriwether, 2001.

2 Create a Sample Mystery Script

Chapter 2 focuses on writing a mystery step-by-step with the basic formula. This chapter looks closely at the *Medieval Murder Mystery* script (chapter 7). This script is a great tie-in to a Middle Ages unit in a school setting or just as a fun public library program at the same time students are studying the Middle Ages in school. Most of the other mystery scripts you will find in this book will follow the same basic sequence of events. Personalize the script so that it fits your own needs.

> The most beautiful thing we can experience is the mysterious. It is the source of all true art and science.
>
> *Albert Einstein*

SCRIPT COVER

Include this information on your script cover:

- Name of Mystery: Medieval Murder Mystery
- Date of Program: _____
- Time of Program: _____
- Location of Program: _____
- Names of Suspects:

  Lord William, played by _____
  Lady Alayne, played by _____
  Harrold the Tutor, played by _____
  Elwyn the Jester, played by _____
  Mad Maggie the Alchemist/Wizard, played by _____
  Rosalynde the Musician, played by _____
  Florinda the Cook, played by _____
  Alyce the Scullery Maid, played by _____
  Gwyneth the Nursemaid, played by _____

- Others on the Scene but Not Suspects, Including the Chief Inspector and the Victim

  Gabriella the Traveling Bard, victim, played by _____
  Brother Bertram, chief inspector, played by _____
  Physician, played by _____
  Guard #1 (optional), played by _____
  Guard #2 (optional), played by _____

PURPOSE

A possible use for this *Medieval Murder Mystery* is for general entertainment in a public library program. In a school, the mystery could be an introduction to a Middle Ages unit. You may narrow your focus to a specific event in the Middle Ages, targeting historical characters or an event such as the bubonic plague.

SETTING

The setting for this script is England in the Middle Ages. Since we are writing a historical script, we need to be familiar with the time period and region and include these details in the writing. We will use a generic setting and invent the holdings of two historical unknowns, Lord William and Lady Alayne. These nobles live in a small castle in the English countryside. The exact year is not stated, but it is during the High Middle Ages.

CRIME

Gabriella is a bard who grew up around the castle but has been away for several years. Now she is famous, and her return to the castle has precipitated a dinner in her honor. There is a somewhat uneasy party atmosphere, and things are about to get ugly. Gabriella's wine has been poisoned and she will soon be dead.

TIMELINE

- Earlier, Gabriella found out that Lord William is practically penniless and she has been blackmailing him. Then Lord William gave Gabriella his wife's heirloom brooch as a bribe to keep her quiet. He also decided to hold a party in Gabriella's honor to try to appease her and stop her threats.
- Gwyneth sneaked into Mad Maggie's laboratory earlier today, stole a vial of red-colored poison, and put a few drops of it in Gabriella's cup at 6:30 p.m. The amount given took about one-half hour to take effect.
- While performing at 7:00 p.m., during the beginning of the program, Gabriella collapsed and died.

SUSPECT BIOGRAPHIES

- Name
- Description of character
- Motivation
- Alibi/weapon
- Other suspect to discuss/discredit and reasons why the suspect thinks this person is guilty of the crime

In our efforts to invent characters that might have lived during the Middle Ages, we will choose suspects from both the noble and serving classes. The castle is prosperous enough to have an entertainment staff. We will also need to develop characterizations for the victim, the chief inspector, and the other miscellaneous characters.

To create a mix of characters that would have interesting interactions in our script, we might decide that we want a suspect with each of these titles: lord, lady, tutor, jester, alchemist/wizard, castle musician, cook, scullery maid, and nursemaid. Our victim will be a traveling bard. The chief inspector will be a monk. Choose names that would be as historically appropriate as possible—or more whimsical, if you choose. Look also in historical books or baby name books for ideas.

The names of our suspects will be Lord William (lord of the castle), Lady Alayne (lady of the castle), Harrold (tutor of Lord William and Lady Alayne's children), Elwyn (jester), Mad Maggie (alchemist/wizard), Rosalynde (castle musician), Florinda (cook), Alyce (scullery maid), and Gwyneth (nursemaid). Our victim is Gabriella (traveling bard). We also have a chief inspector (Brother Bertram), a physician, and guards (optional).

A list of the suspects with character descriptions follows.

Name: Lord William, Lord of the Castle

Description of Character: Since his father died three years ago, Lord William has managed to spend most of the money he inherited, either through gambling or high living. The paltry taxes he collects from his fiefdom are simply not supporting him in the manner to which he has become accustomed. Desperate for any means to make more money, he has grasped onto a get-rich-quick scheme through scientific experiments that will turn cheap metals into gold. He has hired an "expert," Mad Maggie the Alchemist, to carry out this endeavor. In the meantime, Gabriella the Traveling Bard has found out that Lord William's finances are not what they should be. She is blackmailing him for the family jewels to keep her knowledge secret. Earlier today, Lord William gave Gabriella his wife's heirloom brooch to try to keep her quiet. If any of the other lords should find out that he is practically penniless, Lord William's reputation and family prospects will be ruined. He knows that his wife would never forgive him. Lord William hopes Gabriella will stop these threats if he throws this banquet in her honor.

Name: Lady Alayne, Lady of the Castle

Description of Character: The affection Lady Alayne felt for Gabriella as a young child has turned to deep distrust. Several semivaluable items such as old manuscripts and small statues have gone missing from the castle lately. Last week Lady Alayne saw Gabriella slip out of the library with a package under her arm. Before she could question Gabriella, a servant distracted Lady Alayne with a question. Right before the performance this evening, Lady Alayne was shocked to see her own heirloom brooch on Gabriella's dress.

Name: Harrold, Tutor of Lord William and Lady Alayne's Children

Description of Character: Although Harrold is recognized in the castle as a scholar, on the Continent he is infamous for his unsavory activities. He cheated a certain Lord

Prefontaine out of his inheritance while supposedly tutoring that lord's children last year in France. This made it necessary for Harrold to find a quiet, cushy place to lay low for a time, even if it meant teaching more idiot kids. He thought he'd found the perfect spot in Lord William's castle—that is, until Gabriella showed up. Gabriella also performed at Lord Prefontaine's castle and discovered Harrold's scam. Now Gabriella is threatening to tell Lord William about Harrold's past if he doesn't give her half of what he "earned" in France.

NAME: ELWYN THE JESTER

Description of Character: Elwyn and Gabriella grew up together near the castle but they could hardly be called friends. Their families have feuded for generations over an ancient ring that Elwyn's great-grandfather brought back from the Holy Land. It is said that the ring has the power to bless the holder's family. According to Elwyn, his great-grandfather lost the ring to Gabriella's great-grandfather in an unfair game of chance. Elwyn says it is common knowledge that Gabriella's great-grandfather got his great-grandfather intoxicated in order to obtain the ring. Gabriella's family insists that the ring was won fair and square. Gabriella has been flaunting the ring since she came back, and Elwyn has become increasingly angry. His family honor is at stake!

NAME: MAD MAGGIE THE ALCHEMIST

Description of Character: Long before Mad Maggie became an employee of Lord William, she was obsessed with the tales of Merlin and desired to do some magic of her own. She convinced Lord William that, with time and money for experimentation, she would be able to turn base metals into gold. Since she's been at the castle, instead of practicing alchemy, she's tried to learn some real magic. While poring over her magic books and trying some spells last night, Mad Maggie heard a low chuckle and discovered that Gabriella had been spying on her. Gabriella figured out that Mad Maggie had no intention or ability to turn metal into gold and intimated that Lord William might be interested in her real research.

NAME: ROSALYNDE THE MUSICIAN

Description of Character: Rosalynde and Gabriella were trained in music at the same time. Gabriella was always the favorite with the teachers. Rosalynde tried her best not to be envious and was relieved when Gabriella left to travel abroad. Rosalynde became the castle musician. Since Gabriella came back all Rosalynde has heard is "Gabriella this," and "Gabriella that." Rosalynde has not been asked to perform even once by Lord William and Lady Alayne since Gabriella's return. Gabriella even told Rosalynde that she would like to move back to the castle and that she wants Rosalynde's position. Rosalynde isn't up to Gabriella's standard as a musician. If Gabriella takes Rosalynde's job, Rosalynde will be destitute and out sleeping with the pigs.

NAME: FLORINDA THE COOK

Description of Character: Florinda is the head cook in the castle and she takes care of the food marketing. Her only living brother, Freddy, is gravely ill and his family of eight children is starving. Florinda's wages barely feed her own family, let alone her brother's family. She has resorted to the only solution she can think of—to "borrow" the meager amount of money left from the weekly shopping. The master will never miss it, and Freddy has a measure of peace knowing that his poor babies are not starving or in the poorhouse. Last week, Gabriella and Harrold saw Florinda furtively putting the leftover shopping money into her pocket, and she hasn't had a moment of peace since. Harrold said that he won't tell, and Florinda believes him. He's told her about his own problems. However, Gabriella told Florinda that she plans to inform Lord William about the missing money after her performance this evening. Florinda doesn't know why Gabriella hates her, but she suspects that it is because she tries to defend Alyce from Gabriella's insults. Florinda wishes she'd thought of poisoning Gabriella's food, but she didn't. Gabriella got exactly what she deserved.

NAME: ALYCE THE SCULLERY MAID

Description of Character: Gabriella has created a ton of extra work for Alyce since she arrived at the castle. She has singled Alyce out as her victim, publicly humiliating her, calling her "stupid," and tripping her when she brings in trays. More than once Gabriella has gotten Alyce in trouble with the mistress. Alyce feels hopeless and angry at the same time. She told Elwyn that she'd like to "see the hussy dead."

NAME: GWYNETH, NURSEMAID TO LORD WILLIAM AND LADY ALAYNE'S CHILDREN

Description of Character: Gwyneth was not happy when she heard Gabriella was coming back to the castle. Gwyneth and Gabriella grew up together and were more or less friendly. Gwyneth was so happy then, happy and in love with Launce the Goatherd. She thought nothing and no one would ever interfere with their love. Then Gabriella stole Launce from Gwyneth, and made him run away with her across the sea to heathen lands. The last Gwyneth heard, Launce had died from some foreign disease. She will never forgive Gabriella for what she did to her.

MOTIVATION

Our suspects have a variety of possible motivations. Lord William could have poisoned Gabriella to stop her efforts to blackmail him. Lady Alayne could have poisoned Gabriella because she was stealing family jewels and other valuables. Harrold has no wish to leave his hideaway just yet and even less desire to split his take with Gabriella. He realizes there is apparently no money to be earned through Lord William, but he has pocketed several valuable objects such as manuscripts and small statues during his stay. He might have poisoned Gabriella to keep his secret and his money safe. Elwyn's family has had a stroke of bad luck since the ring was lost, and he might have poisoned Gabriella to avenge his family and get the ring back to its rightful owners. Mad Maggie might have poisoned Gabriella to keep her from telling Lord William about her misuse of his money. She also has easy access to poison, as it is in her laboratory. (The laboratory is always unlocked, so everyone else has access as well.) Rosalynde, fearing for her job and livelihood, might have poisoned Gabriella. Florinda could have poisoned

Gabriella to keep up her extra income and thus ensure her brother's family's survival. Alyce might have poisoned Gabriella to get back at her for her insults and humiliation. Gwyneth has never forgiven Gabriella for stealing Launce, her one true love.

ALIBI/WEAPON

In this sample mystery, we will use the basic formula for the simplest case scenario. Each person but the murderer is assigned another suspect as an alibi. The murderer is the person without an alibi. They will be assigned physical locations where they met at the time of the poisoning. The following have alibis: Lord William and Mad Maggie were in the library, Lady Alayne and Rosalynde were in the drawing room, Harrold and Florinda were in the kitchen, and Elwyn and Alyce were in the stables. Gwyneth has no alibi. She will tell the assistant detectives that she was in the nursery.

OTHER SUSPECT(S) TO DISCUSS/DISCREDIT

To make the mystery fun and exciting, suspects should discuss their alibis and discredit their fellow suspects with gusto. It is not always necessary to include the "discuss" element, but always have your suspects discredit another suspect. To make sure that the teams of assistant detectives know about the criminal's motivation, two other suspects are to discuss her. We have assigned the following:

LORD WILLIAM

Discuss Mad Maggie: Lord William had high hopes when he first hired Mad Maggie that she would be able to turn common metals into gold, but now he's just frustrated. Mad Maggie doesn't seem to be trying very hard to accomplish the task. She just seems to be chanting out loud to herself every time Lord William walks past her laboratory. In addition, she never stops asking for more money!

Discredit Alyce: Alyce had reason to hate Gabriella. Lord William noticed that Gabriella treated Alyce a little more cruelly than the rest of the servants, calling her a "stupid, useless lackwit" and other names. While waiting for his horse to be saddled the other day, Lord William heard Alyce tell Elwyn that she'd like to "see the hussy dead."

LADY ALAYNE

Discuss Rosalynde: Rosalynde was whining to Lady Alayne earlier about Gabriella. She droned on and on about how Gabriella was trying to steal her job and worm her way into the castle.

Discredit Elwyn: When Gabriella came to perform, Elwyn changed from a happy-go-lucky jester into a sour young man. Lady Alayne may have to have William terminate him if he doesn't stop with this "family honor" business. For pity's sake—he's only a common jester. He's become obsessed with getting his family's ring back from Gabriella. Apparently, her great-grandfather won it from his great-grandfather in a game of chance. He has become useless as a jester—unless moroseness is the new trend in jesters.

HARROLD

Discuss Florinda: Harrold and Florinda are very close. Harrold thinks fondly of her as the mother he never had. He hates to bring it up, but Gabriella caught Florinda stealing the petty cash from market day. Although it wasn't a lot of money, Florinda has been using it to keep her brother's family from starving. Gabriella was making a big deal about Florinda's dishonesty. She told Florinda that she planned to tell Lord William about it after her performance this evening.

Discredit Gwyneth: Gwyneth was hopping mad when she heard that Lord William and Lady Alayne were bringing Gabriella here. Gabriella stole Gwyneth's one true love, and she has not been the same since.

ELWYN

Discuss Alyce: Alyce has been losing her mind lately with all of the mean treatment she has received from Gabriella. Elwyn guesses she has nothing to worry about anymore now that Gabriella's dead.

Discredit Florinda: The castle gossip on Florinda is that she has been stealing the extra coins from the market money to feed her sick brother's eight kids. Gabriella found out and threatened to tell Lord William right after the performance this evening.

MAD MAGGIE

Discuss Lord William: A few days ago, Mad Maggie overheard Lord William and Gabriella discussing his financial problems. Gabriella was blackmailing Lord William, demanding the family jewels to keep her quiet.

Discredit Harrold: Mad Maggie has noticed some oddities about Harrold. He's no tutor. She could teach those kids more in one day than he does in a month. Mad Maggie has heard rumors about some French lord trying to kill him, but she has no details. It's just a hunch, but she has a feeling that he may be responsible for some of the missing items around the castle.

Discredit Gwyneth: It's no secret that Gabriella stole Gwyneth's first love. Mad Maggie thinks Gwyneth poisoned Gabriella out of her lunatic jealousy and a sense of revenge.

ROSALYNDE

Discuss Lady Alayne: Lady Alayne told Rosalynde that she thought Gabriella was stealing valuable items from the castle such as manuscripts and small statues.

Discredit Lord William: After Lady Alayne first told Rosalynde that she thought Gabriella was stealing jewels, valuable manuscripts, and small statues from the castle, Rosalynde started to notice Gabriella's frequent visits to Lord William's library. Earlier this week, Rosalynde overheard Gabriella telling Lord William that if he didn't give her the brooch, she was going to make everything public. Rosalynde doesn't know what Gabriella was referring to, but she thinks Lord William is hiding something.

FLORINDA

Discuss Harrold: Florinda isn't one to tell tales, but Harrold has told her that he's not really a scholar. Gabriella knew this. She was going to inform Lord William if Harrold didn't pay her a lot of money.

Discredit Rosalynde: Rosalynde has been coming into the kitchen a lot lately. Usually she's too snotty to bother with the likes of kitchen staff, but since Gabriella's been here, she's been out of a job.

ALYCE

Discuss Elwyn: All Elwyn ever talks about is his silly ring. He never defends Alyce when Gabriella is tormenting her. He just goes on about the family honor and how he's going to get that ring back somehow. For a jester, he hasn't been much fun lately.

Discredit Lady Alayne: When Alyce was serving the supper earlier this evening, she heard Lady Alayne tell Lord William that she thought Gabriella was stealing precious household items like the library manuscripts. When Lady Alayne saw Gabriella wearing her heirloom brooch at the very beginning of the evening, she was completely outraged.

GWYNETH

Discuss: Gwyneth is not assigned anyone to discuss.

Discredit Mad Maggie: Mad Maggie is a witch with her spells. She put a spell on Lord William, that's for sure. Last night Gwyneth was walking past her door and Mad Maggie was muttering to herself. At first Gwyneth thought it was one of her spells, but then she heard Mad Maggie say she was going to have to cast a spell to shut up Gabriella forever. She had easy access to the poisons right there in her laboratory.

SUMMARY

Both the scriptwriter and the actors will find it helpful to have a summary of assignments as follows.

Name	Alibi	Discuss	Discredit
Lord William	Mad Maggie	Mad Maggie	Alyce
Lady Alayne	Rosalynde	Rosalynde	Elwyn
Harrold	Florinda	Florinda	Gwyneth
Elwyn	Alyce	Alyce	Florinda
Mad Maggie	Lord William	Lord William	Harrold/Gwyneth
Rosalynde	Lady Alayne	Lady Alayne	Lord William
Florinda	Harrold	Harrold	Rosalynde
Alyce	Elwyn	Elwyn	Lady Alayne
Gwyneth	None	No one	Mad Maggie

OTHERS ON THE SCENE WHO ARE NOT SUSPECTS, INCLUDING THE CHIEF INSPECTOR AND THE VICTIM

For this *Medieval Murder Mystery*, you will also need additional characters who are not suspects. Our victim is Gabriella, the traveling bard. Brother Bertram is the chief inspector. We also need a physician who pronounces the victim dead. If you have an overabundance of volunteers, you could have guards protecting Lord William and/or taking the criminal away at the end. Full characterizations for additional characters are unnecessary since they are not considered suspects.

NAME: GABRIELLA THE TRAVELING BARD

Description of Character: Gabriella is universally disliked and it is unsurprising that she is killed by poison. The death scene occurs while she is in the process of singing a medieval tune (something like "Greensleeves"). Alternatively, she could recite a narrative.

NAME: BROTHER BERTRAM, THE CHIEF INSPECTOR

Description of Character: As the host for the evening, Brother Bertram waits with the physician and ushers the assistant detectives into the room. During the program, he provides information, acts as timekeeper, collects assistant detectives' worksheets, and conducts the final interrogation in Part III.

PHYSICIAN

Description of Character: The physician's role is to verify that the victim, Gabriella, is indeed dead and that she was poisoned precisely one-half hour prior to her death, as that is the length of time needed for the amount of poison gone from the vial to take effect. At the very end, if you choose to have Gwyneth swallow the entire vial of poison, the physician will explain that she died instantly because she swallowed the whole bottle instead of just a few drops.

GUARDS

Description of Character: If guards are used, their role is to guard the doors with Brother Bertram at the beginning of the evening, protect Lord William throughout the program, and escort the criminal out at the end of the evening or chase after her.

PROGRAM SCHEDULE

The duration of our *Medieval Murder Mystery* is 75 minutes. Our sample program is set to begin at 7:00 p.m. At 6:45 p.m., all cast members except Brother Bertram and the physician are in their places at the head table or as wait staff. Brother Bertram will wait for the participants at the room entrance and assign them to a team. Florinda the Cook and Alyce the Scullery Maid will serve the nobles and assistant detectives when they are seated. As soon as any assistant detectives arrive, the program has begun. The cast should start speaking in accented voices and acting the part of their characters at once. For example, Lord William could yell at Alyce to quit lazing around and start working and serve the guests. Alyce will jump up to serve the assistant detectives, all the while muttering about how the master doesn't appreciate how hard she works and how she always gets the jobs no one wants. While she isn't giving out any information about her motivation or anyone else's, she is providing information about her lowly position in the castle. Lord William is setting himself up as the domineering and self-serving lord of the castle.

Part 1 (15 minutes)—Start Time 7:00 p.m.: Information for the Chief Inspector and the Suspects

As participants enter the room, Brother Bertram will divide participants into groups and hand each team a worksheet. To begin the program, Lord William will thank everyone for coming and then introduce Gabriella. She will come up to the stage and start to sing a medieval-sounding song or start to recite something from the period. Before very long, however, it becomes obvious that she is in pain. She will clutch her throat and emit a heart-wrenching scream before collapsing on the floor, dead. The cast will react verbally and/or physically. Brother Bertram will tell everyone to calm down and he will call for a physician. When the physician comes, he or she will declare that Gabriella is dead and has been poisoned with a few drops of poison in her wine glass. The physician will state that Gabriella was poisoned exactly a half-hour ago (at 6:30 p.m.), as the amount and type of poison administered takes effect in precisely one-half hour.

Brother Bertram will introduce the suspects to the assistant detectives. He will then tell them to leave the scene of the crime and to wait for questions in the main room. Suspects are not to leave the castle. Each suspect will be positioned so that he or she will have some interaction—usually animated, heated discussion—during this portion of the program. Brother Bertram will then explain the rules to the assistant detectives. The rules and guidelines for each script are similar and include the following:

- Each suspect will wear a name tag.
- Only one team is allowed to ask questions of a suspect at a time.
- Assistant detectives should not necessarily believe any of the suspects right away when they are told something. The suspect may be lying. Verify statements with another suspect.
- Assistant detectives have a maximum of 45 minutes to solve the mystery, but the first team to turn in the correct answer wins. The chief inspector will mark down the time that each team finishes.
- After a team has turned in the form to the chief inspector, they may return to the meeting room.

Brother Bertram will also explain details on the worksheet. Listed on the worksheet are questions that assistant detectives may start their investigation with, such as

- "Where were you when the crime was committed?"
- "Can anyone confirm your whereabouts?"
- "What were you talking about?"
- "Did you have any reason to dislike the victim?"
- "Do you think any of the other suspects had a reason to benefit from the crime? Why?"

PART II (45 MINUTES)—START TIME 7:15 P.M.: INFORMATION FOR THE CHIEF INSPECTOR AND THE SUSPECTS

At about 7:15 p.m., assistant detectives will question the suspects in another room. Gabriella will disappear into another room until the very end of the program, when she will come out and take a bow with the rest of the cast. During this portion, assistant detectives will ask questions customized to this mystery:

- "Where were you at 6:30 p.m. today when the poison was administered?"
- "Can anyone confirm your whereabouts?"
- "What were you talking about with this person?"
- "Did you have any reason to dislike Gabriella?"
- "Do you think any of the other suspects had a reason to murder Gabriella? Why?"

When assistant detectives have written down the suspect they believe is guilty and have given their worksheet to Brother Bertram (who writes the finishing time and order of completion on each form), they may return to the original room and wait for the suspects to return.

PART III (15 MINUTES)—START TIME 8:00 P.M.: INFORMATION FOR THE CHIEF INSPECTOR AND THE SUSPECTS

At 8:00 p.m. the suspects will return to the original room for Brother Bertram's final interrogation. He will ask questions of the suspects, one by one. Don't try to write these questions until after you have written character descriptions, motives, and alibis. Suspects do not have to memorize their answers. Answers are provided to give the suspect an idea of how to reply. Both the suspects and the chief inspector should be prepared to ad-lib.

Final Interrogation Questions from Brother Bertram

Brother Bertram: Lady Alayne, in the past you truly cared about Gabriella and even invited her to come back to the castle for a visit. How did you feel about her when you saw her wearing your great-grandmother's brooch?

Lady Alayne: I couldn't believe my eyes. I had my suspicions that she was stealing from us, but I hoped I was wrong.

Brother Bertram: Since you thought she stole your family heirlooms, perhaps you thought she deserved punishment?

Lady Alayne: It is not up to me to exact punishment. That is for a higher power.

Brother Bertram: Lord William, isn't it true that since your father died, you've lost most of your inheritance through gambling?

Lord William: Well . . . yes.

Brother Bertram: Why did you hire Mad Maggie?

Lord William: As she is an alchemist, I hoped that she would discover how to turn common metals into gold and thus regain my fortune.

Brother Bertram: What happened when Gabriella found out about your financial problems? Didn't you give her the brooch that belonged to your wife to shut her up?

Lord William: Yes, I must admit that I did. I didn't want anyone to find out what was going on.

Brother Bertram: Harrold, please tell us about your previous employment with Lord Prefontaine in France.

Harrold: I was hired as a tutor for his children.

Brother Bertram: Isn't it true that you cheated Lord Prefontaine out of his inheritance and that you are hiding out here?

Harrold: There's no way you can prove that.

Brother Bertram: What did you decide to do when Gabriella—who knew of your fraudulent activities in France and wanted you to split your "earnings" with her—came to the castle?

Harrold: I didn't do anything to her even though she was threatening me.

Brother Bertram: Did you kill her?

Harrold: No, no. I've never killed anyone.

Brother Bertram: I'd like to clear up another matter. Alyce, as you regularly clean Harrold's room, can you tell us if you have noticed anything suspicious?

Alyce: I have noticed the master's library manuscripts and statues in his room. (Lord William fires Harrold on the spot and the guards pull him to the side of the room. He struggles a bit and a rolled manuscript falls out of his clothing.)

Brother Bertram: Mad Maggie, weren't you hired by Lord William to turn common metals into gold?

Mad Maggie: Yes.

Brother Bertram: Isn't it true that you are much more interested in magic? Tell us about your recent experiments.

Mad Maggie: It is true that I am interested in magical experiments but I'm also an alchemist. Lately, I've been using red plant dyes with imperfect metals to create gold, but I spilled the red dye all over my laboratory.

Brother Bertram: But you really weren't trying to turn common metals into gold, were you? Didn't Gabriella discover your little secret?

Mad Maggie: Yes, it's true! I have no idea how to turn cheap metal into gold! (Lord William motions the guards to take her to the side of the room and also fires her.)

Brother Bertram: As the poisons are stored in your laboratory, you certainly have easy access to them.

Mad Maggie: Yes, but my door is unlocked. Anyone can get in.

Brother Bertram: Did you poison Gabriella?

Mad Maggie: No, I did not.

Brother Bertram: Rosalynde, before Gabriella came back to the castle, what was your position?

Rosalynde: I was the castle musician.

Brother Bertram: And since she's been here?

Rosalynde: I've had nothing to do. It's "Gabriella this" and "Gabriella that." I haven't performed once since she returned.

Brother Bertram: Wouldn't you have done anything to keep your job?

Rosalynde: Of course I want and need my job, but I wouldn't murder for it.

Brother Bertram: Florinda, your brother is very sick, is he not?

Florinda: Yes.

Brother Bertram: In the meantime, you are responsible for feeding his eight children, correct?

Florinda: That is true.

Brother Bertram: A cook does not earn very good wages. How are you able to support them?

31

Florinda: (very hesitantly) I've been sort of "borrowing" the leftover market money to feed my brother's kids.

Brother Bertram: Didn't Gabriella find out about your little scheme?

Florinda: Yes, she saw me and threatened to turn me in to Lord William but I didn't kill her! (Frustrated, Lord William fires Florinda also. The guards come and take her away at Lord William's prompt.)

Brother Bertram: In your job as a castle maid, Alyce, was Gabriella a pleasant person to serve?

Alyce: No. She was always tripping me and calling me stupid and a lackwit. And she gave me this bruise (points to makeup bruise on her face).

Brother Bertram: You were heard to say that you'd really like to see Gabriella dead. Is this really true and did you kill Gabriella?

Alyce: I might have said that in the heat of the moment, but I didn't poison her. I have no time for such goings-on.

Brother Bertram: Elwyn, I understand that you feel strongly about your family's honor.

Elwyn: Yes, family honor is everything.

Brother Bertram: Gabriella was wearing a ring on her finger when she died. Would you care to tell me about how she came to wear it?

Elwyn: That ring belonged to my great-grandfather. Gabriella's great-grandfather cheated it away from my great-grandfather and we've had nothing but bad luck ever since.

Brother Bertram: Wouldn't you have done anything to get that ring back?

Elwyn: It might be tempting, but I didn't kill Gabriella, if that's what you're implying.

Brother Bertram: Mistress Gwyneth, isn't it true that you and Gabriella grew up together?

Gwyneth: Yes.

Brother Bertram: Were you friends?

Gwyneth: We were the best of friends.

Brother Bertram: Tell me about Launce. Why aren't you still with him?

Gwyneth: Launce was my true love. He was my true love until Gabriella stole him from me and took him away across the sea. Now he's dead.

Brother Bertram: Where were you at the time the poison was placed in Gabriella's cup?

Gwyneth: I was in the nursery.

Brother Bertram: With . . . ? (Gwyneth stays silent.)

Brother Bertram: You seem to have no alibi. Let me remind everyone that Mad Maggie was experimenting with red dyes and spilled some in her laboratory. May I see your fingers, Mistress Gwyneth? (Gwyneth's fingers are covered with red dye.) You seem to have red dye on your hands. (He reaches into her pocket.) And the poison vial as well.

Gwyneth (defiantly): Yes, I did it. And I'm glad! Gabriella killed my Launce and now I will join him, too. (Gwyneth grabs the vial of poison from Brother Bertram, drinks the rest of the poison in the vial, and collapses on the floor. The physician might clarify that Gwyneth died instantly because she drank the entire vial of poison instead of just a few drops.)

Brother Bertram thanks all of the assistant detectives for coming to solve the mystery and announces the winning team. While he is giving out prizes, the rest of the cast will stand, wait for Brother Bertram, Gabriella, the physician, and the guards to join them, and bow in unison one time. The cast leaves the room or the curtain closes.

OPTIONAL CLUES AND PROPS
- Expensive-looking brooch for Gabriella
- Ornate ring for Gabriella
- Wooden spoon with reddish stain for Florinda
- Musical instrument like a dulcimer, lute, or recorder for Rosalynde
- Rolled manuscript to fall out of Harrold's tunic
- Vial holding red-colored "poison"
- Wine glass and empty wine bottle
- Red ink to put on Gwyneth's fingers

COSTUMES
When we performed this mystery, we were fortunate to have access to a nice collection of Middle Ages costumes, as the teens do a play every summer based on a different fairy tale. These costumes were made using a variety of techniques: some sewn from scratch, simple costumes glued together, and modified resale shop outfits. See the section on costumes in chapter 1 for specific details on ways to make or acquire costumes. Consult Middle Ages fashion books and the Internet.

Lord William and Lady Alayne dress regally. Make these characters look like the fairy-tale prince and princess without the crown and tiara. Lady Alayne wears a beautiful gown with bell sleeves and a headpiece. Lord William needs to wear a fabulous tunic with tights. Attach a fancy feather to a plain beret to add drama to the costume. Pay attention to detail, from Lord William's belt to Lady Alayne's jewelry. Be bold with color so that these nobles stand out. If you are purchasing fabric, buy fabric that looks and feels rich.

Others who are higher than the serving class level (Harrold, Rosalynde, Mad Maggie, and Gabriella) should be dressed with flair and color, but should not surpass the glory of Lord William and Lady Alayne. Rosalynde and Gabriella wear long, flowing dresses and headpieces such as wreaths. Harrold could wear a long, stately tunic and matching hat (a beret with a feather). For Mad Maggie, you could make her look wizard-like with a pointed hat and graduation gown or dress her more grungily in a long plain dress and make her look a little crazy with wild hair, and so on. This character cares little for her appearance.

Those of the serving class (Gwyneth, Elwyn, Florinda, and Alyce) wear simple clothes made of cotton or cotton blend fabrics in plain colors (white, cream, brown, muted green) so that they will blend into the background. The female actors wear long skirts, aprons, peasant shirts, and cotton caps or kerchiefs. Elwyn and Alyce could go barefoot. Elwyn could wear a loose, long-sleeved cotton shirt over pants that are torn about mid-calf, or he could wear a long tunic, belt, and tights with simple leather shoes. Give Alyce's cheek a bruise with makeup so she can say that Gabriella tripped her and gave her the bruise.

For Brother Bertram, look for a long, natural-colored robe. During one performance, our chief inspector had a striped robe and hat, so he became a more exotic-looking Crusader monk. Dress the physician like the rest of the noble class. For simple guard costumes, you could have the actors wear all black. Make matching sleeveless tunics that will slip over the guards' shoulders. Provide guards with toy or cardboard swords.

DECORATIONS

Set a formal head table with chairs only on the side facing the audience. Set up tables for all of the participants in a big U shape. Invest in cheap tablecloths or use fabric in a rich color like purple or burgundy. Add candelabras if you have them or can borrow them. Butcher paper will work on the participants' tables. Try to find plates, napkins, and cups that don't look too modern. Make medieval-looking flags or pennants from paper or fabric and put those up. Look in books about the Middle Ages for other decorating ideas.

FOOD

Sherrilyn Kenyou has some interesting food suggestions in *The Writer's Guide to Everyday Life in the Middle Ages.* You can serve cheese, bread, and grapes. Suggestions for beverages are sparkling or regular grape juice, ginger ale, water, or mulled cider. Ideas for main course foods are chicken wings, cold cuts, or meat pies. For that sweet tooth, consider toast with honey, gingerbread, cake, apple fritters, pears in syrup, custard, apples, plums, pears, peaches, and nuts. Serve finger food on large platters or trays. Alyce the Scullery Maid and Florinda the Cook can serve the beverages and snacks to the head table and to the assistant detectives. Lord William and Lady Alayne should be demanding of their staff.

GRAPHICS AND PUBLICITY

You will find samples of these forms with the *Medieval Murder Mystery* in chapter 7.

- Recruitment form
- Publicity poster
- Publicity bookmarks
- Assistant Detective Worksheets
  - Who Did It? Worksheet
  - Information, Characters, Guidelines, Sample Questions
- Name tags
- Paper/physical clues, if necessary

> **SHORT NEWS RELEASE**
>
> Gabriella, the traveling bard, has been poisoned! Whodunit? Everyone has a motive, from the scullery maid to the mad alchemist. Come to the library on _____ _____ and interrogate the suspects being held for questioning. It's up to you and your friends to find the criminal and solve the mystery. Form a team or we will assign you to one. Open to students in grades __ to __. Prizes will be awarded to the winning team. Spaces are limited, so sign up now!

TO-DO LIST

- Recruit suspects, chief inspector, and other non-suspects
- Assign places to stand or sit during Parts I–III
  - Parts I and III:

    Seated at the tables: Lord William, Lady Alayne, Gabriella (beginning of Part I only), Rosalynde, Harrold, and Mad Maggie
    Serving: Florinda and Alyce
    Doing jester-ish things: Elwyn
    Sulking unobtrusively nearby: Gwyneth
    Standing at the back: Guards
    The physician will stay in another room until called in to pronounce Gabriella dead.
  - Part II:

    The suspects will stand in a circle with Lord William first, then Alyce, Florinda, Elwyn, Lady Alayne, Mad Maggie, Gwyneth, Harrold, Rosalynde, and back to Lord William.

- Purchase refreshments
- Purchase prizes
- Take pictures, if desired
- Write thank-you notes and/or buy small gifts

Temple, Frances. *The Ramsay Scallop.* Elenor and Tom, a thirteenth century couple, overcome their reluctance to marry after they are sent on a pre-nuptial journey to Spain and learn more about the world and each other.

Tomlinson, Theresa. *The Child of the May.* Magda helps Robin Hood's men rescue Lady Matilda and her daughter Isabelle from the clutches of the Sheriff of Nothingham's evil henchman.

Tomlinson, Theresa. *The Forestwife.* In England during the reign of King Richard I, Marian escapes from an arranged marriage to live with a community of forest folk that includes a daring young outlaw named Robert.

Turner, Ann Warren. *The Way Home.* In 1349, a young girl returns from months of surviving in the marsh, having been "outlawed" for offending the village lord, only to find that her village has been wiped out by "the sickness."

Voigt, Cynthia. *On Fortune's Wheel.* Faced with the prospect of an unhappy life in the Kingdom, Birle accompanies a young runaway nobleman on a journey south and falls into slavery in the citadel of a cruel prince.

Williams, Laura E. *The Executioner's Daughter.* Lily, daughter of the town's executioner living in fifteenth-century Europe, decides whether to fight against her destiny or to rise above her fate.

Yolen, Jane. *Queen's Own Fool.* When Nicola leaves Troupe Brufort and serves as the fool for Mary, Queen of Scots, she experiences the political and religious upheavals in both France and Scotland.

(Your Library's Information Here)

BOOK TIE-INS

Hand out an annotated bibliography of medieval fiction titles. Set up a display of fiction and nonfiction titles on the Middle Ages.

PRODUCTION NOTES

Although some of the suggestions for costumes and decorations will not be perfectly authentic, they will help create a festive atmosphere.

Encourage accents among the cast if they can manage it. A zesty British accent in this script from each cast member would be an excellent accompaniment.

REFERENCES

Kenyou, Sherrilyn. *The Writer's Guide to Everyday Life in the Middle Ages.* Cincinnati, Ohio: Writer's Digest, 1995.

Avi. *Crispin: The Cross of Lead*. When his mother dies, a fourteenth-century peasant boy must flee for his life after being accused of a terrible crime. His only possessions are his newly discovered name and the secret contained in his mother's lead cross.

Barrett, Tracy. *Anna of Byzantium*. Based on the life of Byzantine princess Anna Comnena, this story tells of how a family becomes embroiled in a feud over the power within, as the rights of succession are seized from Anna and given to her brother.

Cadnum, Michael. *The Book of the Lion*. In twelfth-century England, after his master, a maker of coins for the king, is brutally punished for alleged cheating, Edmund finds himself traveling to the Holy Land as squire to a knight crusader.

Cadnum, Michael. *In a Dark Wood*. On orders from the King, the Sheriff of Nottingham seeks to capture the outlaw Robin Hood, but he finds him to be a tricky and elusive foe.

Cushman, Karen. *Catherine, Called Birdy*. Catherine keeps a journal during her fourteenth year. Her descriptions of life on a 13th-century English manor reach through time to speak to modern readers.

Cushman, Karen. *The Midwife's Apprentice*. In medieval England a homeless girl is taken in by a sharp-tempered midwife, and in spite of obstacles, eventually gains the three things she most wants: a full belly, a contented heart, and a place in the world.

De Angeli, Marguerite. *The Door in the Wall*. A boy in fourteenth-century England proves his courage and earns recognition from the King.

Goodman, Joan Elizabeth. *Peregrine*. In 1144, fifteen-year-old Lady Edith, having lost her husband and child and anxious to avoid marrying a man she detests, sets out from her home in Surrey to go on a pilgrimage to Jerusalem.

Haahr, Berit. *The Minstrel's Tale*. When betrothed to a repulsive old man, thirteen-year-old Judith runs away, assumes the identity of a young boy, and hopes to join the King's Minstrels in fourteenth-century England.

Kelly, Eric. *The Trumpeter of Krakow*. A Polish family in the Middle Ages guards a great secret treasure, and a boy's memory of an earlier trumpeter of Krakow makes it possible for him to save his father.

McKinley, Robin. The Outlaws of Sherwood. The author retells the adventures of Robin Hood and his band of outlaws who live in Sherwood Forest in twelfth-century England.

Morris, Gerald. *Parsifal's Page*. In medieval England, Pier's dream comes true when he becomes a page to Parsifal, a peasant whose quest for knighthood reveals important secrets about both their families.

Morris, Gerald. *The Squire's Tale*. In medieval England, Terence finds his tranquil existence suddenly changed when he becomes the squire of the young Gawain of Orkney and accompanies him on a long quest, proving Gawain's worth as a knight and revealing an important secret about his own true identity.

Skurzynski, Gloria. *What Happened in Hamelin*. A novel of the Pied Piper legend told from the standpoint of a baker's assistant who dreams of freedom from his harsh medieval life and of a new life with the piper.

Springer, Nancy. *Rowan Hood*. Rowan has never met her father, the man folks call Robin Hood. With her mother murdered and no one to care for her, she decides to track him down.

MYSTERY PLANNING TIPS

Janet Dickey, well known for her "Anyone's Guess" mystery kits, has put together this useful set of tips for planning mystery theater programs.

1. Decide what kind of mystery you're planning.
   a. A treasure/scavenger hunt designed to teach library skills.
   b. A crime-solving mystery in which the players are investigators.
   c. A crime-solving mystery in which the players are suspects who interact with each other.
   d. Is there a limit to the number of players?
   e. Will players work individually or in teams?
2. Purchase a kit, write a script or basic storyline, or adapt an existing story or play.
   a. Be as simple or elaborate as you need to be.
   b. Start at the end: What was the crime or what is the treasure being sought?

(continued)

MYSTERY PLANNING TIPS (*continued*)

   c. Work backward. List the steps that lead to the treasure or to the true criminal and to other suspects.

   d. Read through the steps and watch for illogical timing or placement.

   e. Estimate the time the mystery will take; cut if it's too long.

3. Ask others to help you.

   a. Enlist the help of staff and/or adult volunteers (parents, community leaders).

   b. Ask older teens, such as library pages or a teen advisory or Junior Friends group, to help (who will not be players in the mystery).

   c. Ask teens to assist in planning the mystery, such as in writing a script or helping to set up an evidence scene.

   d. Ask teens to help during the mystery, as guides, resource persons, or playing the part of suspects or witnesses.

4. Promote your event.

   a. Send announcements to the schools and to local newspapers; use radio and TV spots.

   b. Let players know if they need to prepare costumes or learn a part.

   c. Arrange for registration and parental permission slips, if needed.

5. Decide what prizes you're offering (if any).

   a. Obtain the prizes through donations from business, Friends of the Library funds, or other sources.

   b. Acknowledge the generosity of sponsors.

6. Plan the space you will use.

   a. Will the program be during library hours or after closing?

   b. Will the program be in a meeting room, or spread out over the whole library?

   c. Plan for a place for participants to sit/eat/write and evidence scenes to visit. It is recommended that movement be built into the program!

7. If using suspects, list them and any statements and clues they are to provide.

   a. Will the statement be read to the players by the leader or actors playing the suspects?

   b. Will you give photocopied statements to each player?

   c. Will the statements be scripted and played by actors or the mystery players?

8. If using witnesses or other resource persons, write out their parts and have them practice what they will tell players.

9. Gather necessary props plus others that will add realistic detail.

10. Collect and create evidence and clues.

   a. Determine which evidence, when added up, points to the resolution of the mystery.

   b. Decide whether you want to keep the evidence simple (typewritten, plain black and white) or enhance it to be more realistic (handwriting, use of colored papers, etc.).

   c. If this is a crime-solving mystery, be sure to include red herrings.

11. Plan for dinner or refreshments if these are part of the event.

12. Go through the mystery with everyone helping you.

13. Set up the space and arrange the props and clues/evidence.

14. You're ready to go!

   a. For questions you can't answer yet, just say, "We'll have to see about that!"

   b. Be prepared to help the players. They may not have the level of skill you had expected. Be patient.

15. HAVE FUN!

Part 2

MYSTERY SCRIPTS SET IN LIBRARIES

3
Death in the Library

Death in the Library

Date:

Time:

Place:

SUSPECTS:

Randolph Knightley

Joelle Knightley

Amanda Hennessey

Marnye Classico

Winifred, Head of Housekeeping

Victoria Knightley

Caleb Hennessey

Isaac Classico

Johanna, Housemaid

NON-SUSPECTS:

Inspector Ian Intel

Richard, the Butler & Victim

Laura Knightley

SCRIPT COVER

- Name of Mystery: Death in the Library
- Date of Program: _____
- Time of Program: _____
- Location of Program: _____
- Names of Suspects

  Randolph Knightley, master of the manor, played by _____

  Victoria Knightley, mistress of the manor, played by _____

  Joelle Knightley, their teenage daughter, played by _____

  Caleb Hennessey, houseguest, played by _____

  Amanda Hennessey, houseguest (Caleb's wife), played by _____

  Isaac Classico, houseguest and pianist, played by _____

  Marnye Classico, houseguest and opera singer (Isaac's wife), played by

  _____

  Johanna, Austrian housemaid, played by _____

  Winifred, head of housekeeping, played by _____

- Others on the Scene but Not Suspects, Including the Chief Inspector

  Inspector Ian Intel, chief inspector, played by _____

  Richard, butler and victim, played by _____

  Laura Knightley, the Knightleys' ten-year-old daughter, played by

  _____

PURPOSE

Librarians will find *Death in the Library* most useful for general entertainment. I wrote this as a tribute to the classic murder mystery that takes place in the typical creepy gothic mansion setting.

SETTING

This mystery script is set in a luxurious but dark and dreary manor house. The murder of Richard, the butler, takes place in the Knightleys' library during a weekend house party just before dinner is to be served. It is set during the early twentieth century.

CRIME

While "dusting" in the library (in reality, snooping around), Richard, the butler, received a blow to the head that took his life.

TIMELINE

- Yesterday, Richard agreed to accept money from Joelle in exchange for his silence about her wild party lifestyle.

- This morning, Richard (who is fluent in German) heard Johanna on the library phone. She was blabbing in German about Mr. Knightley's business secrets, thinking no one understood what she was saying. Richard told her that after the dinner party he would be informing Mr. Knightley of her actions.
- Early this afternoon, Richard accidentally discovered that Isaac Classico had lost the majority of his fortune in a risky business venture.
- In addition, this afternoon Richard provoked a very strong response from Caleb Hennessey when talking to him as though they were equals.
- At about 5:30 p.m., Marnye mentioned to Amanda that she was bored and that she was going down to the library for a book. Once in the library, Marnye put a rare book in her bag with the intention of stealing it. Richard was watching. When Marnye tried to explain, Richard stated that the Knightleys did not retain houseguests who stole from them. He turned to the door as if to escort her from the house. At that moment, Marnye grabbed the book from her purse and struck a heavy blow to Richard's head, killing him. In her haste to escape out the side door, Marnye dropped the book at the scene of the crime. A few minutes later, Laura Knightley entered the library through the other door, discovered Richard, and left to get help. Marnye realized that she had forgotten the book and returned to retrieve it. Marnye joined everyone else at the scene of the crime a few minutes later, book in hand.

SUSPECT BIOGRAPHIES

No one has an alibi. Assistant detectives will figure out the mystery based on other criteria. Suspects might say that they were in their rooms, walking around, cleaning, and so on at the time of the crime. When discrediting another suspect, suspects should mention his or her possible weapon.

> Murder is always a mistake. One should never do anything that one cannot talk about after dinner.
>
> *Oscar Wilde*

Name: Randolph Knightley, Master of Mulberry Manor and Businessman

Description of Character: Randolph Knightley is "new money." He earned this money by cheating his former business partner out of the bulk of their assets and then promptly ending the partnership. He hired Richard (whose family had money not too long ago) as his butler, to help him "learn the ropes" of wealthy society, and the arrangement seemed to be working well. Lately, however, Richard has been putting on airs and acting superior toward Randolph. Randolph informed Richard that because of his attitude, he would have to terminate him after the house party. Richard retaliated by saying that if he were terminated, he would personally make sure the rest of society found out how the Knightleys really became wealthy.

Motivation: Randolph may have murdered Richard because of his threat to inform the members of society about how his family became wealthy.

Weapon: Randolph possesses some very large bookends that he may have used to strike Richard over the head.

Discredit Amanda Hennessey: When Caleb and Amanda Hennessey entered the house earlier today, Randolph noticed some tension between Amanda and Richard. Curious, Randolph stayed hidden in another room, and after Caleb went up to their room, his curiosity was rewarded. It turns out that Richard and Amanda dated long ago. When Richard's family lost their money, Amanda dropped him. Richard wanted Amanda to introduce him to her husband Caleb as her former boyfriend. Of course Amanda couldn't do that, given Caleb's insane jealousy and her snobbish attitude. Perhaps Amanda killed Richard with her society planner so that he would not tell Caleb about their former relationship.

Name: Victoria Knightley, Mistress of Mulberry Manor

Description of Character: Victoria Knightley has always loved high society, money, and being fashionable. Perhaps that is why, before her family came into money, when approached by an obviously shady character who wanted to sell her a huge (stolen) diamond necklace, she purchased it instead of turning the thief in. Victoria did not realize that her new necklace actually belonged to Richard's family prior to his reversal of fortune. When Richard saw the necklace on Victoria's neck earlier today, he was shocked. He told Victoria that the necklace was rightfully his and if she didn't give it to him, he would turn her in to the police.

Motivation: Victoria may have murdered Richard so he would stop bothering her about her diamond necklace.

Weapon: Victoria may have used her diamond necklace to knock Richard out. (The diamond is huge!)

Discredit Isaac Classico: Purely by accident, Victoria noticed the Classicos' bedroom door was open this afternoon and decided to greet them. She was surprised to hear Richard laughing maliciously at Isaac Classico and saying that he couldn't wait to share the news that Isaac had lost most of his fortune due to a risky business venture. Even though Isaac practically begged Richard not to say anything to Marnye (because she threatened to leave him if he kept speculating), Richard kept saying he would tell Marnye everything. Perhaps Isaac killed Richard with his cane to keep his secret from Marnye.

Name: Joelle Knightley, Daughter of Mulberry Manor

Description of Character: Joelle is the wild daughter of Randolph and Victoria Knightley. Joelle loves to party with her friends and has been returning home at all hours of the night. Richard had been monitoring her and was planning to tell Mr. and Mrs. Knightley about Joelle's gallivanting until she started bribing him to keep him quiet.

Motivation: Joelle finds it extremely irritating that Richard should have anything on her and that she should have to pay him her allowance to keep him quiet. Joelle may have murdered Richard in order to keep her party life a secret and hang onto her allowance.

Weapon: Joelle has a large rhinestone purse that could have been used to do the deed.

Death in the Library

NEEDED! A team of library staff members and high school teens to help with a Mystery Theatre program for teens. Whodunit? We are now looking for volunteers to play the following roles:

SUSPECTS: Randolph Knightley, Victoria Knightley, Joelle Knightley, Caleb Hennessey, Amanda Hennessey, Isaac Classico, Marney Classico, Johanna, the Austrian Housemaid, Winifred, the Head of Housekeeping

NON-SUSPECTS: Inspector Ian Intel, Richard, the Butler & Victim, Laura Knightley

Be a part of the fun! If you sign up, you are responsible for your own costume and props, but I will provide assistance as necessary.

Rehearsal Date:

Performance Date: Time: Place:

Please return form to _____ by _____.

Name: _____

___ Yes, I would love to help.

___ My first choice of character is _____. My second choice is _____.

___ I need help with my costume!

___ I will help only if you are absolutely desperate.

Discredit Johanna: Ever since Richard has taken to checking up on her, Joelle has decided to do some spying herself. She's determined to get some dirt on him. This morning, she overheard Richard and Johanna arguing. Richard said he heard Johanna talking in German on the phone about Mr. Knightley's private business. Obviously, this is a big no-no. So maybe the maid decided to kill the butler before he could report her! Johanna might have used the phone in the library as a weapon.

Name: Caleb Hennessey, Houseguest and Businessman

Description of Character: Caleb is a powerful businessman. He is controlling of everything and everyone under his care, including his wife, Amanda. He flies into a rage whenever he suspects that anyone is treating him without respect. Earlier today, Caleb felt that Richard talked back to him when he gave him an order. Not very long ago, when Richard had money, he was on the same social level as Caleb was. That may be why Richard cheekily pointed out that Mr. Hennessey was not his master and told him to take up any problems with Mr. Knightley.

Motivation: Unable to bear the idea of a mere servant talking back to him, Caleb may have decided to teach Richard the ultimate lesson.

Weapon: Caleb could have used his brute strength to hit Richard.

Discredit Randolph Knightley: Randolph Knightley is newly wealthy. He hired Richard to help him learn the ropes of society. Caleb noticed Richard putting on airs and acting superior toward Randolph. There is no excuse for uppity servants, no matter what their history. If he were in Randolph's position, Caleb would have fired Richard immediately. Perhaps Richard drove Randolph to murder. Randolph owns those heavy-duty bookends in the library of which he is so proud. He conceivably put them to use on the back of Richard's head.

Name: Amanda Hennessey, Houseguest

Description of Character: Amanda has been a part of high society her entire life. She even dated Richard in her youth when he was still wealthy. She was mortified when Richard answered the door as the butler. She has never told her husband (Caleb) about dating Richard because of Caleb's insane jealousy. She is afraid he would do something rash. Things are a little shaky in their relationship as it is. There have been more petty arguments than there should be lately. When Caleb went up to their room, Amanda talked briefly with Richard. Richard started to make snide insinuations and insisted that she introduce him to Caleb as her old boyfriend, but this is something that Amanda is not prepared to do.

Motivation: Amanda may have murdered Richard so that her husband wouldn't find out that Richard was her old beau.

Weapon: Amanda's planner that she uses to keep up-to-date with all of her society engagements would make a good weapon.

Discredit Marnye Classico: Marnye is a real nut case, a fanatic about rare and antique books. She has been looking for _____ [insert title] for a long time. At 5:30 this evening, she told Amanda that she was going to look for a good book to read in the library. Maybe she saw something. On the other hand, maybe she had a reason to kill Richard herself. A book would make a handy weapon.

Name: Isaac Classico, Houseguest and Pianist

Description of Character: Isaac is a world-renowned pianist with a reputation for risky investments. After the failure of his latest speculation, in which he had risked the majority of his wealth, Isaac was left feeling panicked and frantic. He is desperate to keep the news of his ruined finances from his wife Marnye, who had threatened to leave him if he kept risking their money. While snooping in Isaac's room, Richard came across a telegram with news of Isaac's problem. Isaac discovered Richard reading the telegram. Instead of being embarrassed at being caught, Richard said he wanted a bribe to keep Isaac's secret from Marnye, even if there was only a little bit of money left. Neither Isaac nor Richard saw Victoria Knightley peek into the room and take in the whole scene.

Death in the Library

The butler has been murdered in the library! Whodunit? Your help is needed to solve this mystery. Spaces are limited. Sign up now to be a part of this mystery theatre program! The winning team will be awarded prizes. Refreshments will be served.

LIBRARY NAME
ADDRESS
DATE, TIME

REGISTRATION
INFORMATION
AGE LIMITATIONS

Motivation: Isaac may have murdered Richard to keep him from telling Marnye of their financial ruin.

Weapon: Isaac could have used his cane to strike a blow to Richard's head.

Discredit Caleb Hennessey: Caleb is a control freak. He can't stand it if anyone shows any amount of spine. So when Richard talked back to Caleb earlier today, Caleb freaked. Maybe Caleb became so angry with Richard that he used his brute strength to kill him.

Name: Marnye Classico, Houseguest and Opera Singer

Description of Character: Marnye is an avid collector of antique books. While browsing in the library at 5:30 p.m., she saw a rare first edition of _____ [insert title of a book]. Marnye knew she had to have the book. She had been searching for this title for the last ten years. She knew the Knightleys would never miss it—they purchased the books in the library with the house and have no idea of the book's true value. Marnye looked to the left and right furtively and then placed the book in her bag. It was then that Richard cleared his throat. He had been lurking in the shadows. Marnye stuttered and tried to explain that she was just "borrowing" the book. Richard implied that Marnye's furtive movements indicated that she was stealing the book and that the Knightleys did not retain houseguests who stole from them. He turned to the door as if to escort her from the house. At that moment, Marnye grabbed the book from her purse and struck a heavy blow to Richard's head, killing him. In her haste to escape out the side door, Marnye dropped the book at the scene of the crime. A few minutes later, Laura Knightley entered the library through the main door and observed the scene. She left to get help. Marnye realized that she had forgotten her precious book and quickly returned to retrieve it. She joined everyone else at the scene of the crime a few minutes later.

Motivation: Fearing that Richard would turn her in for stealing the rare book in the library and that she would not be able to acquire the special book to add to her collection, Marnye killed the butler.

Weapon: Marnye used her newly acquired book to strike the butler dead.

Discredit Victoria Knightley: Victoria loves to wear a certain diamond necklace. Anyone who has been in society knows that the necklace was once the property of Richard's family. The necklace was not in the estate sale with the rest of Richard's possessions, so, obviously, Victoria took possession of the necklace by some shady means. Perhaps Richard confronted Victoria about the necklace, and Victoria did something rash. That necklace is big enough to kill someone.

Note: Marnye needs to alert the assistant detectives that she went to the library at 5:30 p.m. She can then lie and say that she left shortly after to mislead the detectives.

Name: Johanna, Austrian Housemaid

Description of Character: A recent immigrant, Johanna is looking to move up in the world. She had been talking on the phone in German about Mr. Knightley's business secrets that she found while "cleaning" his office. Unfortunately for Johanna, Richard is fluent in German and heard her conversation this morning. He threatened to turn her in to the Knightleys after the dinner party this evening.

Motivation: Johanna may have decided to kill Richard before he had a chance to report her activities to Mr. and Mrs. Knightley.

Weapon: Being very familiar with the library phone, Johanna may have used it as a weapon to kill the butler.

Discredit Winifred: Gentle Winifred told Johanna that she has been very angry with Richard lately. Richard has insisted that she work the last two Sundays (her days off), and she hasn't had a chance to visit her family or go to church. This has completely enraged Winifred. Johanna worries that Winifred may have done something that she will regret. Winifred always carries a metal can of cleaning solution. It may have been used as a weapon.

Name: Winifred, Head of Housekeeping

Description of Character: Winifred is a very conscientious employee. The only thing she has ever asked is that she be given Sunday off each week to go to church and to visit her family. For the last two Sundays, however, Richard has denied Winifred's request. He felt that the running of the household did not permit this frivolity. Winifred, though normally reticent and submissive, feels extremely angry toward Richard for his unreasonable attitude.

Motivation: In order to resume her weekly visits to her family, Winifred may have murdered Richard.

Weapon: Winifred could have used her metal bottle of cleaning solution to kill Richard.

Discredit Joelle Knightley: All the servants are aware of Joelle's party lifestyle. Richard had been planning to tell Joelle's parents about her activities. Then yesterday, Winifred heard something that disturbed her very much. Richard agreed to take some money from Joelle in exchange for keeping quiet. Joelle said she will pay Richard out of her allowance, but perhaps she instead decided to take action regarding Richard. Joelle has that huge rhinestone bag that could be used as a weapon.

Summary

Name	Weapon	Discuss/Discredit
Randolph Knightley	Bookends	Amanda Hennessey
Victoria Knightley	Diamond necklace	Isaac Classico
Joelle Knightley	Rhinestone purse	Johanna
Caleb Hennessey	Brute strength	Randolph Knightley
Amanda Hennessey	Society planner	Marnye Classico
Isaac Classico	Cane	Caleb Hennessey
Marnye Classico	Book	Victoria Knightley
Johanna	Phone	Winifred
Winifred	Bottle of cleaning solution	Joelle Knightley

Death in the Library
Assistant
Detective
Worksheet

Suspects:

Randolph Knightley   Victoria Knightley
Joelle Knightley   Caleb Hennessey
Amanda Hennessey   Isaac Classico
Marnye Classico   Johanna (Housemaid)
Winifred (Head of Housekeeping)

Non-Suspects:

Inspector Ian Intel   Richard (Butler & victim)
Laura Knightley

Ask the Suspects:

Where were you at 6:00 p.m. when the Butler
    was murdered?
Can anyone confirm your whereabouts?
Did you have any reason to dislike the Butler?
Do you know anything about any of the other
    suspects that might prove helpful in this investigation?

Guidelines:

- Each Suspect will wear a nametag.
- Only one team is allowed to ask questions of a Suspect at a time.
- Assistant Detectives should not necessarily believe any of the Suspects right away when they are told something. The Suspect may be lying. Verify statements with another Suspect.
- Assistant Detectives have a maximum of 45 minutes to solve the mystery but the first team to turn in the correct answer wins.

OTHERS ON THE SCENE WHO ARE NOT SUSPECTS, INCLUDING THE VICTIM

Name: Inspector Ian Intel, Chief Inspector

Description of Character: Businesslike and to the point, Inspector Intel lives only for his or her work and to get to the crux of every mystery.

Name: Richard, Butler and Victim

Description of Character: Richard's family recently lost all of their money, and he was forced to find employment. The Knightleys, with their newly acquired wealth, needed assistance in breaking into society. Richard helped them make the transition. He had started to feel irritated, however, that he was locked out of society just because he didn't have money, and that these hicks (the Knightleys) were welcomed into society freely because of their cash.

Name: Laura Knightley

Description of Character: The ten-year-old daughter of the Knightleys, Laura discovered Richard in the library. She thought he was unconscious, but he was actually dead. She ran from the room and alerted everyone. Laura thought she remembered seeing a red book on the floor by Richard's body, but when she returned to the room with everyone else, the book was gone.

PROGRAM SCHEDULE

Part 1 (15 minutes): Information for Inspector Intel and the Suspects

Fifteen minutes before the program begins, all cast members except Inspector Intel are in their places. If you have enough cast members to include a body (for Richard), place Richard's body with his face away from the audience at the front of the room. You could also create a tape outline of the body on the floor. Another option would be to reveal the body with the suspects from behind a curtain at the beginning of the program. Inspector Intel will wait for the participants at the room entrance and assign them to a team.

Inspector Intel will introduce the suspects, hand out a worksheet to each team, and explain how it is to be filled out. Inspector Intel will also enlighten assistant detectives as to their role throughout the investigation.

Inspector Intel will talk about the crime: "You have been called here today to solve a mystery. At approximately 6:00 p.m. tonight, Richard, the butler, received a blow to the head that took his life." Inspector Intel will then tell the suspects to leave the scene of the crime and to wait for questions in the main room. Inspector Intel will mention that none of the suspects have alibis. Assistant detectives need to pay attention to possible weapons. He will then explain the rules to the detectives:

- Each suspect will wear a name tag.
- Only one team is allowed to ask questions of a suspect at a time.

- Assistant detectives should not necessarily believe any of the suspects right away when they are told something. The suspect may be lying. Verify statements with another suspect.
- Assistant detectives have a maximum of 45 minutes to solve the mystery, but the first team to turn in the correct answer wins. Inspector Intel will mark down the time that each team finishes.
- After a team has turned in the form to Inspector Intel, it may return to the meeting room.

Part II (45 minutes): Information for Inspector Intel and the Suspects

In another room, suspects will stand in their assigned places and answer questions from the assistant detectives. Assistant detectives may start with the following questions. Suspects should be prepared to answer these questions:

- "Where were you at 6:00 p.m. today when the butler was murdered?"
- "Can anyone confirm your whereabouts?"
- "Did you have any reason to dislike the butler?"
- "Do you know anything about any of the other suspects that might prove helpful in this investigation?"

When assistant detectives have written down the name of the suspect they believe is guilty and have given their worksheet to Inspector Intel (who writes the finishing time and order of completion on each form), they may return to the original room and wait for the suspects to return.

Part III (15 minutes): Information for Inspector Intel and the Suspects

During the third portion of the program, the suspects will return to the original room for the final interrogation. Inspector Intel will ask questions of each suspect, one by one. Although there are suggested questions and answers, both the suspects and Inspector Intel should be prepared to ad-lib. When the criminal is questioned (usually last), a dramatic finish is in order.

Final Interrogation Questions:

Inspector Intel: Joelle Knightley, did you have some kind of arrangement with the deceased?

Joelle Knightley: Why, I don't know what you're talking about!

Inspector Intel: Isn't it true that you were bribing Richard to keep quiet about your nightly partying so he wouldn't tell your parents?

Joelle Knightley: Yes, that is true. He threatened to tell Mother and Father! I had to give him my allowance to keep him quiet.

Inspector Intel: Did you kill the butler so that you wouldn't have to pay him your allowance any longer?

Joelle Knightley: No, of course not. Although I didn't want him to stop my fun, I wasn't about to kill him for it.

Inspector Intel: Johanna, English is not your first language, is it?

Johanna: No, I grew up in Austria.

Inspector Intel: When you make your personal calls, do you speak in English or German?

Johanna: Usually German. It's just more comfortable and easy for me to speak in German.

Inspector Intel: I understand that you were speaking in German this morning to someone on the phone. You didn't realize that Richard was also fluent in German.

Johanna: No, I didn't.

Inspector Intel: When Richard discovered that you were telling your stockbroker all about Mr. Knightley's business secrets, did you kill him?

Johanna: I did not. I want to improve my life, not go to jail!

Inspector Intel: Winifred, Richard hasn't allowed you to take your customary days off lately. How did that make you feel?

Winifred: I've been feeling more and more angry. It's not fair to deny a person her family. I work hard. I deserve to see them.

Inspector Intel: Were you angry enough to kill Richard?

Winifred: No. I am not a violent person.

Inspector Intel: Victoria Knightley, I hear that you have a very distinctive diamond necklace.

Victoria Knightley: Yes, isn't it beautiful? I just adore it!

Inspector Intel: There's a bit of a controversy surrounding the necklace. Some say it belongs to Richard's family, and that you probably purchased it from a thief.

Victoria Knightley: You have the wrong information. I was very upset at Richard when he kept bringing up that story. Why, he even threatened me—I was afraid for my life!

Inspector Intel: Did you kill Richard to protect yourself—or your secret?

Victoria Knightley: I did not! I have no secret and no reason to feel guilty.

Inspector Intel: Just keep telling yourself that. Isaac, Richard discovered something that you desperately need to keep secret. What was that?

Isaac Classico: I suppose you are referring to the fact that I made a slightly poor business decision lately. But I'm not worried. Everything will rally somehow . . .

Inspector Intel: Didn't your wife threaten to leave you if you kept speculating?

Isaac Classico: Well, yes.

Inspector Intel: If Richard were dead, you wouldn't have to worry about Marnye finding out.

Isaac Classico: That is true, but it's just not in my nature to hurt anyone.

Inspector Intel: You, Caleb Hennessey, on the other hand, are known for your controlling nature.

Caleb Hennessey: (with an overly angry reaction) That is a ridiculous statement! I could sue you for saying a thing like that. Where's the phone? I need to call my lawyer!

Inspector Intel: Really, Mr. Hennessey. Please settle down like a good boy and answer the questions. Did you have an argument with the victim earlier today?

Caleb Hennessey: Yes, I did. That *servant* [he says it like it is a dirty word] had the audacity to talk back to me. I was outraged!

Inspector Intel: Outraged enough to kill him?

Caleb Hennessey: Don't be ridiculous. Of course I didn't kill him!

Inspector Intel: Randolph Knightley, you are fairly new to society life. What did you do to ensure that you would fit in?

Randolph Knightley: I hired Richard as our butler. His family used to be rich, and he needed a job, so I thought it would be a good fit. He would work as the butler and would give us tips on how to act in society.

Inspector Intel: How did that work out?

Randolph Knightley: It started out fine, but lately, Richard had been acting pompously and superior to us. It was getting incredibly irritating.

Inspector Intel: I understand you got to the point where you decided to terminate him.

Randolph Knightley: Yes.

Inspector Intel: Did you terminate him completely?

Death in the Library

Who Did It?

Each team fills out
this sheet as they
solve the mystery.

Team Name: _____

Finishing Time: _____

Criminal: _____

Motive (Why they did it): _____

_____

_____

_____

The team that turns in this form with the
correct answer in the fastest time wins
the prize!

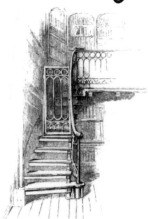

Death
in the
Library

The butler has been
murdered! Whodunit?
Sign up now to solve this
creepy mystery. Prizes
will be awarded to the
winning team.
Refreshments will
be served.
LIBRARY NAME
DATE, TIME
REGISTRATION
INFORMATION
AGE LIMITATIONS

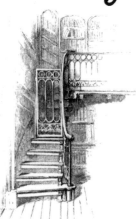

Death
in the
Library

The butler has been
murdered! Whodunit?
Sign up now to solve this
creepy mystery. Prizes
will be awarded to the
winning team.
Refreshments will
be served.
LIBRARY NAME
DATE, TIME
REGISTRATION
INFORMATION
AGE LIMITATIONS

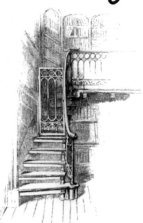

Death
in the
Library

The butler has been
murdered! Whodunit?
Sign up now to solve this
creepy mystery. Prizes
will be awarded to the
winning team.
Refreshments will
be served.
LIBRARY NAME
DATE, TIME
REGISTRATION
INFORMATION
AGE LIMITATIONS

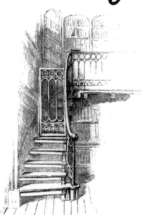

Death
in the
Library

The butler has been
murdered! Whodunit?
Sign up now to solve this
creepy mystery. Prizes
will be awarded to the
winning team.
Refreshments will
be served.
LIBRARY NAME
DATE, TIME
REGISTRATION
INFORMATION
AGE LIMITATIONS

Randolph Knightley: (shocked) Of course not.

Inspector Intel: Amanda Hennessey, would you say that your husband is the jealous type?

Amanda Hennessey: Yes. I hate to say it, but he can be difficult at times.

Inspector Intel: Were you worried he would find out that Richard was your old boyfriend?

Amanda Hennessey: Shhh. Please. I have to go home to him.

Inspector Intel: We can call for a police escort if necessary, Amanda. We need to get to the bottom of this. Did he know about you and Richard?

Amanda Hennessey: No. He had no idea, and I wanted to keep it that way for the happiness of my marriage.

 Randolph Knightley

 Victoria Knightley

 Joelle Knightley

 Caleb Hennessey

 Amanda Hennessey

 Isaac Classico

 Marnye Classico

 Johanna, Austrian Housemaid

 Winifred, Head of Housekeeping

 Inspector Ian Intel

 Richard, Butler

 Laura Knightley

Inspector Intel: Did you murder Richard to keep your secret quiet?

Amanda Hennessey: No, I did not. It would have been easier if Caleb didn't know, but I hope we'll be able to work out our problems.

Inspector Intel: Good luck. Marnye Classico, in addition to being the world's most famous contralto, you are also a collector of fine old books.

Marnye Classico: Yes, I have a lovely collection at home.

Inspector Intel: Laura Knightley, please come forward. When you discovered the body in the library, did you notice anything unusual?

Laura Knightley: Well, the body on the floor was a little creepy, but I also thought I saw a red book on the floor. I went to get help, but when I came back with everyone to the library, the book was gone.

Inspector Intel: Amanda Hennessey, one more question. I understand that Marnye told you this afternoon that she was going to the library to look for a book. About what time did she tell you this?

Amanda Hennessey: Marnye said she was bored and she wanted to get a book. I think it was about 5:30 p.m. or perhaps a little bit later.

Inspector Intel: Interesting. That places Marnye at the scene of the crime right before it happened.

Marnye Classico: Now wait just a minute. I went to the library, got my book, and left.

Inspector Intel: Tell us about this—red—book you are holding.

Marnye Classico: (Marnye forgets herself and gets very excited) It's a wonderful book! I've been looking for this book for ten years now. It's a rare first edition! I knew I had to have it!

Inspector Intel: So you tried to steal it.

Marnye Classico: Why—no—I . . .

Inspector Intel: Is that why, when Richard saw you trying to steal the book, and threatened to throw you out of the house, you hit him on the back of the head with that book—which I'll now take as evidence? (He tries to take the book from Marnye. Marnye resists and starts to run toward the door.)

Inspector Intel: Stop her! The criminal is getting away! (Marnye will still resist, break down, and act outraged, all at the same time.)

After the true criminal has been revealed, Inspector Intel will announce the winning team. While he is giving out prizes, the rest of the cast will stand in a row (or two rows), wait for Inspector Intel to join them, and then bow in unison one time. The cast leaves the room or the curtain closes.

OPTIONAL CLUES AND PROPS
- Ornate "diamond" necklace that would be easy for Richard to identify
- A "rare" book (look for an appropriate aged-looking title, or create a new title and spine for an existing title)
- A metal bottle of cleaning solution
- Bookends
- Rhinestone purse
- Society planner
- Cane
- Phone

COSTUMES

There is no set time period assigned to this mystery other than that it takes place during the early twentieth century or the present. Pick a decade and dress your suspects to reflect the era you choose. Costumes should be formal. The Knightleys and their guests will be dressed in formal evening wear. The servants wear the appropriate aprons, suits, and headwear. Inspector Intel can wear a traditional trench coat with a bowler cap.

DECORATIONS

The atmosphere to try to create for this script is dark and cobwebby (despite repeated cleaning by the maids). There is a very traditional feeling to the house. The owners have not attempted to modernize. The rooms are filled with antiques and leather-bound books. Set up your program room with a couple of armchairs at the front of the room for Randolph and Victoria Knightley to sit on, as well as two or three regular chairs on either side for the houseguests. Arrange a small reading lamp and display a couple of books with a pair of reading glasses on a small table between the chairs. Put out several framed traditional-looking pieces of art. String cobwebs over the chairs and throughout the room. Turn off most of the lights to create a dark, parlor-like feeling.

FOOD

Serve an elaborate meal (such as the meal that would have been served to the Knightleys' guests) early in the evening. If this is not an option for you, serve the usual snacks and pop.

GRAPHICS AND PUBLICITY

A reproducible recruitment form, a publicity poster, publicity bookmarks, Assistant Detective Worksheets, and name tags are included in this chapter.

TO-DO LIST

- Recruit suspects, chief inspector, and other non-suspects
- Assign places to stand or sit during Parts I–III

  o Parts I and III: Set up your meeting room with a couple of armchairs at the front of the room for Randolph and Victoria Knightley to sit on. The Hennesseys and Joelle can sit on regular chairs on one side of the Knightleys. The Classicos can sit on the other side. Johanna and Winifred should stand at attention. Laura Knightley should sit on a chair at the side of the room.
  o Part II: The following should form a large circle: Randolph Knightley, Amanda Hennessey, Marnye Classico, Laura Knightley, Victoria Knightley, Isaac Classico, and Caleb Hennessey. The following should form a smaller circle: Joelle Knightley, Johanna, and Winifred.

- Purchase refreshments
- Purchase prizes
- Take pictures, if desired
- Write thank-you notes and/or buy small gifts

SHORT NEWS RELEASE

The butler is dead! If the butler didn't do it, then whodunit? Everyone has a motive, from the master of the house to the housemaid. Come to the _____ Library on _____ and interrogate the suspects being held for questioning. It's up to you and your friends to find the criminal and solve the mystery. Form a team or we will assign you to one. Open to students in grades ___ to ___. Prizes will be awarded to the winning team. Spaces are limited, so sign up now! Call _____ for details.

BOOK TIE-INS

Pull out great mysteries for both adults and teens. Make up a recommended reading list of mystery books. Put both on a creepy, gothic display. Use plenty of cobwebs and dark colors in the display.

PRODUCTION NOTES

Johanna needs a German accent.

4   A Library Dognapping

It's a Library Dognapping!

Place:

Date:

Time:

SUSPECTS:

Lavinia Binchy

Crofton de la Torre, III

Leanne Love

Rufus Muzzle

Elinor Reade

Coral Crab

Rita Lonelihart

Melody Musick

Rosalie Poormé

NON-SUSPECTS:

Chief Inspector

Danny the Dogcatcher

Zelda Zany

SCRIPT COVER

- Name of Mystery: A Library Dognapping
- Date of Program: _____
- Time of Program: _____
- Location of Program: _____
- Names of Suspects

  Lavinia Binchy, youth services librarian, played by _____
  Coral Crab, adult reference librarian, played by _____
  Crofton de la Torre III, library board member and bank president, played by

  _____
  Rita Lonelihart, technical services librarian, played by _____
  Leanne Love, circulation clerk, played by _____
  Melody Musick, page and music student, played by _____
  Rufus Muzzle, dog aficionado, played by _____
  Rosalie Poormé, library board member, played by _____
  Elinor Reade, library board member, played by _____

- Others on the Scene but Not Suspects, Including the Chief Inspector

  Chief Inspector, played by _____
  Zelda Zany, administrator, played by _____
  Danny, dogcatcher, played by _____
  Zoe, the dog, played by _____

PURPOSE

A Library Dognapping is a fun and entertaining script that will interest teen animal lovers.

SETTING

Your local public library is the setting for this mystery, although it could easily be adapted to a school library setting.

CRIME

The beloved pet dog of Zelda Zany, library administrator, was dognapped from the library at approximately 5:30 p.m. today. (Alter the time for your convenience.)

TIMELINE

- A dog program took place in the late afternoon. At the program, Rufus Muzzle explained to everyone present what a valuable and rare dog Zoe is.
- Zoe was abducted at 5:30 p.m.
- All of the suspects were on library property either for the program or for library business.

SUSPECT BIOGRAPHIES

NAME: LAVINIA BINCHY, YOUTH SERVICES LIBRARIAN

Description of Character: Lavinia has an affected Irish accent. Patrons call Lavinia the "elegant hat lady" because she always wears a fashionable hat with flair and style. Lavinia's claim to fame is that author Maeve Binchy is her third cousin. She has been trying for years to save up enough money to travel to Ireland to visit Maeve but has not been successful so far, supporting herself on her part-time income. She sometimes deludes herself that she will soon have enough money to travel to Ireland.

Motivation: Lavinia may have dognapped Zoe to obtain money to visit Ireland.

Alibi: While in the youth services department, Lavinia was telling Rosalie Poormé about her plans to go to Ireland sometime in the near future.

Discredit Rita Lonelihart: Since Rita's husband died two years ago, she has been very lonely. Rita adores Zoe. She has requested ownership of Zoe if Zelda ever has to give Zoe up. Maybe Rita took Zoe to ease her lonely heart.

NAME: CORAL CRAB, ADULT REFERENCE LIBRARIAN

Description of Character: Coral hates her job, is rude to patrons, and desperately wants Zelda Zany's job. She and Zelda have often argued over one thing or another. Both have worked at the library for years. It has always bothered Coral that Zelda was promoted and she was not. Consequently, over the years, Coral has become bitter and angry about life. Coral directs most of her venom toward Zelda. She hates it that everyone (including Elinor) always sticks up for Zelda.

> The one absolutely unselfish friend that man can have in this selfish world, the one that never deserts him, the one that never proves ungrateful or treacherous, is his dog. . . . When all other friends desert, he remains.
>
> *George Graham Vest*

Motivation: Coral might have taken Zoe to make Zelda crazy with worry and to ease her vengeful nature.

Alibi: In the staff room, Coral and Elinor Reade were having a heated discussion over whether Zelda became administrator because Elinor and Zelda are best friends.

Discredit Rufus Muzzle: When Zelda Zany brought Zoe into Rufus Muzzle's dog program earlier today, Rufus was positively giddy over his discovery of a real Swedish lapdog of New Zealand. He kept ranting about how his critics would have to take him seriously now, and that maybe he'd finally be able to make some money! Obviously, for Rufus to prove himself in the zoological world, he would need to take Zoe with him. He probably dognapped Zoe to get his sagging career back on track.

NAME: CROFTON DE LA TORRE III, LIBRARY BOARD MEMBER AND BANK PRESIDENT

Description of Character: Crofton is pretentious, snobby, and despised by Zelda Zany and Elinor Reade because of his arrogant attitude. During the last library board election, he twisted Elinor's words, implying that she thought the library should be open only one day a week. During a recent board meeting, Crofton was humiliated when Zelda revealed his (up until now) secret plans to dismiss half of the circulation staff in order to provide board members with a yearly stipend. He tried to defend himself with the argument that board members have to provide for their families just like everyone else (right before he drove off in his expensive sports car).

Motivation: Still furious over what Zelda did to him at the last board meeting, Crofton dognapped Zoe out of revenge.

Alibi: None, but Crofton will make up a somewhat believable alibi that does not involve other characters (for example, "I was on my dinner break and went out to eat").

Discredit Elinor Reade: Elinor is obviously unstable. For instance, at the last board meeting, Elinor suggested that the library should be open only one day a week. She is a little crazy and probably took the dog.

Name: Rita Lonelihart, Technical Services Librarian

Description of Character: Rita has often spoken of her admiration for Zoe to other staff members. Rita has told Zelda Zany that if she were to give up Zoe, she would adopt her in a second. It is no secret around the library that since Rita's husband died two years ago, she has been very lonely. Although she is a softie in many ways, Rita's attitude toward libraries is very "old school." She thinks that all library programs should be book-related, so Rufus Muzzle's program was not appropriate. It is hard on her to be "the only one to take a stand on these issues," but she feels it is the ethical thing to do.

Motivation: Rita may have taken Zoe to ease her lonely heart.

Alibi: In the meeting room, Rita was telling Rufus that as much as she loves dogs, non-educational programs do not belong in the library.

Discredit Leanne Love: Leanne is Zelda Zany's daughter. It is common knowledge among staff that Leanne is jealous of all the attention that Zelda gives to Zoe instead of to her, especially now that she needs to talk about her marital problems with her mother. Zelda has no attention to spare for her daughter with Zoe in her life. Perhaps Leanne dognapped Zoe to put the attention back on herself.

Name: Leanne Love, Circulation Clerk

Description of Character: Leanne is Zelda Zany's daughter. She believes that her mother cares more about Zoe than she does for her. Leanne has been having marital troubles during the last year, and every time she has needed to talk, Zelda has been busy walking, grooming, and taking care of the dog.

Motivation: Leanne may have stolen Zoe to get some attention for herself.

Alibi: Leanne was talking to Melody Musick at the circulation desk about how her mother, Zelda Zany, pays more attention to her dog than she does to Leanne.

Discredit: Rosalie Poormé might have done it. She is trying to support her sick brother on her slight wages, but is finding it difficult to pay all of the hospital bills.

Name: Melody Musick, Page and Music Student

Description of Character: Melody wants to make a career on the stage and sing in Broadway musicals. She is optimistic of continuing her musical education in the prestigious Julian School of Music, but unfortunately, her scholarship has just fallen through.

It's a Library Dognapping!

NEEDED! A team of library staff members and high school teens to help with a Mystery Theatre program for teens. Zoe, the beloved pet of the library's head librarian, Zelda Zany, is missing! Authorities have reason to believe that Zoe was abducted from library premises. Whodunit? We are now looking for volunteers to play the following roles:

SUSPECTS: Lavinia Binchy, Coral Crab, Crofton de la Torre, III, Rita Lonelihart, Leanne Love, Melody Musick, Rufus Muzzle, Rosalie Poormé, Elinor Reade

NON-SUSPECTS: Chief Inspector, Zelda Zany, Danny the Dogcatcher

Be a part of the fun! If you sign up, you are responsible for your own costume and props, but I will provide assistance as necessary.

Rehearsal Date:

Performance Date: Time: Place:

Please return form to _____ by _____.

Name: _____

___ Yes, I would love to help.

___ My first choice of character is _____.

    My second choice is _____.

___ I need help with my costume!

___ I will help only if you are absolutely desperate.

Motivation: Melody may have dognapped Zoe to pay for her musical dreams to come true.

Alibi: At the circulation desk, Melody was telling Leanne Love about how she just lost the scholarship to the Julian School of Music, and she doesn't know how she can afford it now.

Discredit Lavinia Binchy: Lavinia has always wanted to travel to Ireland to visit her famous cousin. Melody knows she will never earn enough money working part-time to go to Ireland. It is possible that she took the dog to sell so she could finally afford the trip.

Name: Rufus Muzzle, Dog Aficionado

Description of Character: Once a respected and world-famous zoologist, Rufus's career went downhill when he insisted that there was a breed of dog he dubbed the "Swedish lapdog of New Zealand," even though he had no solid proof. Laughed at by his critics and other zoologists, Rufus has been forced to find employment wherever he can. When he was invited to come and present a program on dog care from 3:30 to 4:30 p.m., he happily accepted. During the program, Zelda Zany brought in Zoe, and Rufus was astounded when he realized that Zoe was, in fact, living proof that the Swedish lapdog of New Zealand did exist! Rufus went on to tell the people gathered for the program that Zoe was therefore worth a lot of money, and so on. At the end of his presentation, Rita Lonelihart entered the room and began raving about how the library should not hold such programs, that the library existed for educational purposes only, not for entertainment. The program soon broke up, with Rita still verbally attacking Rufus Muzzle.

Motivation: Presented with such an unusual breed of dog, the publicity of presenting Zoe to the world could definitely boost his sagging career. Rufus might have taken Zoe in the event that Zelda Zany did not grant him permission.

Alibi: Rita Lonelihart was lecturing Rufus in the meeting room about the evils of non-educational library programs.

Discredit Coral Crab: Coral hired Rufus to do the program. During her phone call to Rufus to book him, Coral ended up telling Rufus all about how unfair promotion policies are in the library. Rufus did not solicit any of the information. He was told how Coral was overlooked in favor of Zelda Zany for the administrator position just because Zelda is friends with Elinor Reade, an influential board member. Coral sounded very angry with Zelda Zany. Perhaps she dognapped Zoe (Zelda's dog) out of revenge because she did not get the promotion.

Name: Rosalie Poormé (pronounced "Pore-may"), Circulation Clerk

Description of Character: Rosalie is having a hard time right now trying to make ends meet since she alone is supporting her sickly younger brother. She doesn't know how she can begin to pay for all of the hospital bills that are adding up.

Motivation: She could definitely use the money from the sale of Zoe to pay all of the hospital bills.

Alibi: Rosalie was in the youth services department, confiding in Lavinia Binchy about her financial problems.

Discredit Melody Musick: Melody also has financial problems. A career in librarianship is not Melody's calling. She wished to attend the Julian School of Music. Although she had applied for a scholarship, that didn't work out. Perhaps Melody took Zoe to pay for her college expenses.

Name: Elinor Reade, Library Board Member

Description of Character: Elinor is Zelda Zany's best friend. She despises Crofton de la Torre III. During the last library board election, Crofton made it appear that Elinor thought the library should be open only one day a week instead of six days. Because of this, Elinor pressured Zelda into revealing Crofton's plans to fire half of the circulation staff at the last board meeting. Elinor secretly dislikes all dogs and Zoe in particular. She knows that Zelda would stop being her friend if she knew about her aversion to animals.

Motivation: Elinor could have dognapped Zoe and deposited her at the pound, in order to avoid "getting licked to death" when she visits Zelda.

Alibi: Elinor and Coral Crab were having a heated discussion in the staff room over whether Zelda became administrator because Elinor and Zelda are best friends.

Discredit Crofton de la Torre III: Crofton was very angry with Zelda Zany at the last board meeting. She revealed his plans to dismiss half of the circulation staff in order to provide board members with a yearly stipend. Crofton hardly needs a stipend when he makes so much money at the bank. Just look at the expensive sports car he drives!

Summary

Name	Alibi	Discredit
Lavinia Binchy	Rosalie Poormé	Rita Lonelihart
Coral Crab	Elinor Reade	Rufus Muzzle
Crofton de la Torre III	No alibi	Elinor Reade
Rita Lonelihart	Rufus Muzzle	Leanne Love
Leanne Love	Melody Musick	Rosalie Poormé
Melody Musick	Leanne Love	Lavinia Binchy
Rufus Muzzle	Rita Lonelihart	Coral Crab
Rosalie Poormé	Lavinia Binchy	Melody Musick
Elinor Reade	Coral Crab	Crofton de la Torre III

Others on the Scene Who Are Not Suspects, Including the Chief Inspector and the Victim

Name: Chief Inspector

Description of Character: Businesslike and to the point, the Chief Inspector lives only for his or her work and to get to the crux of every mystery.

NAME: ZELDA ZANY, ADMINISTRATOR

Description of Character: Zelda was walking her dog, Zoe, in the library parking lot about 5:30 p.m. An unidentifiable person with a black stocking over his or her head hit Zelda on the head, knocking her unconscious. When she awoke, Zoe was gone. During the program, Zelda will be wearing bandages around her head.

NAME: DANNY, THE DOGCATCHER

Description of Character: The dogcatcher will bring Zoe in at the end of the program, stating that she was found tied up to a blue BMW with license plate TORRE3, about two blocks away.

NAME: ZOE, THE DOG

Description of Character: Since there is no such dog as the Swedish lapdog of New Zealand, any well-behaved dog will do.

PROGRAM SCHEDULE

PART 1 (15 MINUTES): INFORMATION FOR THE CHIEF INSPECTOR AND THE SUSPECTS

Fifteen minutes before the program begins, all cast members except the chief inspector are in their places. The chief inspector will wait for the participants at the room entrance and assign them to a team.

The chief inspector will introduce the suspects, hand out a worksheet to each team, and explain how it is to be filled out. The chief inspector will also enlighten assistant detectives as to their role throughout the investigation.

The chief inspector will talk about the crime that has occurred: "The beloved pet dog of Administrator Zelda Zany was dognapped from the library at approximately 5:30 p.m. today." The chief inspector will then tell the suspects to leave the scene of the crime and to wait for questions in the main room. He or she will then explain the rules to the detectives:

- Each suspect will wear a name tag.
- Only one team is allowed to ask questions of a suspect at a time.
- Assistant detectives should not necessarily believe any of the suspects right away when they are told something. The suspect may be lying. Verify statements with another suspect.
- Assistant detectives have a maximum of 45 minutes to solve the mystery, but the first team to turn in the correct answer wins. The chief inspector will mark down the time that each team finishes.
- After a team has turned in the form to the chief inspector, it may return to the meeting room.

It's a Library Dognapping!

Zoe, the beloved pet of the library's head librarian, Zelda Zany, is missing! Authorities have reason to believe that Zoe was abducted from library premises. Whodunit? Spaces are limited. Sign up now to be a part of this mystery theatre program! The winning team will be awarded prizes. Refreshments will be served.

LIBRARY NAME
ADDRESS
DATE, TIME
REGISTRATION
INFORMATION
AGE LIMITATIONS

Library Dognapping
Assistant Detective Worksheet

Suspects:

Lavinia Binchy
Coral Crab
Crofton de la Torre, III
Rita Lonelihart
Leanne Love

Melody Musick
Rufus Muzzle
Rosalie Poormé
Elinor Reade

Non-Suspects:

Chief Inspector
Zelda Zany

Danny the Dogcatcher

Ask the Suspects:

Where were you at this afternoon when the crime was committed?
Can anyone confirm your whereabouts?
Is there any reason you would want to dognap Zoe?
Do you think any of the other Suspects had a reason to dognap
    Zoe? Why?

Guidelines:

- Each Suspect will wear a nametag.
- Only one team is allowed to ask questions of a Suspect at a time.
- Assistant Detectives should not necessarily believe any of the Suspects right away when they are told something. The Suspect may be lying. Verify statements with another Suspect.
- Assistant Detectives have a maximum of 45 minutes to solve the mystery but the first team to turn in the correct answer wins. The Chief Inspector will mark down the time that each team finishes.
- After a team has turned in the form to the Chief Inspector, it may return to the meeting room.

Part II (45 minutes): Information for the Chief Inspector and the Suspects

In another room, suspects will stand in their assigned places and answer questions from the assistant detectives. Suspects should be prepared to answer the following questions:

- "Where were you this afternoon when the crime was committed?"
- "Can anyone confirm your whereabouts?"
- "Is there any reason you would want to dognap Zoe?"
- "Do you think any of the other suspects had a reason to dognap Zoe? Why?"

When assistant detectives have written down the name of the suspect they believe is guilty and have given their worksheet to the chief inspector (who writes the finishing time and order of completion on each form), they may return to the original room and wait for the suspects to return.

Part III (15 minutes): Information for the Chief Inspector and the Suspects

During the third portion of the program, the suspects will return to the original room for the final interrogation. The chief inspector will ask questions of each suspect, one by one. Although there are suggested questions and answers, both the suspects and the chief inspector should be prepared to ad-lib. When the criminal is questioned (usually last), a dramatic finish is in order.

Final Interrogation Questions

Chief Inspector: Rita Lonelihart, isn't it true that your husband died two years ago, and ever since then, you have felt lonely and sad?

Rita Lonelihart: Yes, it's true that I've felt very much alone.

Chief Inspector: Didn't you tell library staff that Zoe's eyes reminded you of your dearly departed husband's?

Rita Lonelihart: Why, yes!

Chief Inspector: A dog like Zoe would make a good companion to a lonely person.

Rita Lonelihart: That's true, but it wouldn't be right to take Zoe away from her home. I wouldn't like it if someone did that to me.

Chief Inspector: Melody Musick, aren't you trying to raise money to go to the Julian School of Music?

Melody Musick: Yes, I am.

Chief Inspector: Is that because your scholarship wasn't approved?

Melody Musick: Yes. Unfortunately, I didn't get the scholarship, so now I will have to get the money some other way.

Chief Inspector: You could get a lot of money from the sale of a rare dog like Zoe.

Melody Musick: I could if I were a criminal—which I'm not!

Chief Inspector: Rosalie Poormé, I understand that your younger brother is often ill. Do you have unpaid hospital bills?

Rosalie Poormé: That is unfortunately true.

Chief Inspector: When you heard how much Zoe was worth, were you tempted to take her to pay for your debts that keep piling up?

Rosalie Poormé: Everyone in this room could probably find a reason to be tempted, but no, I did not. I'll find the money some other way.

Chief Inspector: Rufus Muzzle, you have been the laughingstock of the U.S. Zoologists' Foundation for some time, have you not?

Rufus Muzzle: Yes. They didn't take my theory seriously.

Chief Inspector: And your theory is—was?

Rufus Muzzle: That the Swedish lapdog of New Zealand really exists.

Chief Inspector: Now that you have discovered Zoe, the temptation to take Zoe with you and prove her existence to all of your foes must be incredible.

Rufus Muzzle: I suppose so, but I'm not a dishonest person. I would ask permission first.

Chief Inspector: Lavinia Binchy, isn't it true that your cousin is Maeve Binchy, the famous author?

Lavinia Binchy: Yes. I'm so lucky to be related to her.

Chief Inspector: I hear that you have been trying for years to raise enough money to go and visit her, but you have not been able to because you only have a part-time income.

Lavinia Binchy: That is the sad truth.

Chief Inspector: And that you have been faking your Irish accent for years?

Lavinia Binchy: Why, I never!

Chief Inspector: Leanne Love, please identify your mother.

Leanne Love: My mother is Zelda Zany.

Chief Inspector: What do you think of Zoe being missing?

Leanne Love: My *mother* is very upset.

Library Dognapping

Who Did It?

Each team fills out this sheet as they solve the mystery.

Team Name: _____

Finishing Time: _____

Criminal: _____

Motive (Why they did it): _____

_____

_____

_____

The team that turns in this form with the correct answer in the fastest time wins the prize!

It's a Library Dognapping!

Have you seen this dog?

The librarian's dog has been stolen! Whodunit? We need your help to solve this mystery! Prizes will be given to the winning team. Refreshments will be served. Sign up now.

LIBRARY NAME, ADDRESS, PHONE, DATE, TIME, REGISTRATION INFORMATION, AGE LIMITATIONS

It's a Library Dognapping!

Have you seen this dog?

The librarian's dog has been stolen! Whodunit? We need your help to solve this mystery! Prizes will be given to the winning team. Refreshments will be served. Sign up now.

LIBRARY NAME, ADDRESS, PHONE, DATE, TIME, REGISTRATION INFORMATION, AGE LIMITATIONS

It's a Library Dognapping!

Have you seen this dog?

The librarian's dog has been stolen! Whodunit? We need your help to solve this mystery! Prizes will be given to the winning team. Refreshments will be served. Sign up now.

LIBRARY NAME, ADDRESS, PHONE, DATE, TIME, REGISTRATION INFORMATION, AGE LIMITATIONS

It's a Library Dognapping!

Have you seen this dog?

The librarian's dog has been stolen! Whodunit? We need your help to solve this mystery! Prizes will be given to the winning team. Refreshments will be served. Sign up now.

LIBRARY NAME, ADDRESS, PHONE, DATE, TIME, REGISTRATION INFORMATION, AGE LIMITATIONS

Chief Inspector: Isn't it true that you have told other staff members that your mother cares more about her dog than she cares about you?

Leanne Love: Well, it certainly seems that way.

Chief Inspector: Aren't you jealous over the attention your mother showers on her dog?

Leanne Love: I have to admit that I am jealous of Zoe, but I didn't dognap her! I just wish my mother would care a little bit about the problems I am going through right now.

Chief Inspector: Coral Crab, isn't it true that you were very upset when Zelda was promoted to administrator and you weren't?

Coral Crab: It wasn't fair. I deserved the promotion more than she.

Chief Inspector: It's common knowledge that you are always putting Zelda down and talking about her behind her back. (Coral Crab shrugs.)

 Lavinia Binchy

 Coral Crab

 Crofton de la Torre III

 Rita Lonelihart

 Leanne Love

 Melody Musick

 Rufus Muzzle

 Rosalie Poorne

 Elinor Reade

 Chief Inspector

 Zelda Zany

 Dogcatcher

Chief Inspector: In your jealous state, you could very well have taken Zoe to get back at Zelda, couldn't you?

Coral Crab: Very tempting. I wish I'd thought of it myself.

Chief Inspector: Elinor Reade, Zelda is your best friend, is she not? You would do anything for her, right?

Elinor Reade: Of course.

Chief Inspector: Isn't it true, though, that when Zelda acquired Zoe, you weren't too thrilled?

Elinor Reade: Well . . . (she shrugs)

Chief Inspector: Isn't it true that you hate dogs—the smell, the drool, the licking?

Elinor Reade: Yes, yes! It's true!

Chief Inspector: Didn't you get rid of Zoe to have some peace of mind when you visit Zelda?

Elinor Reade: No, of course I didn't. If my friend wants a drooling, smelly animal in her home, it is not my place to complain.

Chief Inspector: Crofton de la Torre III, during the last board meeting, you were humiliated when Zelda revealed your secret plans to get rid of over half the circulation staff so that you could have a stipend. Isn't your $200,000 banking salary enough?

Crofton de la Torre III: I was just thinking of the other board members.

Chief Inspector: You are known for always being well dressed, yet you seem so casually dressed today. Where is your tie?

Crofton de la Torre III: I seem to have misplaced it.

Chief Inspector: I had a chance to look at Zelda's head earlier, underneath the bandages. There was bruising in just the shape of (reaches into Crofton's pocket) this stapler. How do you explain this?

Crofton de la Torre III: I really couldn't say.

Chief Inspector: Isn't it true that you were consumed by fury, and in your anger, you dognapped Zoe?

Crofton de la Torre III: Of course not. I—(At this point, the Dogcatcher enters the room with Zoe. Zoe has Crofton's tie around her neck.)

Chief Inspector: Crofton, is this your tie?

Crofton de la Torre III: Yes! I admit it all! I dognapped Zoe and I'm happy I did it. It serves Zelda Zany right. How dare she humiliate me in front of the other board members!

The Chief Inspector pushes Crofton down into his chair and concludes the investigation by announcing the winning team. Crofton should continue to whine and complain. While the chief inspector is giving out prizes, the rest of the cast will stand in a row—or two rows—wait for the chief inspector to join them, and then bow in unison one time. The cast leaves the room or the curtain closes.

OPTIONAL PROPS AND CLUES
- Stapler
- Crofton's tie around Zoe's neck
- Bandages for Zelda Zany's head/injury

COSTUMES

Dress as library staff and board members in their respective stations would dress. Crofton de la Torre III needs to be in business clothes (minus the tie). Lavinia Binchy needs a hat.

DECORATIONS

No special decorations are needed for this script.

FOOD

Serve your choice of snacks, dessert, and drinks.

GRAPHICS AND PUBLICITY

A reproducible recruitment form, a publicity poster, publicity bookmarks, Assistant Detective Worksheets, and name tags are included in this chapter.

TO-DO LIST

- Recruit suspects, chief inspector, and other non-suspects
- Assign places to stand or sit during Parts I–III

  ○ Parts I and III: Arrange suspects in chairs at the front of the room in this order: Melody Musick, Rita Lonelihart, Rosalie Poormé, Rufus Muzzle, Leanne Love, Lavinia Binchy, Coral Crab, Crofton de la Torre III, and Elinor Reade.

○ Part II: Arrange suspects in a large circle around the room starting with Melody Musick, Rita Lonelihart, Rosalie Poormé, Rufus Muzzle, Leanne Love, Lavinia Binchy, Coral Crab, Crofton de la Torre III, Elinor Reade, and back to Melody Musick.

- Purchase refreshments
- Purchase prizes
- Take pictures, if desired
- Write thank-you notes and/or buy small gifts

BOOK TIE-INS

Put out an assortment of dog and other pet-care books and fiction books about pets. You could also hand out an annotated bibliography with your library's holdings of dog fiction and nonfiction.

PRODUCTION NOTES

If you have a staff member who owns a well-behaved dog, find out if you could use the dog for your program. You could change Zoe's name to the name of the real dog you are using. Insert real photographs in place of the graphics used in the provided publicity to make the mystery more real. The owner of the dog could act as the dogcatcher and bring the dognapped dog in at the end of the program. Adjust the times in this script to your own convenience.

SHORT NEWS RELEASE

Zoe, the beloved pet of the library's head librarian, Zelda Zany, is missing! Authorities have reason to believe that Zoe was abducted from library premises. Whodunit? Everyone has a motive, from the librarians to the board members. Come to the _____ Library on _____ and interrogate the suspects being held for questioning. It's up to you and your friends to find the criminal and solve the mystery. Form a team or we will assign you to one. Open to students in grades __ to __. Prizes will be awarded to the winning team. Spaces are limited, so sign up now! Call _____ for details.

5

Mysterious Mona

Mysterious Mona

SUSPECTS:

Professor Sirfaraz   Madame LaFarge

Dirk Death   Sally Sunshine

Eddie Monette   Julia Chill

Maria Mantalbano   Heather Readbetter

Della Bert

NON-SUSPECTS:

Chief Inspector

Place:

Date:

Time:

SCRIPT COVER

- Name of Mystery: Mysterious Mona
- Date of Program: _____
- Time of Program: _____
- Location of Program: _____
- Names of Suspects

  Professor Sirfaraz, tour coordinator, played by _____
  Madame LaFarge, Louvre Museum curator, played by _____
  Dirk Death, assistant maintenance person, played by _____
  Sally Sunshine, youth services assistant, played by _____
  "Fast" Eddie Monette, adult services librarian, played by _____
  Julia Chill, cooking guru, played by _____
  Maria Mantalbano, foreign exchange student and page, played by _____
  _____

  Heather Readbetter, Friends of the Library chairperson, played by _____
  _____

  Della Bert, library patron, played by _____

- Others on the Scene but Not Suspects, Including the Chief Inspector

  Chief inspector, played by _____

PURPOSE

The purpose of this mystery is to entertain and possibly to introduce students to great works of art.

SETTING

The setting of this mystery is your public library. Adapt it for a school library by changing some of the characters to teachers, volunteers, PTA members, and student volunteers.

CRIME

Leonardo da Vinci's famous painting, the *Mona Lisa*, was visiting libraries across the country in the "Libraries of _____ [fill in a country] and *Mona*" tour until it was stolen from the _____ Library.

TIMELINE

- At 4:30 p.m. (or whatever time works for your programming schedule), Sally Sunshine and Dirk Death were heard arguing in the youth services department.
- At 5:00 p.m., when everyone else was busy, Sally Sunshine sneaked into the front entryway where the *Mona Lisa* was being displayed, grabbed the painting, and hid it in the youth services storage closet. Remembering that she had forgotten to

wear gloves, Sally tried to remove her fingerprints with a handkerchief. Sally went back to the crime scene and planted Dirk's cleaning solution to try to incriminate him. Sally was not aware that she dropped her handkerchief at the scene of the crime. Shortly after this, the *Mona Lisa* was discovered missing, and assistant detectives were called in.

SUSPECT BIOGRAPHIES

NAME: PROFESSOR SIRFARAZ

Description of Character: Professor Sirfaraz is the coordinator for the "Libraries of _____ [fill in a country] and *Mona*" tour. She is trying to make the great works of art available to the common person and so has set up a national tour, to which Madame LaFarge is so opposed. Professor Sirfaraz feels that a painting should be admired and seen, not made available to only a select few.

> Heaven has no rage like love to hatred turned, nor hell a fury like a woman scorned.
>
> *William Congreve*

Motivation: Professor Sirfaraz has completely mismanaged the finances for the tour. She knows people and has connections, however, and it would be easy for her to get rid of the *Mona Lisa* to settle the debts and save her reputation.

Alibi: Professor Sirfaraz and Maria Mantalbano were discussing the *Mona Lisa* in the staff lounge. Professor Sirfaraz was pleased to discover such an art aficionado in Maria.

Discredit Madame LaFarge: Professor Sirfaraz wouldn't be surprised if Madame LaFarge managed to steal the *Mona Lisa*. Madame LaFarge is always talking about how the *Mona Lisa* belongs only in the Louvre Museum.

NAME: MADAME LAFARGE

Description of Character: Madame LaFarge is the curator of the Louvre Museum. She is sick and tired of tourists who come to the Louvre unappreciative of the great works of art, tourists who do not see the *Mona Lisa*'s true value and significance.

Motivation: Madame LaFarge could have stolen the *Mona Lisa* to stop the painting from traveling with the "Libraries of _____ [fill in a country] and *Mona*" tour.

Alibi: In the maintenance room, Madame LaFarge was lecturing Dirk Death about how he really must do a better job of cleaning around the *Mona Lisa*. Absolutely no dust must settle on the painting.

Discredit Professor Sirfaraz: Sirfaraz probably had the *Mona Lisa* removed. The professor—if she indeed is a professor—is just the type of person to do something this outrageous. First Professor Sirfaraz subjected poor *Mona* to this tour and now she has bungled the budget as well. There is absolutely no money left.

NAME: DIRK DEATH

Description of Character: Dirk Death is assistant maintenance person at the library. He is obsessed with _____ [insert current band], dreams of going on tour with them, and will do anything he needs to do to fulfill this dream. Unfortunately, he has no cash. As far as his personal life is concerned, Dirk and Sally used to date. Sally Sunshine drove Dirk crazy with all of her whining and he broke up with her. He and she had another blowup today.

Motivation: Dirk could have stolen the *Mona Lisa* in order to get enough cash to go on tour with the band.

Alibi: Dirk Death and Madame LaFarge were talking in the maintenance room. Madame LaFarge was yakking on about the necessity of cleanliness around the *Mona Lisa*, and Dirk was trying to tell her that she had no right to boss him around.

Discredit Heather Readbetter: While dusting, Dirk heard Della Bert and Heather Readbetter whispering in the shelves. Heather was begging Della not to say anything, that she would have the money for her soon. Della said something about "extortion," whatever that means, and something about the Friends of the Library book sale.

Name: Sally Sunshine

Description of Character: Sally is a youth services assistant. Ever since she first met Dirk, she has had a big crush on him. She was thrilled when he asked her out. Then Dirk dumped Sally, and since then she has lived only for revenge. Her hatred for Dirk consumes her, and she has publicly vowed to get him back. Despite this dark, mostly secret side of her personality, Sally comes off as a sweet, caring individual. Earlier today, she had another fight with Dirk.

Motivation: Sally might have stolen the *Mona Lisa* to frame Dirk, and . . . she did.

Alibi: Sally has no alibi. She will state that she was working at the youth services reference desk. When everyone else was otherwise occupied, she sneaked into the front entryway where the *Mona Lisa* was being displayed, grabbed the painting, and hid it away in what she thought was a safe place. Remembering that she had forgotten to wear gloves, she tried to remove her fingerprints with a handkerchief. Sally then planted Dirk's cleaning solution at the scene of the crime to try to incriminate him.

Discredit Dirk Death: Dirk probably did it. All he ever thinks about is _____ ____ [insert current band] and he probably stole the *Mona Lisa* to get some money to go on tour with the band. Sally is sick and tired of hearing about _____ [insert current band]. Sally should also point out that Dirk's cleaning solution was found at the scene of the crime, even though the chief inspector did not mention this fact in Part I.

Name: "Fast" Eddie Monette

Description of Character: Eddie works as an adult reference librarian in the library. He is the nephew of Julia Chill (of cooking fame). His notorious gambling addiction has gotten him into trouble more than once and has affected other library staff negatively as well.

Motivation: Eddie might have stolen the *Mona Lisa* in order to pay off his heavy debts to loan sharks incurred because of his compulsive gambling sprees.

Alibi: Eddie was at the reference desk talking with Julia Chill.

Discredit Della Bert: Eddie doesn't think any sane person would steal the *Mona Lisa*. He thinks Della Bert—the bane of the adult services department—probably did it. She's been extremely obsessed with the *Mona Lisa* ever since she found out about the tour. It would be just like her to do something crazy.

Name: Julia Chill

Description of Character: Julia is a famous cooking guru who was visiting her favorite nephew (Eddie Monette) in the library when the *Mona Lisa* was stolen. Lately Julia has been feeling depressed. Her last cooking show was a bit of a flop, but she is trying to convince herself that the future will be brighter, especially if she can get another TV show going. Right now, however, no network wants to take a chance on her.

Motivation: With the idea of starting her own cooking network and proving to the world that she is no failure, Julia Chill could have stolen the painting for the money to get her career back on track.

Alibi: Julia Chill and Eddie Monette were talking at the reference desk.

Discredit Maria Mantalbano: Maria should stop spreading rumors about Julia's nephew Eddie. Eddie wouldn't hurt a fly, but Maria keeps saying that she lost all of her money by going to a riverboat casino with Eddie and now she can't get back home to Spain. He didn't force her to spend her money, did he?

Name: Maria Mantalbano

Description of Character: Maria is a foreign exchange student from Spain who works part-time in the library as a page. About a month ago, she went with Eddie to a riverboat casino and lost all of her money that was meant to pay for her ticket home to Spain. She is afraid to tell her father what she has done because of his volatile temper. She feels hurt and upset at Eddie for taking her to the casino in the first place. She tried to talk to Eddie about his responsibility in the matter, but today she received a note from Eddie telling her to stop bugging him about money. She doesn't know what to do. The only thing that consoles Maria lately is the time she spends during her breaks admiring the *Mona Lisa*. It is a pleasant reminder of her family vacations to the Louvre Museum in Paris as a child.

Alibi: Maria Mantalbano and Professor Sirfaraz were discussing the *Mona Lisa* in the staff lounge. Maria was happy that she could talk about her childhood memories in relation to the painting to someone who understood.

Motivation: Maria desperately needs money to pay for her plane ticket home. She could have stolen the *Mona Lisa* to obtain it.

Discredit Sally Sunshine: Earlier today—at about 4:30 p.m., when Maria was shelving books in the youth services department, she overheard Sally telling Dirk to make sure not to forget to dump the garbage. Dirk told Sally to stop nagging at him. Soon they were yelling at each other. Sally got all upset and ran from the room. When she came back later, Sally seemed fine. She even had a smile on her face.

NAME: HEATHER READBETTER

Description of Character: Heather is the chairperson for the Friends of the Library. Heather's dream has been to write the Great American Novel, but unfortunately, her eyesight is failing and she finds it difficult to read anymore. At the last Friends of the Library book sale last week, which turned a large profit, Heather quietly pocketed most of the money to pay for part of her eye surgery. No one knows that Heather's eyesight is failing and that corrective eye surgery is the only way to fix the problem. To cover her tracks, Heather turned in a figure indicating that the sale did not go well at all. Inconveniently, a patron, Della Bert, has somehow managed to find out Heather's scheme, and so Heather had to give Della Bert part of her eye surgery money to keep her quiet. Now Heather does not have enough money to pay to have her eyesight corrected.

Motivation: Facing possible blindness, Heather Readbetter might have stolen the *Mona Lisa* to pay for surgery. In addition, Della Bert has gone back on her word to keep quiet and is threatening to tell the library board everything if she doesn't get more money from Heather.

Alibi: Heather Readbetter and Della Bert were whispering in the stacks.

Discredit Eddie Monette and Julia Chill: While Heather was looking for a book in the adult services department, she overheard Julia Chill and her nephew Eddie Monette talking. Julia was telling Eddie of her desire to start her own cooking network on cable since no one will hire her anymore (as her last cooking show was such a flop). Eddie asked Julia if he could borrow some money when her show became a success, as he had a few debts he needed to pay off. Just a few? It's a serious problem for Eddie. Maria told Heather that Eddie lost $7,500 in one sitting. Both Eddie and Julia obviously need money. Heather is sure the two of them are in cahoots. They probably stole the *Mona Lisa*.

NAME: DELLA BERT

Description of Character: Della has an annoying, over-the-edge type of personality. She is fascinated with different things and drives library staff crazy with her obsessions. For the last month, she has been asking reference librarians for every detail about the *Mona Lisa*. This has continued, even though they've given her everything there is to be found about the painting.

Motivation: Della Bert is obsessed with the *Mona Lisa* and may have stolen it for that reason.

Alibi: Della Bert and Heather Readbetter were whispering in the stacks.

Discredit Sally Sunshine: Sally pretends to be all sweetness and light, but Della knows there's something darker there. It's common knowledge that Dirk Death dumped Sally. Perhaps Sally is trying to frame Dirk. She does keep mentioning Dirk's cleaning solution. Now why is that?

Mona Lisa is missing!

NEEDED!

A team of library staff members and high school teens to help with a Mystery Theatre program for teens. Leonardo daVinci's famous painting, the Mona Lisa, has been stolen! The Mona Lisa was visiting libraries across the country in the "Libraries of (fill in country) and Mona" tour until it was stolen from the library! Whodunit? We are now looking for volunteers to play the following roles:

SUSPECTS: Professor Sirfaraz, Madame LaFarge, Dirk Death, Sally Sunshine, Eddie Monette, Julia Chill, Maria Mantalbano, Heather Readbetter, Della Bert

NON-SUSPECTS: Chief Inspector

Be a part of the fun! If you sign up, you are responsible for your own costume and props, but I will provide assistance as necessary.

Rehearsal Date: Performance Date:

Time: Place:

Please return form to _____ by _____ .

Name: _____

___ Yes, I would love to help.

___ My first choice of character is _____ .

      My second choice is _____ .

___ I need help with my costume!

___ I will help only if you are absolutely desperate.

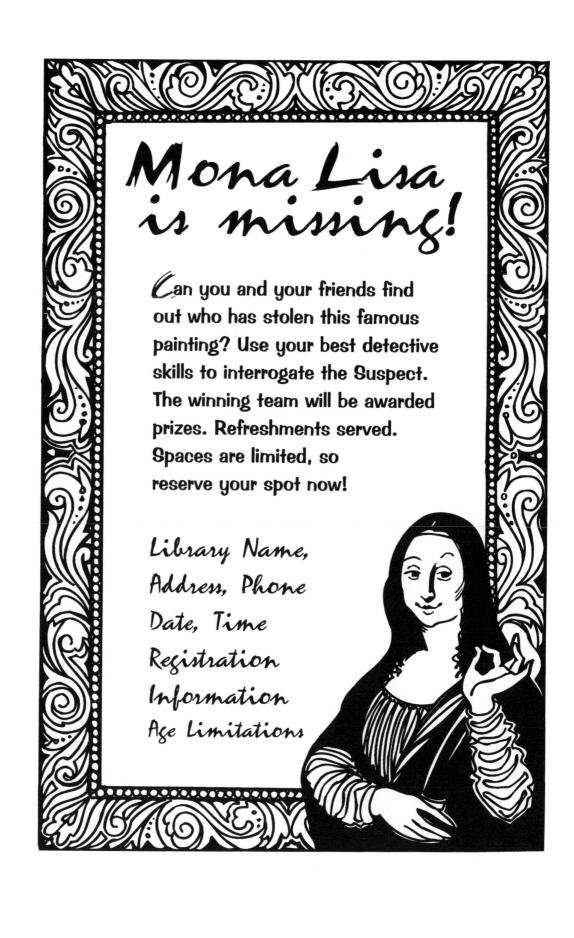

Mona Lisa is missing!

Can you and your friends find out who has stolen this famous painting? Use your best detective skills to interrogate the Suspect. The winning team will be awarded prizes. Refreshments served. Spaces are limited, so reserve your spot now!

Library Name,
Address, Phone
Date, Time
Registration
Information
Age Limitations

Summary

Name	Alibi	Discredit
Professor Sirfaraz	Maria Mantalbano	Madame LaFarge
Madame LaFarge	Dirk Death	Professor Sirfaraz
Dirk Death	Madame LaFarge	Heather Readbetter
Sally Sunshine	No alibi	Dirk Death
Eddie Monette	Julia Chill	Della Bert
Julia Chill	Eddie Monette	Maria Mantalbano
Maria Mantalbano	Professor Sirfaraz	Sally Sunshine/Dirk Death
Heather Readbetter	Della Bert	Julia Chill/Eddie Monette
Della Bert	Heather Readbetter	Sally Sunshine

OTHERS ON THE SCENE WHO ARE NOT SUSPECTS, INCLUDING THE CHIEF INSPECTOR

NAME: CHIEF INSPECTOR

Description of Character: Businesslike and to the point, the chief inspector lives only for his or her work and to get to the crux of every mystery.

PROGRAM SCHEDULE

PART I (15 MINUTES): INFORMATION FOR THE CHIEF INSPECTOR AND THE SUSPECTS

Fifteen minutes before the program begins, all cast members except the chief inspector are in their places. The chief inspector will wait for the participants at the room entrance and assign them to a team.

The chief inspector will introduce the suspects, hand out a worksheet to each team, and explain how it is to be filled out. The chief inspector will also enlighten assistant detectives as to their role throughout the investigation.

The chief inspector will talk about the crime that has occurred: "Leonardo da Vinci's famous painting, the *Mona Lisa*, was visiting libraries across the country in the 'Libraries of _____ [fill in a country] and *Mona*' tour until it was stolen from the _____ Library. You have been called here today to try to solve this crime. This handkerchief was found at the scene of the crime." The chief inspector will then tell the suspects to leave the scene of the crime and to wait for questions in the main room. He or she will then explain the rules to the detectives:

- Each suspect will wear a name tag.
- Only one team is allowed to ask questions of a suspect at a time.
- Assistant detectives should not necessarily believe any of the suspects right away when they are told something. The suspect may be lying. Verify statements with another suspect.

- Assistant detectives have a maximum of 45 minutes to solve the mystery, but the first team to turn in the correct answer wins. The chief inspector will mark down the time that each team finishes.
- After a team has turned in the form, it may return to the meeting room.

PART II (45 minutes): Information for the Chief Inspector and the Suspects

In another room, suspects will stand in their assigned places and answer questions from the assistant detectives. Suspects should be prepared to answer the following questions:

- "Where were you at 5:00 p.m. today when the *Mona Lisa* was discovered missing?"
- "Can anyone confirm your whereabouts at 5:00 p.m. today?"
- "Have you needed extra money for any reason lately? Do you know if any of the other suspects have been in need of money?"
- "Did you see or hear anything suspicious earlier today?"

When assistant detectives have written down the name of the suspect they believe is guilty and have given this worksheet to the chief inspector (who writes the finishing time and order of completion on each form), they may return to the original room and wait for the suspects to return.

PART III (15 minutes): Information for the Chief Inspector and the Suspects

During the third portion of the program, the suspects will return to the original room for the final interrogation. The chief inspector will ask questions of each suspect, one by one. Although there are suggested questions and answers, both the suspects and the chief inspector should be prepared to ad-lib. When the criminal is finally questioned, a dramatic finish is in order.

Final Interrogation Questions

Chief Inspector: Madame LaFarge, do you approve of the "Libraries of _____ ____ [fill in a country] and *Mona*" tour?

Madame LaFarge: I certainly do not! Idiots thought up this idea! It's obvious that it was a mistake, since now our beloved *Mona Lisa* is missing.

Chief Inspector: Perhaps you took the *Mona Lisa* yourself so that she would be put back in the Louvre?

Madame LaFarge: I did no such thing. Professionals are in charge of handling the *Mona Lisa* at each step of her move. She's very fragile. I would not want to damage her.

Chief Inspector: Professor Sirfaraz, are the finances in order for this tour?

Professor Sirfaraz: Well, perhaps not perfectly in order, but I'm taking steps to correct the problems.

Mysterious Mona
Assistant
Detective
Worksheet

Suspects:

Professor Sirfaraz

Madame LaFarge

Dirk Death

Sally Sunshine

Eddie Monette

Julia Chill

Maria Mantalbano

Heather Readbetter

Della Bert

Non-Suspect: Chief Inspector

Ask the Suspects:

Where were you at 5:00 p.m. today when the Mona Lisa was discovered missing?

Can anyone confirm your whereabouts at 5:00 p.m. today?

Have you needed extra money for any reason lately? Do you know if any of the other Suspects have been in need of money?

Did you see or hear anything suspicious earlier today?

Guidelines:

- Each Suspect will wear a nametag.
- Only one team is allowed to ask questions of a Suspect at a time.
- Assistant Detectives should not necessarily believe any of the Suspects right away when they are told something. The Suspect may be lying. Verify statements with another Suspect.
- Assistant Detectives have a maximum of 45 minutes to solve the mystery but the first team to turn in the correct answer wins. The Chief Inspector will mark down the time that each team finishes.
- After a team has turned in the form to the Chief Inspector, it may return to the meeting room.

Mysterious Mona
Who Did It?

Each team fills out this sheet as they solve the mystery.

Team Name: _____

Finishing Time: _____

Criminal: _____

Motive (Why they did it): _____

_____

_____

_____

The team that turns in this form with the correct answer in the fastest time wins the prize!

Chief Inspector: These financial problems are of no small consequence. Perhaps you took the *Mona Lisa* to settle the debts incurred from the tour and to save your managerial reputation?

Professor Sirfaraz: No, I am being open and honest with all of the problems. By the time we finish the tour, everything will work out, I'm sure.

Chief Inspector: Dirk Death, what is the name of your favorite band?

Dirk Death: _____ [insert current band]. They rock!

Chief Inspector: I understand that you would love to follow the band around on its next tour, but that you lack the cash.

Dirk Death: Yeah, I'm broke. It really stinks. I need to go on that tour.

Chief Inspector: Did you take the painting in order to exchange it for some cash?

Dirk Death: No, man. I hadn't thought of that.

Chief Inspector: Sally Sunshine, tell us about your relationship with Dirk.

Sally Sunshine: We used to go out, but then I found out he was a jerk and I broke up with him.

Dirk Death: No way. I'm the one who broke it off with you.

Sally Sunshine: You are such a liar. You know I can't stand you. (Dirk Death and Sally Sunshine should ad-lib until the chief inspector breaks it up.)

Chief Inspector: All right, you two. That's enough for now.

Chief Inspector: Heather Readbetter, is your sight what it used to be?

Heather Readbetter: Unfortunately, I am finding it difficult to see the small print these days.

Chief Inspector: I think you are minimizing the problem. I understand that you are in danger of losing your sight completely and that you need money to have corrective eye surgery.

Heather Readbetter: (breaking down) Yes, it's true. I'm practically blind. I really need to have surgery, but it costs so much, and now with Della Bert threatening me— (Heather stops, appalled that she has said so much.)

Chief Inspector: Yes, Della Bert is threatening to tell the library board about your little scam last week when you stole most of the profit from the last Friends of the Library book sale, isn't she? You've had to bribe her with that money to keep quiet, haven't you? (Heather nods.) Now, despite everything, you still don't have the money to keep from going blind, do you?

Mona Lisa is missing!

Can you and your friends find out who has stolen this famous painting? Use your best detective skills to interrogate the suspects. The winning team will receive a prize. Refreshments served. Spaces are limited, so reserve your spot now for **Mysterious Mona!**

Library Name
Address, Phone
Date, Time
Registration
Information
Age Limitations

Mona Lisa is missing!

Can you and your friends find out who has stolen this famous painting? Use your best detective skills to interrogate the suspects. The winning team will receive a prize. Refreshments served. Spaces are limited, so reserve your spot now for **Mysterious Mona!**

Library Name
Address, Phone
Date, Time
Registration
Information
Age Limitations

Mona Lisa is missing!

Can you and your friends find out who has stolen this famous painting? Use your best detective skills to interrogate the suspects. The winning team will receive a prize. Refreshments served. Spaces are limited, so reserve your spot now for **Mysterious Mona!**

Library Name
Address, Phone
Date, Time
Registration
Information
Age Limitations

Mona Lisa is missing!

Can you and your friends find out who has stolen this famous painting? Use your best detective skills to interrogate the suspects. The winning team will receive a prize. Refreshments served. Spaces are limited, so reserve your spot now for **Mysterious Mona!**

Library Name
Address, Phone
Date, Time
Registration
Information
Age Limitations

Heather Readbetter: No, I don't.

Chief Inspector: Did you steal the *Mona Lisa* so that you could pay for corrective eye surgery?

Heather Readbetter: No. I felt bad enough after I stole the money from the book sale, and I will pay that back somehow, I promise.

Chief Inspector: Julia Chill, what happened with your last cooking show?

Julia Chill: It unfortunately was not the big success I had hoped.

Chief Inspector: It flopped, didn't it? (Julia nods.) What do you hope to do now?

Julia Chill: My dream is to start my own cooking network, but unfortunately, that will cost a lot of money.

Chief Inspector: Money you will get from the sale of the *Mona Lisa*?

 **Professor Sirfaraz**

 **Madame LaFarge**

 Dirk Death

 **Sally Sunshine**

 **Eddie Monette**

 **Julia Chill**

 **Maria Mantalbano**

 **Heather Readbetter**

 **Della Bert**

 **Chief Inspector**

Julia Chill: Of course not! I believe in doing things honestly, unlike some people.

Chief Inspector: Maria Mantalbano, what happened when you went with Eddie to a riverboat casino?

Maria Mantalbano: I lost all of the money for my ticket back to Spain. Now I'm stuck here and my father is going to kill me! Eddie won't help even though this is all his fault!

Chief Inspector: Perhaps you took the *Mona Lisa* so that you could buy a ticket home?

Maria Mantalbano: No. I admire the painting too much to do something like that.

Chief Inspector: Eddie Monette, your gambling debts have led to some unpleasant interactions with loan sharks, is that correct?

Eddie Monette: Yes, unfortunately I've gotten myself into a bit of financial trouble. However, when I get my next big win, I'll be able to pay everything off.

Chief Inspector: It might be easier just to steal the *Mona Lisa*.

Eddie Monette: I'm a gambler, not a thief.

Chief Inspector: Della Bert, lately you've seemed especially obsessed with the *Mona Lisa*. You're driving library staff crazy with all of your questions.

Della Bert: It's their job to answer all of my questions, isn't it? I pay taxes. They're supposed to work for me.

Chief Inspector: Nevertheless, it seems odd that you are so interested in the *Mona Lisa*.

Della Bert: I'm interested in fine art. That's all.

Chief Inspector: Sally Sunshine, let's come back to you. I didn't get a chance to ask you all of my questions. Where were you when the painting was stolen?

Sally Sunshine: I was sitting at the youth services reference desk, doing my work.

Chief Inspector: I understand that you had just had a fight with Dirk Death.

Sally Sunshine: Yes, that is true, but what does that have to do with anything?

Chief Inspector: Haven't you hated Dirk Death since he dumped you?

Sally Sunshine: I told you. I dumped him. (At this point, everyone disagrees verbally. Everyone knows that Dirk dumped Sally.)

Chief Inspector: Apparently, that is only your side of the story. Everyone knows how fragile and temperamental you have been since you and Dirk broke up. You practically hate him.

Sally Sunshine: Yes, I do hate him! He made me look like a fool.

Chief Inspector: Is that why you tried to frame him by putting his cleaning solution by the painting?

Sally Sunshine: I . . . I . . . I didn't do anything like that!

Chief Inspector: Sally, we found your fingerprints on the bottle of cleaning solution that you so kindly made everyone aware of, even though it was not presented as evidence, and we found this (pulls out the *Mona Lisa* painting) in the youth services storage closet! (Sally sinks into her chair, defeated.)

Sally Sunshine: I just wanted him to stop working here. I never wanted to see his face again. I wanted revenge! (She slowly gets angrier as she talks.)

Chief Inspector: It looks like we have our criminal, ladies and gentlemen.

After Sally Sunshine has been revealed as the true criminal, the chief inspector will announce the winning team. While he is giving out prizes, the rest of the cast will stand in a row (or two rows), wait for the chief inspector to join them, and then bow in unison one time. The cast leaves the room or the curtain closes.

OPTIONAL CLUES AND PROPS
- Handkerchief left at the scene of the crime
- Cleaning solution left at the scene of the crime with the word "Death" on it
- A replica of the *Mona Lisa* to be brought out at the end of the program

COSTUMES
Attention should be paid to each suspect's station in life as far as the type of modern-day clothing to wear. Dirk Death could wear a T-shirt with the logo of his favorite band imprinted on it. Julia Chill might wear a chef's hat or apron.

DECORATIONS

As the setting is your library, no special decorations are necessary.

FOOD

It would be fun to go with French cuisine for this script. Serve baguettes, croissants, cheese, fruit, sparkling grape juice, and fine pastries.

GRAPHICS AND PUBLICITY

A reproducible recruitment form, a publicity poster, publicity bookmarks, Assistant Detective Worksheets, and name tags are included in this chapter.

PUBLICITY POSTER

To advertise the event, we placed an empty frame with police tape in the front lobby with our publicity poster, and this generated a lot of interest.

TO-DO LIST

- Recruit suspects, chief inspector, and other non-suspects
- Assign places to stand or sit during Parts I–III

  o Parts I and III: Suspects should sit in a row as follows: Heather Readbetter, Julia Chill, Eddie Monette, Madame LaFarge, Professor Sirfaraz, Sally Sunshine, Maria Mantalbano, Dirk Death, and Della Bert.

  o Part II: Suspects should form a large circle in the interrogating area starting with Madame LaFarge, Professor Sirfaraz, Dirk Death, Sally Sunshine, Heather Readbetter, Julia Chill, Maria Mantalbano, Eddie Monette, Della Bert, and back to Madame LaFarge

- Purchase refreshments
- Purchase prizes
- Take pictures, if desired
- Write thank-you notes and/or buy small gifts

SHORT NEWS RELEASE

Leonardo da Vinci's famous painting, the *Mona Lisa*, has been stolen! The *Mona Lisa* was visiting libraries across the country in the "Libraries of _____ [fill in country] and *Mona*" tour until it was taken from the _____ Library [fill in your library]. Whodunit? Everyone has a motive, from the librarians to the maintenance man. Come to the _____ _____ Library on _____ _____ and interrogate the suspects being held for questioning. It's up to you and your friends to find the criminal and solve the mystery. Form a team or we will assign you to one. Open to students in grades __ to __. Prizes will be awarded to the winning team. Spaces are limited, so sign up now! Call _____ for details.

BOOK TIE-INS

For this script, focus on great artists, including Leonardo da Vinci. You could also put drawing and painting instruction books in your display.

THE CASE OF THE LOONEY LIBRARIAN

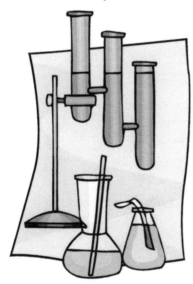

Place:

Date:

Time:

SUSPECTS:

Natalie Neurato

Dolores Desperado

Dr. Jonathan Squash

Madeleine Madde

Matthew Harmony

Jessica the Janitor

Betty Bidder

Susan Sly

NON-SUSPECTS:

Chief Inspector

Janie Madde

Lola Latchkey

SCRIPT COVER

- Name of Mystery: The Case of the Looney Librarian
- Date of Program: _____
- Time of Program: _____
- Location of Program: _____
- Names of Suspects

  Natalie Neurato, teenage patron, played by _____
  Matthew Harmony, teenage patron, played by _____
  Dolores Desperado, teenage patron, played by _____
  Jessica, janitor, played by _____
  Dr. Jonathan Squash, scientist, played by _____
  Betty Bidder, adult patron, played by _____
  Madeleine Madde, adult patron, played by _____
  Susan Sly, administrator, played by _____

- Others on the Scene but Not Suspects, Including the Chief Inspector and the Victim

  Chief Inspector, played by _____
  Lola Latchkey, head of youth services and victim, played by _____
  Janie Madde, daughter of Madeleine Madde, played by _____

PURPOSE

This mystery theater script is intended for entertainment purposes and to entice teens to come to the library.

SETTING

Although written for a public library setting, this mystery could be converted to a school library media center setting.

CRIME

A crime has been committed. Lola Latchkey, head of youth services, was preparing for a program for the young people of her community. Just before the program began, she mysteriously lost the ability to talk in anything but a garbled mumbo-jumbo. Dr. Squash, who is a horticultural researcher for the government, believes he knows what caused Lola to lose her speech. He has been testing out a new type of vegetable serum to increase plant growth and productivity in one-quarter of the time usually required; he has dubbed his secret blend "Summergreen" (as it is similar in smell to wintergreen). Dr. Squash's research is well known in the community. Everyone is also aware that if Summergreen were ever to be ingested by a human, the result would be incomprehensible speech for several hours and possibly for life. Dr. Squash believes someone took the vial of Summergreen that he absentmindedly left on a table and poured it on Lola's jelly doughnut, because

- Everyone knows what a liking Lola has for jelly doughnuts.
- Lola was heard to wonder why the jelly doughnut she was eating right before she became incapacitated tasted minty.

> The first step towards vice is to shroud innocent actions in mystery, and whoever likes to conceal something sooner or later has reason to conceal it.
>
> *Jean Jacques Rousseau*

TIMELINE

- Susan Sly purchased doughnuts for the library staff. Lola took a doughnut and absentmindedly left it outside her office on a counter.
- Lola was trying to prepare for her American Girls program, but then Madeleine Madde and Betty Bidder began to argue with Lola. After giving them both her best diplomatic attitude (for about half an hour), Lola went into her office to avoid them. They remained outside her office.
- Outside the library, Dr. Squash heard Susan Sly talking on her cell phone to someone. Dr. Squash then went to see Lola in her office. They promptly began to argue loudly.
- In the meantime, Natalie Neurato and Matthew Harmony came to talk to Lola. They joined Madeleine and Betty, who were also waiting outside Lola's office.
- Dolores Desperado was working in the youth services area.
- Jessica the Janitor was in the youth services department just doing her job.
- While all of this was going on, Susan Sly quietly poured the Summergreen onto Lola's jelly doughnut. There were no witnesses. Lola walked out of her office to supervise the American Girl program, took a bite of her doughnut, wondered why it tasted minity, and was immediately rendered speechless.

SUSPECT BIOGRAPHIES

Obvious alibis are unnecessary in this script. This will make the mystery more difficult to solve.

NAME: NATALIE NEURATO, TEENAGE PATRON

Description of Character: Natalie is a somewhat unstable teenager. She believes that everyone (with the exception of Lola Latchkey) hates her and that her only friend is found in her mirror, "Mimi." She speaks with Mimi constantly. She had thought that the only person she could talk to was Lola Latchkey. However, that was before Dolores Desperado (another youth services librarian) told her that Lola really didn't like her and always talked among library staff about what an annoying girl Natalie was. When Natalie went to ask Lola if that was true, Lola was having a heated discussion with Dr. Squash and told Natalie to come back later.

Motivation: Natalie might have laced Lola's jelly doughnut with Summergreen to get her for supposedly not liking her and ignoring her.

Alibi: Natalie was in the youth services area with everyone else waiting to speak with Lola. Her mirror, Mimi, accompanied her. Mimi can vouch for her innocence.

Discredit Matthew Harmony: Matthew is an idiot. He can't hear anything anyone tells him because he has lost his hearing (due to years of exposure to really loud music). Lola—who used to tell Natalie everything—told her how bad she felt that she couldn't recommend Matthew as a page because she knew he would refuse to turn off his music. Now he's furious at Lola. Natalie thinks he may have poured Summergreen on the doughnut.

Name: Matthew Harmony, Teenage Patron

Description of Character: Matthew is already hard of hearing because he listens to excessively loud music on his MP3 player all of his waking hours. He is also a teen with a grudge. Since Lola Latchkey is his neighbor, he thought he was a shoe-in for a library job. Ever since Matthew found out that Lola recommended to the library's director that he *not* be given a job as a page, he has been angry and upset with her. Lola talked Matthew into coming to see her before her program to explain her reasons—namely that he wouldn't be able to play his music while he is working because it would disturb patrons as well as his concentration. Lola knew he wouldn't want to give up his music for a mere job.

Motivation: In a vengeful spirit, Matthew may have poured the Summergreen solution onto Lola's doughnut.

Alibi: Matthew was hanging out in youth services listening to his tunes and waiting to speak to Lola.

Discredit Natalie Neurato: Natalie is a weird one. While Matthew was waiting to talk to Lola, he overheard her talking to herself (and her mirror). She was raving about how Lola doesn't love her anymore, how all she wanted was a friend, and now she has no one. He heard her say, "Mimi, how could Lola do this to me?" She was sounding more and more frantic. She seemed capable of doing something crazy.

Name: Dolores Desperado, Part-Time Youth Services Librarian

Description of Character: Dolores is a part-time youth services librarian who likes to run the show and would do just about anything to get Lola's job. Ever since she started working at the library, she has been jealous of Lola.

Motivation: Dolores would like nothing better than to have Lola permanently out of the picture so that she could take Lola's position as head of youth services.

Alibi: Dolores was helping patrons in the youth services area while Lola was working in her office.

Discredit Jessica the Janitor: By Dolores's standards, Jessica is a bit nutty, always talking about positive and negative energy and feng shui. Dolores thinks Jessica committed the crime because earlier in the day she heard Jessica telling her assistant that if Lola didn't move the furniture around in a more harmonious way, she was going to have to do something about it herself.

THE CASE OF THE LOONEY LIBRARIAN

NEEDED!

A team of library staff members and high school teens to help with a Mystery Theatre program for teens. Lola Latchkey, the Youth Services Librarian, has lost the ability to speak coherently. In fact, she sounds downright nutty! Whodunit? We are now looking for volunteers to play the following roles:

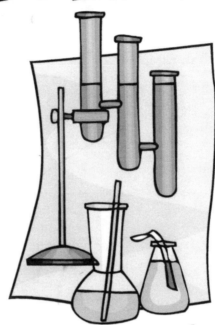

SUSPECTS: Natalie Neurato, Matthew Harmony, Dolores Desperado, Jessica the Janitor, Dr. Jonathan Squash, Betty Bidder, Madeleine Madde, Susan Sly

NON-SUSPECTS: Chief Inspector, Lola Latchkey, Janie Madde

BE A PART OF THE FUN! IF YOU SIGN UP, YOU ARE RESPONSIBLE FOR YOUR OWN COSTUME AND PROPS, BUT I WILL PROVIDE ASSISTANCE AS NECESSARY.

Rehearsal Date:

Performance Date: Time: Place:

Please return form to _____ by _____.

Name: _____

____ Yes, I would love to help.

____ My first choice of character is _____.

      My second choice is _____.

____ I need help with my costume!

____ I will help only if you are absolutely desperate.

THE CASE OF THE LOONEY LIBRARIAN

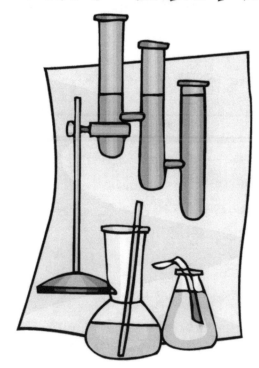

Lola Latchkey, the Youth Services Librarian, has lost the ability to speak coherently. In fact, she sounds downright nutty! Whodunit? Sign up to solve this peculiar mystery. Prizes will be given to the winning team. Refreshments will be served.

LIBRARY NAME, ADDRESS, PHONE, DATE, TIME, REGISTRATION INFORMATION, AGE LIMITATIONS

Name: Jessica, the Janitor

Description of Character: Jessica is a hippie who believes in love and peace for all. It really irks her when people like Lola ignore the principles of feng shui. Jessica has repeatedly explained to Lola that the furniture is placed in a completely unacceptable way and that she is throwing the whole library scheme off balance by messing with the patterns of yin and yang. Jessica's work is suffering as a result. Lola simply laughs at Jessica's concerns. Normally a free and accepting person, Jessica has found herself experiencing negative feelings of rage toward Lola. She also has a bit of a martyr complex in regard to the amount of work that she is expected to do in the library.

Motivation: If Lola were permanently incapacitated, then Jessica would be free to make the entire library a positive, calming zone.

Alibi: Jessica was working very hard cleaning, as usual (no one else in the library ever seems to do any work). She was in the youth services area.

Discredit Dolores Desperado: It's a well-known fact that Dolores Desperado wants Lola's job. How convenient for Dolores that since Lola can't talk anymore, the job will most likely fall to Dolores.

Name: Dr. Jonathan Squash, Scientist

Description of Character: As a horticultural researcher for the government with an experimental new plant serum called Summergreen, Dr. Squash is on the pathway to success. Things aren't going so well with his girlfriend (Lola Latchkey), however. Earlier today, he and Lola had a big fight. Lola said that he spent more time with his plants than he ever did with her and she was feeling neglected. He then got angry because he thought she understood how close he was to perfecting the serum. Both said some mean things and he left without resolving the matter. Dr. Squash came back to talk to Lola before her program to try to clear the air, but unfortunately, Lola was still angry and kept pressing her point.

Motivation: Dr. Squash might have given Lola the serum to shut her up for a while so he could get a word in edgewise.

Alibi: As he is its inventor, Dr. Squash had easy access to the Summergreen serum, but of course he could have given it to Lola at any time if he truly harbored ill feelings toward her. He was in the youth services area with everyone else.

Discredit Susan Sly: When Dr. Squash walked up to the library earlier today, he dropped some papers and bent to pick them up. Susan Sly, the library administrator, was nearby, talking on her cell phone. He couldn't help but overhear her speaking agitatedly to someone. She said, "If I can get rid of her, then you can have her job and you and your kids won't have to move in with me." Dr. Squash didn't know who she was talking to, but her whole plan to get rid of some female sounded very suspicious.

Name: Betty Bidder, Library Patron

Description of Character: Betty does a lot of online shopping. Right now, her laptop is on the fritz, so she went to the library to use their computers. Library policy states that adults can only use the computers in the adult area of the library. When Betty went to adult services to use a computer, she was told that they were all in use. Desperate to use any computer to get onto eBay to bid on a special Hannah Montana doll worth thousands of dollars but going for just hundreds, Betty begged Lola to let her use a computer in the youth services department. Lola explained the library's policy and said she couldn't let Betty on, even though there was a computer available. At that point, Betty started yelling at Lola. Lola tried to calm Betty, but having no luck, she went into her office to put some space between them. Dr. Squash soon joined her, and Betty was forced to wait to speak with Lola to convince her to let her get on a computer.

Motivation: Because she could not get onto a computer, Betty missed her chance on eBay and lost out on the Hannah Montana doll. Betty was very angry. She may have put the serum on Lola's doughnut out of revenge.

Alibi: Betty was waiting outside Lola's office in the youth services area.

Discredit Madeleine Madde: Madeleine might have done it. Betty has never met anyone who is so self-centered. She wouldn't shut up about how she needed to get her daughter into some American Girls doll program. Betty asked Madeleine if she could speak to Lola first, but Madeleine wouldn't let Betty go ahead of her even though there was obviously a severe time restriction for the Hannah Montana doll.

Name: Madeleine Madde, Library Patron

Description of Character: Madeleine's daughter, Janie, just adores the American Girls dolls and books. Janie wanted to attend the library's American Girls party. Unfortunately, Madeleine waited too long to register her daughter and the program filled up. Now Janie won't be able to attend. Madeleine asked Lola, very reasonably, to make an exception and let her daughter attend. After all, her family has lived in this town for generations, and her family pays Lola's salary. She would hate to disappoint Janie.

Motivation: Ticked off at Lola because she wouldn't make an exception and add her daughter to the already-filled-to-capacity American Girls program, Madeleine may have put the serum on Lola's doughnut.

Alibi: Madeleine was outside Lola's office in the youth services area waiting to speak with her.

Discredit Betty Bidder: Betty is a rude woman. She forced her way ahead of Madeleine to wait to talk to Lola Latchkey in her office about letting her get on a youth services computer to go on eBay and buy some kind of doll. She is obviously older than 17 [or whatever your library's age limit is]. Some people just refuse to follow the rules.

Name: Susan Sly, Library Administrator

Description of Character: Although Susan has no problem with the quality of Lola's work, she is now sorry that she hired Lola. Susan's sister, an unemployed single mother whose benefits will soon run out, is in need of a job. If her sister doesn't find a job soon, Susan is worried that she and her kids will be moving in with her.

Motivation: Worried that her sister and family will soon be moving in to her home, Susan purposely spilled Summergreen on Lola's jelly doughnut. Dr. Squash and Lola, engrossed in their conversation just inside Lola's office door, did not notice Susan. Madeleine Madde and Betty Bidder did not notice either, as they were arguing about who was next in line to speak with Lola. Natalie and Matthew were glaring at each other from across the room. Lola came out, took a bite out of her jelly doughnut, and shortly thereafter became incomprehensible.

Alibi: Although Susan is guilty of having put Summergreen on Lola's doughnut, she will state that she was in the youth services department just like everyone else, checking on things.

Discredit Dr. Squash: Susan heard Lola and Dr. Squash arguing very loudly when she was checking on things in the youth services department earlier today. Lola wouldn't let Dr. Squash get a word in edgewise. Perhaps in anger, Dr. Squash decided to shut her up. Who would know more about the effects of Summergreen than the person who invented it? Who would have better access to the serum?

SUMMARY

Name	Discredit
Natalie Neurato	Matthew Harmony
Matthew Harmony	Natalie Neurato
Dolores Desperado	Jessica the Janitor
Jessica the Janitor	Dolores Desperado
Dr. Jonathan Squash	Susan Sly
Betty Bidder	Madeleine Madde
Madeleine Madde	Betty Bidder
Susan Sly	Dr. Jonathan Squash

OTHERS ON THE SCENE WHO ARE NOT SUSPECTS, INCLUDING THE CHIEF INSPECTOR AND THE VICTIM

NAME: CHIEF INSPECTOR

Description of Character: Businesslike and to the point, the chief inspector lives only for his or her work and to get to the crux of every mystery.

NAME: LOLA LATCHKEY, HEAD OF YOUTH SERVICES AND VICTIM

Description of Character: Normally a kind and loving person, Lola reached her wits' end today when she was accosted by patrons (Madeleine Madde, Betty Bidder, Matthew Harmony, and Natalie Neurato) and friends (Dr. Squash) alike. Her co-workers were not helping the situation either, with Jessica the Janitor going on about harmony and balance and Dolores Desperado shooting daggers at her. Only her administrator, Susan Sly, seemed to be showing her support. Today, Susan even purchased Lola's favorite food: jelly doughnuts!

Name: Janie Madde, daughter of Madeleine Madde (Optional Character)

Description of Character: Janie is Madeleine Madde's daughter. She is dressed just like the American Girl doll that she is carrying.

Program Schedule

Part 1 (15 minutes): Information for the Chief Inspector and the Suspects

Fifteen minutes before the program begins, all cast members except the chief inspector are in their places. The chief inspector will wait for the participants at the room entrance and assign them to a team. Library staff should go about doing their jobs. Jessica the Janitor will make a big deal about being the only one who apparently does any work. Susan Sly will look benignly upon the teenagers as they enter and welcome them to the library. As patrons, Madeleine Madde and Betty Bidder will sit in the audience with assistant detectives. Dr. Squash can sit at the back of the room and pretend to be working on paperwork. As teens come to the meeting room, the chief inspector should form them into teams and then call everyone to come and gather round. The chief inspector will ask Lola to come forward. "Lola, would you please say a few words?" Lola will reply in a garbled manner. "This woman, ladies and gentlemen, is the victim of our crime today."

The chief inspector will then read aloud this information about the crime: "A crime has been committed. Lola Latchkey, head of youth services, was preparing for a program for the young people of her community. Just before the program began, she mysteriously lost the ability to talk in anything but a garbled mumbo-jumbo. Dr. Squash, who is a horticultural researcher for the government, believes he knows what caused Lola to lose her speech. He has been testing a new type of vegetable serum to increase plant growth and productivity in one-quarter of the time with a secret blend he has dubbed Summergreen (as it is similar in smell to wintergreen). Dr. Squash's research is well known in the community. Everyone is also aware that if Summergreen were ever to be ingested by a human, the result would be incomprehensible speech for several hours and possibly for life. Dr. Squash believes that someone took the vial of Summergreen he absentmindedly left on a table and poured it on Lola's jelly doughnut. Here is the infamous jelly doughnut—notice the bite taken out of it. We also know this information:

- Everyone knows what a liking Lola has for jelly doughnuts.
- Lola was heard to wonder why the jelly doughnut she had gotten from the staff room right before she became incapacitated tasted minty.

After presenting the evidence, the chief inspector will introduce the suspects. The suspects are Natalie Neurato, Matthew Harmony, Dolores Desperado, Jessica the Janitor, Dr. Jonathan Squash, Susan Sly, Madeleine Madde, and Betty Bidder. Suspects should act somewhat surprised that they are being singled out, but then file to the front of the room to sit on chairs.

The chief inspector will then send the suspects to the main room. Suspects should wait in their assigned places for the assistant detectives to interrogate them. After suspects leave, the chief inspector will give teams their worksheets and pencils. He or she will explain the rules:

- Each suspect will wear a name tag.
- Only one team is allowed to ask questions of a suspect at a time.
- Assistant detectives should not necessarily believe any of the suspects right away when they are told something. The suspect may be lying. Verify statements with another suspect.
- When a team believes it knows who the murderer is, it will turn in the "Who Did It?" worksheet to the chief inspector.
- Assistant detectives have a maximum of 45 minutes to solve the mystery, but the first team to turn in the correct answer wins. The chief inspector will mark down the time that each team finishes.
- After a team has turned in the form to the chief inspector, it may return to the meeting room.

Part II (45 minutes): Information for the Chief Inspector and the Suspects

In another room, suspects will stand in their assigned places and answer questions from the assistant detectives. Suspects should be prepared to answer the following questions:

- "Where were you earlier today when the Summergreen serum was poured onto Lola's jelly doughnut?"
- "Can anyone confirm your whereabouts?"
- "Did you have any reason to dislike Lola?"
- "Do you think any of the other suspects had a reason to perform a criminal act against Lola? Why?"

When assistant detectives have written down the name of the suspect they believe is guilty and have given their worksheet to the chief inspector (who writes down the finishing time and order of completion on each form), they may return to the original room and wait for the suspects to return.

Part III (15 minutes): Information for the Chief Inspector and the Suspects

During the third portion of the program, the suspects will return to the original room for the final interrogation. The chief inspector will ask questions of each suspect one by one. Although there are suggested questions and answers, both the suspects and the chief inspector should be prepared to ad-lib. When the criminal is questioned (usually last), a dramatic finish is in order. After each person states his or her relationship with Lola, Lola will try to communicate her true feelings through gestures, and so on.

Final Interrogation Questions

Chief Inspector: Natalie Neurato, I am under the impression that you have very few friends. Is this true?

Natalie Neurato: Yes, but though everyone may desert me, I will still have my mirror, Mimi.

Chief Inspector: Until tonight, you believed that Lola Latchkey was your friend, correct?

Natalie Neurato: Yes.

Chief Inspector: What happened to make you think she had deserted you?

Natalie Neurato: Dolores Desperado told me that Lola said I was annoying.

Chief Inspector: Perhaps you gave Lola the Summergreen to get back at her?

Natalie Neurato: No. Even if she hates me, I would never hurt her.

Chief Inspector: Matthew Harmony, is it true that you wished to get a job here at the library and that you thought Lola would recommend you?

Matthew Harmony: What?

Chief Inspector: (more loudly) Is it true that you wished to get a job here at the library and that you thought Lola would recommend you?

Matthew Harmony: You don't need to yell. Yeah, I thought she would recommend me, but she didn't.

Chief Inspector: Were you angry enough when you heard she told the administrator not to hire you that you poured Summergreen on her jelly doughnut?

Matthew Harmony: I might have been angry, but I would never do anything like that.

Chief Inspector: Dolores Desperado, you work in youth services with Lola, correct?

Dolores Desperado: Yes.

Chief Inspector: It's no secret that you have wanted Lola's job from the start. Perhaps you laced her doughnut with Summergreen to get her position?

Dolores Desperado: It's true that I deserve to be head of the department, but I wouldn't stoop to such levels for a mere job.

THE CASE OF THE LOONEY LIBRARIAN
Who Did It?

Each team fills out this sheet as they solve the mystery.

Team Name: _____

Finishing Time: _____

Criminal: _____

Motive (Why they did it): _____

_____

_____

_____

The team that turns in this form with the correct answer in the fastest time wins the prize!

THE CASE OF THE LOONEY LIBRARIAN
Assistant Detective Worksheet

SUSPECTS:

Natalie Neurato

Matthew Harmony

Dolores Desperado

Jessica the Janitor

Dr. Jonathan Squash

Betty Bidder

Madeleine Madde

Susan Sly

NON-SUSPECTS:

Chief Inspector

Lola Latchkey

Janie Madde (child)

ASK THE SUSPECTS:

? Where were you earlier today when the Summergreen serum was poured onto Lola's jelly donut?

? Can anyone confirm your whereabouts?

? Did you have any reason to dislike Lola?

? Do you think any of the other suspects had a reason to perform a criminal act against Lola and why?

GUIDELINES:

- Each Suspect will wear a nametag.
- Only one team is allowed to ask questions of a Suspect at a time.
- Assistant Detectives should not necessarily believe any of the Suspects right away when they are told something. The Suspect may be lying. Verify statements with another Suspect.
- Assistant Detectives have a maximum of 45 minutes to solve the mystery but the first team to turn in the correct answer wins.

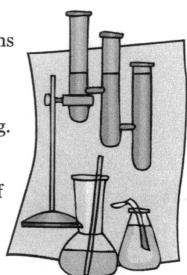

Chief Inspector: Jessica, what is your idea of a good work environment?

Jessica the Janitor: It occurs when all of the principles of feng shui are observed.

Chief Inspector: Have they been observed?

Jessica the Janitor: Unfortunately, one person was holding back everyone in this building from experiencing balance and harmony.

Chief Inspector: And that was . . .

Jessica the Janitor: Lola.

Chief Inspector: It obviously bothers you to work in such an environment. Perhaps you put the Summergreen on Lola's doughnut to get her out of the library?

Jessica the Janitor: Any sort of violent act would go against my principles. That suggestion is absurd.

Chief Inspector: Dr. Jonathan Squash, tell us the topic of your argument with Lola earlier tonight.

Dr. Squash: We were discussing some issues. She said I spend too much time with my plants. I was trying to explain that I'm very close to perfecting my serum and just need a little more time.

Chief Inspector: You were heard to say that she wouldn't listen to you and that she just kept talking and talking. Perhaps you gave her the serum to shut her up?

Dr. Squash: Of course not. We may have been fighting, but I love Lola and would never do anything to hurt her.

Chief Inspector: Betty, please tell us why you wanted to use a computer.

Betty Bidder: I needed to get onto eBay to bid on a very special Hannah Montana doll for my collection.

Chief Inspector: And this Hannah Montana doll is worth a lot of money?

Betty Bidder: Thousands!—but I could have gotten it for mere hundreds.

Chief Inspector: When Lola wouldn't let you on the children's computers, perhaps you were angry enough to do something nasty?

Betty Bidder: Yes, I was angry, but I'm not a violent person by nature.

Chief Inspector: Madeleine, why were you in the youth services department today?

Madeleine Madde: I was trying to register my daughter for the American Girls party, but she (pointing to Lola) wouldn't let me.

THE CASE OF THE LOONEY LIBRARIAN

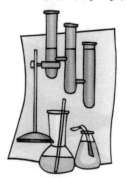

Lola Latchkey, the Youth Services Librarian, has lost the ability to speak coherently. In fact, she sounds downright nutty! Whodunit? Sign up to solve this peculiar mystery. Prizes will be given to the winning team. Refreshments will be served.

LIBRARY NAME, ADDRESS, PHONE, DATE, TIME, REGISTRATION INFORMATION, AGE LIMITATIONS

THE CASE OF THE LOONEY LIBRARIAN

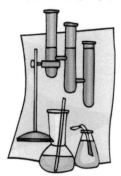

Lola Latchkey, the Youth Services Librarian, has lost the ability to speak coherently. In fact, she sounds downright nutty! Whodunit? Sign up to solve this peculiar mystery. Prizes will be given to the winning team. Refreshments will be served.

LIBRARY NAME, ADDRESS, PHONE, DATE, TIME, REGISTRATION INFORMATION, AGE LIMITATIONS

THE CASE OF THE LOONEY LIBRARIAN

Lola Latchkey, the Youth Services Librarian, has lost the ability to speak coherently. In fact, she sounds downright nutty! Whodunit? Sign up to solve this peculiar mystery. Prizes will be given to the winning team. Refreshments will be served.

LIBRARY NAME, ADDRESS, PHONE, DATE, TIME, REGISTRATION INFORMATION, AGE LIMITATIONS

THE CASE OF THE LOONEY LIBRARIAN

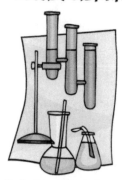

Lola Latchkey, the Youth Services Librarian, has lost the ability to speak coherently. In fact, she sounds downright nutty! Whodunit? Sign up to solve this peculiar mystery. Prizes will be given to the winning team. Refreshments will be served.

LIBRARY NAME, ADDRESS, PHONE, DATE, TIME, REGISTRATION INFORMATION, AGE LIMITATIONS

Chief Inspector: How did you feel about that?

Madeleine Madde: I couldn't believe it, of course. My husband and I always give our daughter, little Janie, everything she wants. I don't know how to tell her that she can't attend the party. We've never disappointed her before. That librarian was just being pigheaded.

Chief Inspector: Were you mad enough at Lola to make her lose her speech?

Madeleine Madde: Mad, but not insane. I have no wish to go to jail.

Chief Inspector: Susan Sly, tell us about your sister.

Susan Sly: My sister has fallen on some hard times. She is out of a job and her benefits will run out soon.

Chief Inspector: Does Lola do a good job at the library?

Susan Sly: Her work is fine.

 **CHIEF INSPECTOR**

 **LOLA LATCHKEY**

 **NATALIE NEURATO**

 **MATTHEW HARMONY**

 **DOLORES DESPERADO**

 **JESSICA THE JANITOR**

 **DR. JONATHAN SQUASH**

 **BETTY BIDDER**

 **MADELEINE MADDE**

 **SUSAN SLY**

 **JANIE MADDE**

Chief Inspector: It seems odd, then, for you to want to offer Lola's job to your sister, when Lola does a satisfactory job. Unless, of course, you knew that Lola would soon be unable to communicate with her staff and library patrons.

Susan Sly: What are you suggesting?

Chief Inspector: I'm suggesting that in the fear that your sister and her children would be moving in with you if she did not find a job soon, you were willing to disable Lola and replace her with your sister.

Susan Sly: That is ridiculous! I'd never do anything like that to Lola!

Chief Inspector: Then how do you explain this? (The chief inspector reaches behind a piece of furniture and pulls out a small vial with the word "Summergreen" on it. Susan gasps.) I found this under the cushion of a chair and dusted it for fingerprints.

It obviously had Dr. Squash's fingerprints on it, but yours were also there. (Susan Sly breaks down into hysterics, describing how she doesn't like kids and didn't want her happy home invaded.)

Lola Latchkey: (suddenly regaining her voice) How could you? I've always been a good employee! (With shock and happy surprise, she states that she's cured, and so on.)

The chief inspector thanks the assembled detectives and takes Susan Sly away.

OPTIONAL CLUES AND PROPS
- Jelly doughnut with a bite taken out of it as evidence
- MP3 player to play loudly for Matthew Harmony
- Handheld/compact mirror for Natalie Neurato
- Plant vial filled with "Summergreen." (Tint liquid with green food coloring.) Dr. Squash might also carry another larger vial of Summergreen with him.
- A laptop computer for Betty Bidder (optional)
- An 18-inch doll for Madeleine Madde
- A broom or mop for Jessica the Janitor

COSTUMES
Since this is a modern-day script, you will not need to create any elaborate costumes. Dr. Squash could wear a white lab coat. Library staff should be dressed professionally. Teen patrons should be dressed in age-appropriate clothing.

DECORATIONS

There is no need for special decorations in this script.

FOOD

Serve jelly doughnuts and soft drinks.

GRAPHICS AND PUBLICITY

A reproducible recruitment form, a publicity poster, publicity bookmarks, Assistant Detective Worksheets, and name tags are included in this chapter.

TO-DO LIST

- Recruit suspects, chief inspector, and other non-suspects
- Assign places to stand or sit during Parts I–III
  - Parts I and III: Suspects should sit in a row as follows: Dr. Jonathan Squash, Susan Sly, Natalie Neurato, Dolores Desperado, Matthew Harmony, Jessica the Janitor, Betty Bidder, and Madeleine Madde.
  - Part II: Suspects should form a large circle, starting with Natalie Neurato, Matthew Harmony, Madeleine Madde, Betty Bidder, Susan Sly, Dr. Jonathan Squash, Jessica the Janitor, Dolores Desperado, and back to Natalie Neurato.
- Purchase refreshments
- Purchase prizes
- Take pictures, if desired
- Write thank-you notes and/or buy small gifts

BOOK TIE-INS

In addition to displaying general mystery books, you could also create a display called "The Suspects Recommend . . ." Pull books that each of the suspects might select to recommend to your teen readers. Make a bookmark that says, "This book was recommended by _____" [fill in appropriate suspect's name]. Some examples of subject areas might include books on feng shui from Jessica the Janitor, titles on computer use and eBay from Betty Bidder, books on plants from Dr. Jonathan Squash, and books on popular bands from Matthew Harmony.

Part 3

GENERAL MYSTERY SCRIPTS

7 Medieval Murder Mystery

Place:

Time:

Date:

Suspects:

Lord William

Harrold, Tutor

Florinda, Cook

Gwyneth, Nursery Maid

Mad Maggie, Alchemist/Wizard

Lady Alayne

Rosalynde, Musician

Alyce, Scullery Maid

Elwyn, Jester

Non-Suspects:

Brother Bertram, Chief Inspector

Physician

Guards #1, 2

SCRIPT COVER

- Name of Mystery: Medieval Murder Mystery
- Date of Program: _____
- Time of Program: _____
- Location of Program: _____
- Names of Suspects

    Lord William, played by _____
    Lady Alayne, played by _____
    Harrold the Tutor, played by _____
    Elwyn the Jester, played by _____
    Mad Maggie the Alchemist/Wizard, played by _____
    Rosalynde the Musician, played by _____
    Florinda the Cook, played by _____
    Alyce the Scullery Maid, played by _____
    Gwyneth the Nursemaid, played by _____

- Others on the Scene but Not Suspects, Including the Chief Inspector and the Victim

    Brother Bertram, chief inspector, played by _____
    Gabriella the Traveling Bard, victim, played by _____
    Physician, played by _____
    Guard #1 (optional), played by _____
    Guard #2 (optional), played by _____

PURPOSE

Our purpose in choosing *Medieval Murder Mystery* is general entertainment. It would also be a good introduction to a Middle Ages unit in a school.

SETTING

The setting for the script is England in the Middle Ages. We will use a generic setting and invent the holdings of two historical unknowns, Lord William and Lady Alayne. These nobles live in a small castle in the English countryside during the High Middle Ages.

CRIME

Gabriella is a bard who grew up around the castle but has been away for several years. Now she is famous, and her return to the castle has precipitated a dinner in her honor. There is a somewhat uneasy party atmosphere, and things are about to get ugly. Gabriella's wine has been poisoned and she will soon be dead.

TIMELINE

- Gabriella found out earlier that Lord William is practically penniless and she has been blackmailing him. Earlier today, Lord William gave Gabriella his wife's heirloom brooch as a bribe to keep her quiet. He also decided to hold a party in Gabriella's honor to try to appease her and stop her threats.
- Gwyneth sneaked into Mad Maggie's laboratory earlier today, stole a vial of red-colored poison, and put a few drops of it in Gabriella's cup at 6:30 p.m. The amount given took about one-half hour to take effect.
- While performing at 7:00 p.m., during the beginning of the program, Gabriella collapsed and died.

SUSPECT BIOGRAPHIES

> If you poison us, do we not die?
> *William Shakespeare*

Name: Lord William, Lord of the Castle

Description of Character: Since his father died three years ago, Lord William has managed to spend most of the money he inherited, either through gambling or high living. The paltry taxes he collects from his fiefdom are simply not supporting him in the manner to which he has become accustomed. Desperate for any means to make more money, he has grasped onto a get-rich-quick scheme through scientific experiments that will turn base metals into gold. He has hired an "expert," Mad Maggie the Alchemist, to carry out this endeavor. In the meantime, however, Gabriella the Traveling Bard has somehow found out that Lord William's finances are not what they should be. She is blackmailing him for the family jewels to keep her knowledge secret. Earlier today, Lord William gave Gabriella his wife's heirloom brooch to try to keep her quiet. If any of the other lords find out that he is practically penniless, Lord William's reputation and family prospects will be ruined. Certainly, he also knows that his wife would never forgive him. Lord William hopes Gabriella will stop these threats if he throws this banquet in her honor.

Motivation: Lord William could have poisoned Gabriella to stop her efforts to blackmail him.

Alibi: Lord William was consulting with Mad Maggie in his library about the progress of her experiments to turn base metals into gold.

Discuss Mad Maggie: Lord William had high hopes when he first hired Mad Maggie that she would be able to turn base metals into gold, but now he's just frustrated. Mad Maggie doesn't seem to be trying very hard to accomplish the task. She always just seems to be chanting out loud to herself every time Lord William walks past her laboratory. In addition, she never stops asking for more money!

Discredit Alyce: Alyce had reason to hate Gabriella. Lord William noticed that Gabriella treated Alyce a little more cruelly than the rest of the servants, calling her a "stupid, useless lackwit" and other names. While waiting for his horse to be saddled the other day, Lord William heard Alyce tell Elwyn that she'd like to "see the hussy (Gabriella) dead."

NAME: LADY ALAYNE, LADY OF THE CASTLE

Description of Character: The affection Lady Alayne felt for Gabriella as a young child has turned to deep distrust. Several semi-valuable items such as old manuscripts and small statues have gone missing from the castle lately. Last week Lady Alayne saw Gabriella slip out of the library with a package under her arm. Before she could question Gabriella, a servant distracted Lady Alayne with a question. Right before the performance this evening, Lady Alayne was shocked to see her own heirloom brooch on Gabriella's dress.

Motivation: Lady Alayne could have poisoned Gabriella because she was stealing family jewels and other valuables.

Alibi: Lady Alayne was conferring with Rosalynde in the drawing room. Rosalynde was sharing her fears that Gabriella might be stealing from the household.

Discuss Rosalynde: Rosalynde was whining to Lady Alayne earlier about Gabriella. She droned on and on about how Gabriella was trying to steal her job and worm her way into the castle.

Discredit Elwyn: When Gabriella came to perform, Elwyn changed from a happy-go-lucky jester into a sour young man. Lady Alayne may have to have William terminate him if he doesn't stop with this "family honor" business. For pity's sake—he's only a common jester. He's become obsessed with getting his family's ring back from Gabriella. Apparently, her great-grandfather won it from his great-grandfather in a game of chance. He has become useless as a jester—unless moroseness is the new trend in jesters.

NAME: HARROLD, TUTOR OF LORD WILLIAM AND LADY ALAYNE'S CHILDREN

Description of Character: Although Harrold is recognized at the castle as a scholar, on the Continent he is infamous for his less savory activities. He cheated a certain Lord Prefontaine out of his inheritance while supposedly tutoring that lord's children last year in France. This made it necessary for Harrold to find a quiet, cushy place to lay low for a time, even if it meant teaching more idiot kids. He thought he'd found the perfect spot in Lord William's castle—that is, until Gabriella showed up. Gabriella also performed at Lord Prefontaine's castle and discovered Harrold's scam. Now Gabriella is threatening to tell Lord William about Harrold's past if he doesn't give her half of what he "earned" in France.

Motivation: Harrold has no wish to leave his hideaway just yet and even less desire to split his take with Gabriella. Although there is apparently no money to be earned through Lord William, Harrold has been pocketing several valuable objects such as manuscripts and small statues during his stay. He might have poisoned Gabriella to keep his secret and his money safe.

Alibi: At the time of the poisoning, Harrold was commiserating with Florinda in the kitchen about Gabriella's threats to report Florinda to Lord William.

Discuss Florinda: Harrold and Florinda are very close. Harrold thinks fondly of her as the mother he never had. He hates to bring it up, but Gabriella caught Florinda stealing the petty cash from market day. Although it wasn't a lot of money, Florinda had been using it to keep her brother's family from starving. Gabriella was making a big deal about Florinda's dishonesty. She told Florinda that she planned to tell Lord William about it after her performance this evening.

Discredit Gwyneth: Gwyneth was hopping mad when she heard that Lord William and Lady Alayne were bringing Gabriella here. Gabriella stole Gwyneth's one true love, and she has not been the same since.

Name: Elwyn the Jester

Description of Character: Elwyn and Gabriella grew up together near the castle but they could hardly be called friends. Their families have feuded for generations over an ancient ring that Elwyn's great-grandfather brought back from the Holy Land. It is said that the ring has the power to bless the holder's family. According to Elwyn, in an unfair game of chance, his great-grandfather lost the ring to Gabriella's great-grandfather. Elwyn says it is common knowledge that Gabriella's great-grandfather got his great-grandfather intoxicated in order to obtain the ring. Gabriella's family, however, always insisted that the ring was won fair and square. Gabriella has been flaunting the ring for the entire time she has been back and Elwyn has become more and more angry. His family honor is at stake!

Motivation: Elwyn's family has had a stroke of bad luck since the ring was lost and he may have poisoned Gabriella to avenge his family and get the ring back to its rightful owners.

Alibi: Elwyn was telling Alyce how he planned to get his family ring back when they talked in the stables.

Discuss Alyce: Alyce has been losing her mind lately with all of the mean treatment she has received from Gabriella. Elwyn guesses she has nothing to worry about anymore now that Gabriella's dead.

Discredit Florinda: The castle gossip on Florinda is that she has been stealing the extra coins from the market money to feed her sick brother's eight kids. Gabriella found out and threatened to tell Lord William right after the performance this evening.

Name: Mad Maggie, Alchemist

Description of Character: Long before Mad Maggie became an employee of Lord William, she was obsessed with the tales of Merlin and wished to do some magic of her own. She convinced Lord William that, given time and money for experimentation, she would be able to turn base metals into gold. Since she's been at the castle, instead of practicing alchemy, Mad Maggie has instead tried to learn some real magic. While poring over her magic books and trying some spells last night, Mad Maggie heard a low chuckle and discovered that Gabriella had been spying on her. Clever Gabriella figured out that Mad Maggie had no intention or ability to turn metals into gold and intimated that Lord William might be interested in her real research.

Motivation: Mad Maggie might have poisoned Gabriella to keep her from telling Lord William about her misuse of his money. She also has easy access to poison as it is in her laboratory. Of course, with the laboratory always unlocked, everyone else does as well.

Alibi: Mad Maggie was trying to convince Lord William in his library that she was near a breakthrough with her experiments and that she needed more money.

Discuss Lord William: A few days ago, Mad Maggie overheard Lord William and Gabriella discussing his financial problems. Gabriella was blackmailing Lord William, demanding the family jewels to keep her quiet.

Discredit Harrold: Mad Maggie has noticed some oddities about Harrold. He's no tutor. She could teach those kids more in one day than he does in a month. Mad Maggie has heard rumors about some French lord trying to kill him, but she has no details. It's just a hunch, but she has a feeling that he may be responsible for some of the missing items around the castle.

Discredit Gwyneth: It's no secret that Gabriella stole Gwyneth's first love. Mad Maggie thinks Gwyneth poisoned Gabriella out of her lunatic jealousy and a sense of revenge.

Name: Rosalynde, Castle Musician

Description of Character: Rosalynde and Gabriella were trained in music at the same time. Unfortunately, Gabriella was always the favorite with the teachers. Rosalynde tried her best not to be envious, and was relieved when Gabriella left to travel abroad. Rosalynde became the castle musician. Then Gabriella came back and all Rosalynde has heard since then is "Gabriella this," and "Gabriella that." Rosalynde has not been asked to perform even once by Lord William and Lady Alayne since Gabriella's return. Gabriella even told Rosalynde that she would like to move back to the castle and that she wants Rosalynde's position. Rosalynde really isn't up to Gabriella's standard as a musician. If Gabriella takes Rosalynde's job, Rosalynde will be destitute and out sleeping with the pigs.

Motivation: Fearing for her job and livelihood, Rosalynde may have poisoned Gabriella.

Alibi: Rosalynde was conferring with Lady Alayne in the drawing room about her current lack of status in the castle.

Discuss Lady Alayne: Lady Alayne told Rosalynde that she thought Gabriella was stealing valuable items from the castle such as manuscripts and small statues.

Discredit Lord William: After Lady Alayne first told Rosalynde that she thought Gabriella was stealing jewels and other valuable items such as manuscripts from the castle, Rosalynde started to notice Gabriella's frequent visits to Lord William's library. Earlier this week, Rosalynde overheard Gabriella telling Lord William that if he didn't give her the brooch, she was going to make everything public. Rosalynde doesn't know what she was referring to, but she thinks Lord William is hiding something.

Place:

Time:

Date:

Suspects:

Lord William

Harrold, Tutor

Florinda, Cook

Gwyneth, Nursery Maid

Mad Maggie, Alchemist/Wizard

Lady Alayne

Rosalynde, Musician

Alyce, Scullery Maid

Elwyn, Jester

Non-Suspects:

Brother Bertram, Chief Inspector

Physician

Guards #1, 2

HEAR YE! HEAR YE!

Library staff members and high school students are needed to assist with a Mystery Theatre program for teens. Someone has poisoned Gabriella, the traveling bard! Whodunit? We are now looking for volunteers to play the following roles:

SUSPECTS: Lord William, Lady Alayne, Harrold (Tutor), Rosalynde (Musician) Florinda (Cook), Alyce (Scullery Maid), Gwyneth (Nursery Maid), Mad Maggie (Alchemist/Wizard), Elwyn (Jester)

NON-SUSPECTS: Brother Bertram (Chief Inspector), Physician, Guards #1, 2

Be a part of the fun! If you sign up, you are responsible for your own costume and props, but I will provide assistance if necessary.

Rehearsal Date:

Performance Date: Time: Place:

Please return form to _____ by _____.

Name: _____

____ Yes, I would love to help.

____ My first choice of character is _____. My second choice is _____.

____ I need help with my costume!

____ I will help only if you are absolutely desperate.

Name: Florinda the Cook

Description of Character: Florinda is the head cook in the castle and she takes care of the food marketing. Her only living brother, Freddy, is deathly ill and his family is starving. Florinda's wages barely feed her own family, let alone her brother's family of eight. She has resorted to the only solution she can think of—to "borrow" the meager amount of money left from the weekly shopping. The master will never miss it, and Freddy has a measure of peace knowing that his poor babies are not starving or in the poorhouse. Last week, Gabriella and Harrold saw Florinda furtively putting the leftover shopping money into her pocket and she hasn't had a moment of peace since. Harrold said that he won't tell, and Florinda believes him. He's told her about his own problems. However, Gabriella told Florinda that she planned to inform Lord William about the missing money after her performance this evening. Florinda doesn't know why Gabriella hates her, but she suspects that it is because she tried to defend Alyce from Gabriella's insults. Florinda wishes she'd thought of poisoning Gabriella's food, but she didn't. Anyway, Gabriella got exactly what she deserved.

Motivation: Florinda could have poisoned Gabriella to keep her extra income and thus ensure her family's survival.

Alibi: Florinda was talking with Harrold in the kitchen about his problems with Gabriella and Gabriella's threat to inform Lord William about the missing market money.

Discuss Harrold: Florinda isn't one to tell tales, but Harrold has told her that he's not really a scholar. Gabriella knew this. She was going to inform Lord William if Harrold didn't pay her a lot of money.

Discredit Rosalynde: Rosalynde has been coming into the kitchen a lot lately. Usually she's too snotty to bother with the likes of kitchen staff, but since Gabriella's been here, she's probably out of a job.

Name: Alyce, Scullery Maid

Description of Character: Gabriella has created a ton of extra work for Alyce since she arrived at the castle. For some reason, she has singled Alyce out as her victim, publicly humiliating her, calling her "stupid," and tripping her when she was bringing in trays. More than once Gabriella has gotten Alyce in trouble with the mistress for purely vindictive reasons. Alyce feels hopeless and angry at the same time. She told Elwyn that she'd like to "see the hussy dead."

Motivation: Alyce may have poisoned Gabriella to get back at her for her insults and humiliation.

Alibi: Alyce was talking with Elwyn in the stables about what she would like to do to Gabriella for humiliating her.

Discuss Elwyn: All Elwyn ever talks about is his silly ring. He never defends Alyce when Gabriella is tormenting her. He just goes on about the family honor and how he's going to get that ring back somehow. For a jester, he hasn't been much fun lately.

Discredit Lady Alayne: When Alyce was serving the supper earlier this evening, she heard Lady Alayne tell Lord William that she thought Gabriella was stealing precious household items like the library manuscripts. When Lady Alayne saw Gabriella wearing her own brooch at the very beginning of the evening, she was completely outraged.

NAME: GWYNETH, NURSEMAID TO LORD WILLIAM AND LADY ALAYNE'S CHILDREN

Description of Character: Gwyneth was not happy when she heard Gabriella was coming back to the castle. Gwyneth and Gabriella grew up together and were more or less friendly. Gwyneth was so happy then, happy and in love with Launce the Goatherd. She thought nothing and no one would ever interfere with their love. Then Gabriella stole Launce from Gwyneth, and made him run away with her across the sea to heathen lands. The last Gwyneth heard, Launce had died from some foreign disease. She will never forgive Gabriella for what she did to her.

Motivation: Gwyneth has never forgiven Gabriella for stealing her one true love, Launce.

Alibi: Gwyneth has no alibi. She will tell the assistant detectives that she was in the nursery.

Discredit Mad Maggie: Mad Maggie is a witch with her spells. She put a spell on Lord William, that's for sure. Last night Gwyneth was walking past her door and Mad Maggie was muttering to herself. At first Gwyneth thought it was one of Mad Maggie's spells, but then she heard Mad Maggie say she was going to have to cast a spell to shut up Gabriella forever. Mad Maggie had easy access to the poisons right there in her laboratory.

SUMMARY

Name	Alibi	Discuss	Discredit
Lord William	Mad Maggie	Mad Maggie	Alyce
Lady Alayne	Rosalynde	Rosalynde	Elwyn
Harrold	Florinda	Florinda	Gwyneth
Elwyn	Alyce	Alyce	Florinda
Mad Maggie	Lord William	Lord William	Harrold/Gwyneth
Rosalynde	Lady Alayne	Lady Alayne	Lord William
Florinda	Harrold	Harrold	Rosalynde
Alyce	Elwyn	Elwyn	Lady Alayne
Gwyneth	None	No one	Mad Maggie

OTHERS ON THE SCENE WHO ARE NOT SUSPECTS, INCLUDING THE CHIEF INSPECTOR AND THE VICTIM

NAME: GABRIELLA, THE TRAVELING BARD AND VICTIM

Description of Character: Gabriella is universally disliked and it is unsurprising that she is killed by poison. The death scene occurs while she is in the process of singing a medieval tune (something like "Greensleeves"). Alternatively, she could recite a narrative.

Name: Brother Bertram, Chief Inspector

Description of Character: As the host for the evening, Brother Bertram waits with the physician and the assistant detectives outside of the room before everyone is allowed in. During the program, he provides information, acts as timekeeper, collects assistant detectives' worksheets, and conducts the final interrogation in Part III.

Name: Physician

Description: The physician's role is to verify that the victim, Gabriella, is indeed dead and that she was poisoned precisely one-half hour prior to her death. At the very end, if you choose to have Gwyneth swallow the entire vial of poison, the physician will explain that she died instantly because she swallowed the whole bottle instead of just a few drops.

Name: Guards (optional)

Description: If guards are used, their role is to guard the doors with Brother Bertram at the beginning of the evening, protect Lord William throughout the program, and escort the criminal out at the end of the evening or chase after her.

PROGRAM SCHEDULE

Part I (15 minutes): Information for the Chief Inspector and the Suspects

Brother Bertram will act as the chief inspector. He will wait for the participants at the room entrance and assign them to a team. The chief inspector will also hand out a worksheet to each team and explain how it is to be filled out.

Lord William and Lady Alayne are presiding at a long banquet table. Other nobility sits at the table, while the serving staff waits on the table.

At the beginning of the program, Lord William will thank everyone for coming and then introduce Gabriella. She will come up to the stage and start to sing a medieval-sounding song or recite something from the period. Before very long, however, it becomes obvious that Gabriella is in pain. She will clutch her throat and emit a heart-wrenching scream before collapsing on the floor, dead. The cast will react verbally and/or physically to this occurrence. Brother Bertram will tell everyone to calm down and he will call for a physician. When the physician comes, he or she will declare that Gabriella is dead and has been poisoned with a few drops of poison in her wine glass. He/she states that Gabriella was poisoned exactly a half-hour ago, as the amount and type of poison administered takes effect in precisely one-half hour.

Brother Bertram will introduce the suspects to the assistant detectives. He will then tell them to leave the scene of the crime and to wait for questions in the main room. Suspects are not to leave the castle. Each suspect will be positioned so that he or she will have some interaction—usually animated, heated discussion—during this portion of the program. Brother Bertram will explain the rules to the assistant detectives:

- Each suspect will wear a name tag.
- Only one team is allowed to ask questions of a suspect at a time.
- Assistant detectives should not necessarily believe any of the suspects right away when they are told something. The suspect may be lying. Verify statements with another suspect.
- Assistant detectives have a maximum of 45 minutes to solve the mystery, but the first team to turn in the correct answer wins. The chief inspector will mark down the time that each team finishes.
- After a team has turned in the form to the chief inspector, they may return to the meeting room.

Part II (45 minutes): Information for the Chief Inspector and the Suspects

In another room, suspects will stand in their assigned places and answer questions from the assistant detectives. Suspects should be prepared to answer the following questions:

- "Where were you at _____ p.m. today when the poison was administered?"
- "Can anyone confirm your whereabouts?"
- "What were you talking about?"
- "Did you have any reason to dislike Gabriella?"
- "Do you think any of the other suspects had a reason to murder Gabriella? Why?"

When assistant detectives have written down the name of the suspect they believe is guilty and have given their worksheet to Brother Bertram (who writes the finishing time and order of completion on each form), they may return to the original room and wait for the suspects to return.

Part III (15 minutes): Information for the Chief Inspector and the Suspects

During the third portion of the program, the suspects will return to the original room for the final interrogation. Brother Bertram will ask questions of each suspect, one by one. Although there are suggested questions and answers, both the suspects and Brother Bertram should be prepared to ad-lib. When the criminal is questioned, a dramatic finish is in order.

Final Interrogation Questions:

Brother Bertram: Lady Alayne, in the past you truly cared about Gabriella and even invited her to come back to the castle for a visit. How did you feel about her when you saw her wearing your great-grandmother's brooch?

Someone has poisoned Gabriella, the traveling bard, and it is up to you to determine whodunit! Prizes will be given to the winning team.

Sign up now to attend the Medieval Banquet at Lord William's castle. Join in the festivities as you unravel this Middle Ages Mystery. Refreshments will be served.

LIBRARY NAME, ADDRESS
PHONE, DATE, TIME
REGISTRATION INFORMATION
AGE LIMITATIONS

Lady Alayne: I couldn't believe my eyes. I had my suspicions that she was stealing from us, but I hoped I was wrong.

Brother Bertram: Since you thought she stole your family heirlooms, perhaps you thought she deserved punishment?

Lady Alayne: It is not up to me to exact punishment. That is for a higher power.

Brother Bertram: Lord William, isn't it true that since your father died, you've spent most of your inheritance through gambling?

Lord William: Well . . . yes.

Brother Bertram: Why did you hire Mad Maggie?

Lord William: As she is an alchemist, I hoped that she would discover how to turn common metals into gold and thus regain my fortune.

Brother Bertram: What happened when Gabriella found out about your family problems? Didn't you give her the brooch that belonged to your wife to shut her up?

Lord William: Yes, I must admit that I did. I didn't want anyone to find out what was going on.

Brother Bertram: Harrold, please tell us about your previous employment with Lord Prefontaine in France.

Harrold: I was hired as a tutor to his children.

Brother Bertram: Isn't it true that you cheated Lord Prefontaine out of his inheritance and that you are hiding out here?

Harrold: There's no way you can prove that.

Brother Bertram: What did you decide to do when Gabriella—who knew of your fraudulent activities in France and wanted you to split your "earnings"—came to the castle?

Harrold: I didn't do anything to her even though she was threatening me.

Brother Bertram: Did you kill her?

Harrold: No, no. I've never killed anyone.

Brother Bertram: I'd like to clear up another matter. Alyce, as you regularly clean Harrold's room, can you tell us if you have noticed anything suspicious?

Alyce: I have noticed the master's library manuscripts and statues and such. (Lord William fires Harrold on the spot and the guards pull him to the side of the room. He struggles a bit and a rolled manuscript falls out of clothing.)

Medieval Murder Mystery
Assistant Detective Worksheet

Suspects:

Lord William
Lady Alayne
Harrold the Tutor
Elwyn the Jester
Mad Maggie the Alchemist/Wizard

Rosalynde the Musician
Florinda the Cook
Alyce the Scullery Maid
Gwyneth the Nursery Maid

Non-Suspects:

Brother Bertram
Physician

Guard #1 (optional)
Guard #2 (optional)

Ask the Suspects:

Where were you at _____ p.m. today when the poison was administered?

Can anyone confirm your whereabouts?

What were you talking about?

Did you have any reason to dislike Gabriella?

Do you think any of the other Suspects had a reason to murder Gabriella and why?

Guidelines:

- Each Suspect will wear a nametag.
- Only one team is allowed to ask questions of a Suspect at a time.
- Assistant Detectives should not necessarily believe any of the Suspects right away when they are told something. The Suspect may be lying. Verify statements with another Suspect.
- Assistant Detectives have a maximum of 45 minutes to solve the mystery but the first team to turn in the correct answer wins.

Medieval Murder Mystery

Who Did It?

Each team fills out this sheet as they solve the mystery.

Team Name: _____

Finishing Time: _____

Murderer: _____

Motive (Why they did it): _____

_____

_____

_____

The team that turns in this form with the correct answer in the fastest time wins the prize!

Brother Bertram: Mad Maggie, weren't you hired by Lord William to turn common metals into gold?

Mad Maggie: Yes.

Brother Bertram: Isn't it true that you are much more interested in magic? Tell us about your recent experiments.

Mad Maggie: It is true that I am interested in magical experiments but I'm also an alchemist. Lately, I've been using red plant dyes with imperfect metals to create gold, but I spilled the red dye all over my laboratory.

Brother Bertram: But you really weren't trying to turn common metals into gold, were you? Didn't Gabriella discover your little secret?

Mad Maggie: Yes, it's true! I have no idea how to turn base metals into gold! (Lord William motions the guards to take her to the side of the room and also fires her.)

Brother Bertram: As the poisons are stored in your laboratory, you certainly have easy access to them.

Mad Maggie: Yes, but my door is unlocked. Anyone can get in.

Brother Bertram: Did you try to poison Gabriella?

Mad Maggie: No, I did not.

Brother Bertram: Rosalynde, before Gabriella came back to the castle, what was your position?

Rosalynde: I was the castle musician.

Brother Bertram: And since she's been here?

Rosalynde: I've had nothing to do. It's "Gabriella this" and "Gabriella that." I haven't performed once since she returned.

Brother Bertram: Wouldn't you have done anything to keep your job?

Rosalynde: Of course I want and need my job, but I wouldn't murder for it.

Brother Bertram: Florinda, your brother is very sick, is he not?

Florinda: Yes.

Brother Bertram: In the meantime, you are responsible for feeding his eight children, correct?

Florinda: That is true.

Brother Bertram: A cook does not earn very good wages. How are you able to support them?

Medieval Murder Mystery

Someone has poisoned Gabriella, the traveling bard, and it is up to you to determine whodunit! The winning team will receive prizes. Refreshments will be served.
LIBRARY NAME
ADDRESS, PHONE, DATE
TIME, REGISTRATION
INFORMATION
AGE LIMITATIONS

Medieval Murder Mystery

Someone has poisoned Gabriella, the traveling bard, and it is up to you to determine whodunit! The winning team will receive prizes. Refreshments will be served.
LIBRARY NAME
ADDRESS, PHONE, DATE
TIME, REGISTRATION
INFORMATION
AGE LIMITATIONS

Medieval Murder Mystery

Someone has poisoned Gabriella, the traveling bard, and it is up to you to determine whodunit! The winning team will receive prizes. Refreshments will be served.
LIBRARY NAME
ADDRESS, PHONE, DATE
TIME, REGISTRATION
INFORMATION
AGE LIMITATIONS

Medieval Murder Mystery

Someone has poisoned Gabriella, the traveling bard, and it is up to you to determine whodunit! The winning team will receive prizes. Refreshments will be served.
LIBRARY NAME
ADDRESS, PHONE, DATE
TIME, REGISTRATION
INFORMATION
AGE LIMITATIONS

Florinda: (very hesitantly) I've been sort of "borrowing" the leftover market money to feed my brother's kids.

Brother Bertram: Didn't Gabriella find out about your little scheme?

Florinda: Yes, she saw me and threatened to turn me in to Lord William, but I didn't kill her! (Frustrated, Lord William fires Florinda also. The guards come and take her away at Lord William's prompt.)

Brother Bertram: In your job as a castle maid, Alyce, was Gabriella a pleasant person to serve?

Alyce: No. She was always tripping me and calling me stupid and a lackwit. She gave me this bruise (points to makeup bruise on her face).

Brother Bertram: You were heard to say that you'd really like to see Gabriella dead. Is this really true and did you kill Gabriella?

Alyce: I might have said that in the heat of the moment, but I didn't poison her. I have no time for such goings on.

 Brother Bertram

 Lord William

 Lady Alayne

 Harrold, Tutor

 Elwyn, Jester

 Mad Maggie, Alchemist

 Rosalynde, Musician

 Florinda, Cook

 Alyce, Scullery Maid

 Gwyneth, Nursery Maid

 Physician

 Guard

Brother Bertram: Elwyn, I understand that you feel strongly about your family's honor.

Elwyn: Yes, family honor is everything.

Brother Bertram: Gabriella was wearing a ring on her finger when she died. Would you care to tell me about how she came to wear it?

Elwyn: That ring belonged to my great-grandfather. Gabriella's great-grandfather cheated it away from my great-grandfather and we've had nothing but bad luck ever since.

Brother Bertram: Wouldn't you have done anything to get that ring back?

Elwyn: It might be tempting, but I didn't kill Gabriella, if that's what you're implying.

Brother Bertram: Isn't it true, Mistress Gwyneth, that you and Gabriella grew up together?

Gwyneth: Yes.

Brother Bertram: Were you friends?

Gwyneth: We were the best of friends.

Brother Bertram: Tell me about Launce. Why aren't you still with him?

Gwyneth: Launce was my true love. He was my true love until Gabriella stole him from me and took him away across the sea. Now he's dead.

Brother Bertram: Where were you at the time the poison was placed in her cup?

Gwyneth: I was in the nursery.

Brother Bertram: With . . . (Gwyneth stays silent).

Brother Bertram: You seem to have no alibi. Let me remind everyone that Mad Maggie was experimenting with red dyes and spilled some in her laboratory. May I see your fingers? (Gwyneth's fingers are covered with red dye. She hadn't noticed that there was red dye on her fingers from the dye that Mad Maggie spilled in her laboratory.) You seem to have red dye on your hands. (He reaches in her pocket.) And the poison vial as well.

Gwyneth (defiantly): Yes, I did it. And I'm glad! Gabriella killed my Launce and now I will join him, too. (She grabs the vial of poison from Brother Bertram, drinks the rest of the poison in the vial, and collapses on the floor.) The physician might clarify that Gwyneth died instantly because she drank the entire vial of poison instead of just a few drops.

Brother Bertram will then thank all of the assistant detectives for coming to solve the mystery and announce the winning team. While he is giving out prizes, the rest of the cast will stand in a row (or two rows), wait for Brother Bertram, Gabriella, the physician, and the guards to join them, and bow in unison one time. The cast leaves the room or the curtain closes.

OPTIONAL CLUES AND PROPS
- Expensive-looking brooch for Gabriella
- Ornate ring for Gabriella
- Wooden spoon with reddish stain for Florinda
- Musical instrument like a dulcimer, lute, or recorder for Rosalynde
- Rolled manuscript to fall out of Harrold's tunic
- Vial to hold red-colored "poison"
- Wine glass and empty wine bottle
- Red ink to put on Gwyneth's fingers

d be dressed regally. If you have money for cos-
mes. Make these characters look like the fairy-
own and tiara. Lady Alayne wears a beautiful
am needs to wear a fabulous tunic with tights.
ortant. Be bold with color so that these nobles
buy richly textured fabric.
ng class level (Harrold, Rosalynde, Mad Mag-
ed with flair and color, but should not surpass
Alayne. Rosalynde and Gabriella should wear
such as wreaths. Gabriella needs to wear a

ic and matching hat (take a beret and sew on
ly made her look wizard-like with pointed hat
be dressed more grungily in a long, plainer
ress. She should look a little crazy with wild hair, and so on. This character cares
little for her appearance.

Those of the serving class (Gwyneth, Elwyn, Florinda, and Alyce) need to wear
simple clothes made of cotton or cotton blend fabrics in plain colors (white, cream,
brown, muted green) so that they will blend into the background. The female actors
can get away with long skirts, aprons, peasant shirts, and cotton mobcaps or kerchiefs.

Elwyn and Alyce could go barefoot. Elwyn could wear a loose, long-sleeved cotton shirt over pants that are torn up about mid-calf, or he could wear a long tunic, belt, and tights with plain leather shoes. Paint a bruise with makeup on Alyce's cheek so that she can say that Gabriella tripped her and caused her to have the bruise.

For Brother Bertram, look for a long, plain-colored robe. Dress the physician like the rest of the noble class. For simple guard costumes, you could have the actors wear all black. Make matching sleeveless tunics that will slip over the guards' shoulders. Provide them with fake swords.

DECORATIONS

You could really make a decorating statement with this script. Make a formal head table with chairs only on one side, facing the audience. Set up tables for all of the participants in a big "U" shape. Invest in cheap tablecloths or fabric on a bolt in a rich color like purple or burgundy. Add candelabras if you have these or can borrow them. You could also put butcher paper on the participants' tables. Try to find plates, napkins, and cups that don't look too modern. You could make medieval-looking flags or pennants from paper or fabric and put those up. Look in books about the Middle Ages for other ideas.

FOOD

Do some research on medieval cookery. For a very basic menu, serve cheese, bread, and grapes. Some suggestions for beverages are sparkling or regular grape juice, ginger ale, water, or mulled cider. In addition to the suggestions above, ideas for main course foods that are more or less teen-friendly are chicken wings, cold cuts, and perhaps meat pies. For that sweet tooth, consider toast with honey, gingerbread, cake, apple fritters, pears in syrup, custard, apples, plums, peaches, and nuts. Serve finger food on large platters or trays. Alyce the Scullery Maid and Florinda the Cook can serve the beverages and snacks to the head table and to the assistant detectives. Lord William and Lady Alayne should be demanding of their staff.

GRAPHICS AND PUBLICITY

A reproducible recruitment form, a publicity poster, publicity bookmarks, Assistant Detective Worksheets, and name tags are included in this chapter.

SHORT NEWS RELEASE

Gabriella the Traveling Bard has been poisoned! Whodunit? Everyone has a motive, from the scullery maid to the mad alchemist. Come to the _____ _____ Library on _____ and interrogate the suspects being held for questioning. It's up to you and your friends to find the criminal and solve the mystery. Form a team or we will assign you to one. Open to students in grades ___ to ___. Prizes will be awarded to the winning team. Spaces are limited, so sign up now! Call _____ for details.

TO-DO LIST

- Recruit suspects, chief inspector, and other non-suspects
- Assign places to stand or sit during Parts I–III

  - Parts I and III: Seated at the tables: Lord William, Lady Alayne, Gabriella (beginning of Part I only), Rosalynde, Harrold, and Mad Maggie. Serving: Florinda and Alyce. Doing jester-ish things: Elwyn. Sulking unobtrusively nearby: Gwyneth. Standing at the back: Guards. The physician will stay in another room until called in to pronounce Gabriella dead.
  - Part II: The suspects will stand in a circle with Lord William first, then Alyce, Florinda, Elwyn, Lady Alayne, Mad Maggie, Gwyneth, Harrold, Rosalynde, and back to Lord William.

- Purchase refreshments
- Purchase prizes
- Take pictures, if desired
- Write thank-you notes and/or buy small gifts

BOOK TIE-INS

Hand out an annotated bibliography with medieval fiction titles. Set up a display of fiction and nonfiction titles on the Middle Ages.

PRODUCTION NOTES

Although some of the suggestions for costumes and decorations will not be perfectly authentic, they will help create a festive atmosphere.

Ask your cast if they can try to use British accents for this mystery theater program.

8

The Highbrow Curse Mystery
In Memory of Grandpa Beard

Location:

Date:

Time:

Suspects:

Dan Ahman

Rhoda Bordtuteers

Jackie Gruj

Athena Highbrow

Bethany Holiday

Professor Peter Linton

Linda Lonsuffrin

Rebecca Eberhardt

Shawn Steele

Non-Suspects:

Inspector La Rue and Sir Edward Highbrow

SCRIPT COVER

- Name of Mystery: The Highbrow Curse Mystery
- Date of Program: _____
- Time of Program: _____
- Location of Program: _____
- Names of Suspects

  Professor Peter Linton, American tycoon, played by _____
  Rhoda Bordtuteers, Highbrow's head archaeologist, played by _____
  Athena Highbrow, daughter of Sir Edward Highbrow, played by _____
  Linda Lonsuffrin, Athena's governess, played by _____
  Dan Ahman, site worker, played by _____
  Shawn Steele, Interpol agent, played by _____
  Rebecca Eberhardt, Nazi spy, played by _____
  Jackie Gruj, tour guide, played by _____
  Bethany Holiday, archaeology student, played by _____

- Others on the Scene but Not Suspects, Including the Chief Inspector

  Inspector La Rue, played by _____
  Sir Edward Highbrow, British millionaire, played by _____

PURPOSE

This mystery script could be used for several purposes. It could be used in a social studies class to introduce political concerns—current or historical—in the Middle East. It could also be used to discuss the process archaeologists use when doing a dig.

SETTING

This mystery is set at the site of an archaeological excavation in the Middle East in the mid-1930s.

CRIME

An archaeological team as well as some other individuals is gathered at the site of a dig where ancient manuscripts are believed to exist. The infamous British millionaire, Sir Edward Highbrow, has been funding a dig in the Middle East. Thus far, the dig has proved anything but rewarding. Suspicious accidents abound, and locals have taken to calling the site and the site leader (Rhoda Bordtuteers) "cursed." Among several suspicious occurrences are collapsing tunnels, injured team members, missing tools, and expensive but dysfunctional brand-new equipment. After much insistence by Sir Edward Highbrow, local officials have called in a special detective, Inspector La Rue, to investigate who—or what—has been sabotaging the dig. Sir Edward does not believe in any curse. It is his opinion that the criminal is definitely a human.

TIMELINE

Over the past several weeks, Bethany Holiday has been sabotaging the dig in various ways. Her escapades have taken place in the dead of night with no witnesses. The exact times of these events are irrelevant.

SUSPECT BIOGRAPHIES

Alibis: Since the crimes have occurred at various times, alibis are irrelevant. Assistant detectives will need to solve the mystery based on evidence that they "dig" up.

> It began in mystery, and it will end in mystery, but what a savage and beautiful country lies in between.
>
> *Diane Ackerman*

NAME: PROFESSOR PETER LINTON

Description of Character: Peter Linton is a young, brilliant, but unscrupulous American tycoon who will stop at nothing to make a buck. Like Sir Edward Highbrow, he is also an investor in the archaeological world and is Sir Edward's archrival. Linton has no difficulty in exploiting the workers he hires at low wages or in selling the artifacts his team finds to whoever pays top dollar, although he pretends otherwise. He would love it if Sir Edward's dig were thwarted somehow, since his sources tell him that Sir Edward is searching in the right spot to find the ancient manuscripts everyone is looking for. He is delighted that Highbrow is having so many difficulties with this dig. Perhaps if Highbrow continues to have difficulties, he will give up and move on.

Motivation: Linton might have thwarted the dig so that Highbrow would pull out and Linton's own people would be able to move in and transfer the profit.

Discredit Dan Ahman: Linton feels that Dan Ahman is a bad egg. He drifts from job to job, all the time complaining that foreigners are exploiting the land and that they should not be allowed to remain. He might have sabotaged the dig in an attempt to get everyone to leave.

NAME: RHODA BORDTUTEERS, HEAD ARCHAEOLOGIST

Description of Character: Rhoda Bordtuteers is the head archaeologist hired by Sir Edward Highbrow to lead his expedition. As one of the few female archaeologists in the field, Bordtuteers has adopted a blasé façade to hide her emotional nature, so detested in a male-dominated world. Bordtuteers turned down another dig in Peru because Sir Edward promised her a big find (ancient manuscripts) at this site. So far, she's had nothing but problems on the site. Rumors are circulating that she doesn't know what she is doing. She now believes the dig she is on is pointless and that they will find nothing. Furthermore, the job she turned down has proved very lucrative for her friends, who have found dwellings dating to 2000 B.C.

Motivation: Rhoda's archaeologist friends on the dig at the ancient Incan city of Cuzco have invited her to join them, but she made a promise to Sir Edward. She can't go back on that. She does feel betrayed by Sir Edward, however. She may have sabotaged the site so that Sir Edward will fire her, and then she will be free to join her friends.

Discredit Linda Lonsuffrin: As Athena Highbrow's governess, Linda Lonsuffrin was forced to come to the Middle East, and she misses her quaint English cottage. Sir Edward Highbrow refuses to release Linda from her contract, even though she has begged him to let her go back to England. She is very angry and may have destroyed the dig to get back at Sir Edward.

Name: Athena Highbrow, Daughter of Sir Edward Highbrow

Description of Character: The spoiled teenage daughter of Sir Edward Highbrow, Athena usually gets her own way. She dragged her governess to the dig so she could pursue her latest crush, Professor Linton. It does not matter that Professor Linton is her father's archrival in the archaeological world or that her governess is obviously unhappy away from England. Linton just ignores her, believing that she is pursuing him just to spite her father, with whom she is always arguing about something or other.

Motivation: Athena has been sending Professor Peter Linton love letters stating, among other things, that she is responsible for all of the site problems and saying that she is doing it for him. In reality, she is not guilty. If assistant detectives question her about this, she will tell them that she just made up that rumor to try to impress Professor Linton.

Discredit Jackie Gruj: Jackie is a lady with a grudge. She harbors deep resentment toward Sir Edward Highbrow because he took advantage of her (with a stolen kiss and no promise of marriage). In her anger, Jackie may have tried to get back at Sir Edward Highbrow by damaging his dig.

Name: Linda Lonsuffrin, Athena's Governess

Description of Character: Linda has just about had it working as Athena Highbrow's governess. Not only does she have to put up with Athena's spoiled ways, but she was also forced (by Sir Edward) to come to this forsaken piece of land from her sweet little English cottage. Linda has been trying to get out of her contract as governess, but Sir Edward is firmly holding her to it, stating that she has to stay with Athena at least until she turns 18—in 12 long months!—or he will guarantee that she never finds another governess job in England again.

Motivation: In anger and frustration, Linda may have decided to destroy the dig.

Discredit Athena Highbrow: Linda honestly doesn't know if she believes it or not, but Athena Highbrow has told her in secret that she is the one who is wrecking things on the dig site. Athena wants to win Professor Peter Linton, and in her warped mind, she thinks this is the way to do it.

Name: Dan Ahman, Site Worker

Description: Dan Ahman is a local hired by Sir Edward Highbrow. After some trying times with his previous employer (Professor Peter Linton), he defected to Sir Edward Highbrow's camp, hoping for a better situation. Unfortunately, Sir Edward has proved nearly as impossible as Linton. Dan is beginning to feel as if all foreigners—who exploit the land and people as they choose—should be made to leave.

Motivation: In his belief that the area should be rid of foreigners, Dan may have sabotaged the dig.

Discredit Professor Peter Linton: Professor Linton wants to get in on Sir Edward Highbrow's dig. It would be just like the professor to sabotage a dig so that he could clean up the mess afterward. Dan should know. He used to work for Professor Linton and the man is a piece of work, all right.

Name: Shawn Steele, Interpol Agent

Description of Character: Shawn Steele, although pretending to be part of the dig, is actually a member of Interpol (the International Criminal Police Organization). Interpol has reason to suspect that a German spy is trying to access secrets that will be found in the ancient manuscripts that are being searched for on this site. Shawn has been planted to discover if this is really the case.

Motivation: Shawn has no motivation to sabotage the site. His furtive movements have caused others to be suspicious of him, however.

Discredit Rebecca Eberhardt: Shawn believes that Rebecca Eberhardt is a Nazi spy. He saw Rebecca looking through the manuscripts deep into the night when everyone else was sleeping. She was taking copious notes. With all of the confusion at the dig, no one has noticed that some of the ancient manuscripts recovered so far are missing. Shawn knows they are in Rebecca's tent. Rebecca may have caused the various sabotages in order to create a diversion.

Name: Rebecca Eberhardt, Nazi Spy

Description of Character: Rebecca is a Nazi spy trying to find ancient secrets for the Führer. Because she grew up in Germany, the Nazi ideology is second nature to her.

Motivation: Rebecca is stealing some of the manuscripts that have been recovered in the dig to take back to the Führer. All of the problems on the site are creating a nice diversion for Rebecca's secret activities. Perhaps she is the source of the sabotage.

Discredit Shawn Steele: Rebecca doesn't trust Shawn Steele. There is something suspicious about him. Instead of working on the dig, he always seems to be sneaking around and startling Rebecca.

Name: Jackie Gruj, Tour Guide

Description of Character: Jackie Gruj is a local tour guide who brought Athena Highbrow and Linda Lonsuffrin out to the excavation site. Although Sir Edward Highbrow has no recollection of it, he actually met Jackie while on vacation, 50 years earlier. She says he made a promise to marry her if she would give him a kiss. She kept her end of the bargain, but after the kiss, he disappeared and left her brokenhearted. That was the last time she saw him.

Motive: Having held a grudge against Sir Edward for 50 years, Jackie may have finally found a way to repay his heartless behavior by destroying his site.

Discredit Bethany Holiday: Bethany pretends to adore her mentor, Rhoda Bordtuteers, but the reality is something quite different. She is constantly talking about Rhoda behind her back and telling anyone who will listen how Rhoda is mismanaging the dig. Bethany does not want to have to work her way up the ladder the hard way. Anytime something strange happens on the dig, Bethany Holiday is never far away. Perhaps she is cooking up some scheme so that she can get to the top the easy way.

Name: Bethany Holiday, Archaeology Student

Description of Character: A Canadian archaeology student, Bethany has taken up an apprenticeship with Rhoda Bordtuteers, whom she says she adores. She gushes constantly about what a wonderful role model Miss Bordtuteers is and how she wants to be just like her someday. The only problem is that Bethany does not want to pay her dues like Bordtuteers did and work her way up the ranks. She believes that if Sir Edward Highbrow thinks Bordtuteers is doing a bad job managing the dig (because of the numerous accidents and problems), he will have no choice but to fire her and hire Bordtuteers's assistant (Bethany) for the job.

Motivation: By sabotaging the dig, Bethany thinks she will be able to skip all of the menial work, not have to follow someone else's orders, and get all of the glory for herself! Bethany rigged all of the equipment so that it wouldn't work. She has also caused all of the minor accidents to occur. She started the rumor about the curse to throw people off track and to cast the blame on Rhoda Bordtuteers. She also left a slick of oil on a bedsheet, manipulated the camera so it wouldn't work, and has been pilfering needed tools and storing them in her backpack.

Alibi: Bethany Holiday has no alibi or weapon per se. However, she does possess knowledge of how to use a camera, and there is a missing bedsheet and several tools in her backpack.

Discredit Rhoda Bordtuteers: Rhoda really wants to go to another dig in Peru with her friends. If Rhoda sabotaged the dig, Sir Edward might fire Rhoda and she would be free to leave to excavate the ancient city of Cuzco. Rhoda should just leave. It's all her fault that bad things are happening to the dig.

Summary

Name	Discredit
Professor Peter Linton	Dan Ahman
Rhoda Bordtuteers	Linda Lonsuffrin
Athena Highbrow	Jackie Gruj
Linda Lonsuffrin	Athena Highbrow
Dan Ahman	Professor Peter Linton
Shawn Steele	Rebecca Eberhardt
Rebecca Eberhardt	Shawn Steele
Jackie Gruj	Bethany Holiday
Bethany Holiday	Rhoda Bordtuteers

The Highbrow Curse Mystery

NEEDED!

A team of library staff members and high school teens to help with a Mystery Theatre program for teens. Whodunit? We are now looking for volunteers to play the following roles:

SUSPECTS: Professor Peter Linton, Rhoda Bordtuteers, Athena Highbrow, Linda Lonsuffrin, Dan Ahman, Shawn Steele, Rebecca Eberhardt, Jackie Gruj, Bethany Holiday

NON—SUSPECTS: Inspector La Rue

Be a part of the fun! If you sign up, you are responsible for your own costume and props, but I will provide assistance as necessary.

Rehearsal Date:

Performance Date: Time: Place:

Please return form to _____by _____.

Name:_____

___ Yes, I would love to help.

___ My first choice of character is _____.

     My second choice is _____.

___ I need help with my costume!

___ I will help only if you are absolutely desperate.

The Highbrow Curse Mystery

Travel back in time to the 1930's — your help is needed!
Lord Highbrow's archaeological site is said to be
cursed — mysterious accidents, equipment that won't
work. Is the site really cursed or is it a matter of
sabotage? Spaces are limited. Sign up now to be a
part of this mystery theatre program! The winning team
will be awarded prizes. Refreshments will be served.

LIBRARY NAME

DATE

TIME

AGE LIMITATIONS

REGISTRATION

INFORMATION

OTHERS ON THE SCENE WHO ARE NOT SUSPECTS, INCLUDING THE CHIEF INSPECTOR

NAME: INSPECTOR LA RUE

Description of Character: Businesslike and to the point, Inspector La Rue lives only for his or her work and to get to the crux of every mystery.

NAME: SIR EDWARD HIGHBROW

Description of Character: Sir Edward is a tough old man who usually gets what he wants. Right now he wants answers! He will do anything necessary to get his dig back on track.

PROGRAM SCHEDULE

PART 1 (15 MINUTES): INFORMATION FOR THE CHIEF INSPECTOR AND THE SUSPECTS

Fifteen minutes before the program begins, all cast members except Inspector La Rue are in their places. The chief inspector will wait for the participants at the room entrance and assign them to a team. Inspector La Rue will introduce the suspects, hand out a worksheet to each team, and explain how it is to be filled out. He or she will also enlighten assistant detectives as to their role throughout the investigation.

Inspector La Rue will talk about the crime that has occurred:

"We are here at the dig of British millionaire Sir Edward Highbrow in the Middle East. Unfortunately, instead of finding any historical artifacts, plenty of suspicious accidents are occurring. Locals have taken to calling the site and the site leader (Rhoda Bordtuteers) 'cursed.' Among the suspicious occurrences are collapsing tunnels, injured team members, missing tools, and expensive, brand-new equipment that fails to work. You have been called here to investigate who—or what—has been sabotaging the dig."

Inspector La Rue will then tell the suspects to leave the scene of the crime and to wait for questions in the main room. Inspector La Rue will then show the assistant detectives the evidence or clues in hand and explain the rules:

- Each suspect will wear a name tag.
- Only one team is allowed to ask questions of a suspect at a time.
- Assistant detectives should not necessarily believe any of the suspects right away when they are told something. The suspect may be lying. Verify statements with another suspect.
- Assistant detectives have a maximum of 45 minutes to solve the mystery, but the first team to turn in the correct answer wins. Inspector La Rue will mark down the time that each team finishes.
- After a team has turned in the form to Inspector La Rue, it may return to the meeting room.

PART II (45 MINUTES): INFORMATION FOR THE CHIEF INSPECTOR AND THE SUSPECTS

In another room, suspects will stand in their assigned places and answer questions from the assistant detectives. Suspects should be prepared to answer the following questions:

- "Do you have any reason to dislike Sir Edward Highbrow or a reason to want to destroy the dig?"
- "Do you think any of the other suspects had a reason to commit the crime? Why?"
- "Do you know how to operate a camera?"
- "Is there anything in your pockets?" (Bethany will have an oilcan lid in her pocket.)
- "Do you know anything about the missing archaeological tools?"

When assistant detectives have written down the suspect they believe is guilty and have given their worksheets to Inspector La Rue, they may return to the original room and wait for the suspects to return. As Inspector La Rue collects the "Who Did It?" forms from teams of teens, he or she marks the time that each form was turned in and order of completion.

PART III (15 MINUTES): INFORMATION FOR THE CHIEF INSPECTOR AND THE SUSPECTS

During the third portion of the program, the suspects will return to the original room for the final interrogation. Inspector La Rue will ask questions of each suspect, one by one. Although there are suggested questions and answers, both the suspects and Inspector La Rue should be prepared to ad-lib. When the criminal is questioned, a dramatic finish is in order.

Final Interrogation Questions

Inspector La Rue: Professor Linton, how would you describe your relationship with Sir Edward Highbrow?

Peter Linton: He is my archrival.

Inspector La Rue: What have you heard from your sources about his current dig?

Peter Linton: (in a whisper) He is definitely in the right spot to find the ancient manuscripts.

Inspector La Rue: So it would be to your advantage to sabotage his dig?

Peter Linton: Financially, yes—but of course I wouldn't do such a thing because valuable items might be destroyed. I place too high a historical and cultural value on such items to think about inadvertently damaging or destroying them.

The Highbrow Curse Mystery

Assistant Detective Worksheet

Suspects:

Professor Peter Linton

Rhoda Bordtuteers

Athena Highbrow

Linda Lonsuffrin

Dan Ahman

Shawn Steele

Rebecca Eberhardt

Jackie Gruj

Bethany Holiday

Non-Suspects:

Inspector La Rue

Ask the Suspects:

Do you have any reason to dislike Sir Edward Highbrow or a reason to want to destroy the dig?

Do you think any of the other Suspects had a reason to commit the crime? Why?

Do you know how to operate a camera?

Is there anything in your pockets?

Do you know anything about the missing archaeological tools?

Guidelines:

- Each Suspect will wear a nametag.
- Only one team is allowed to ask questions of a Suspect at a time.
- Assistant Detectives should not necessarily believe any of the Suspects right away when they are told something. The Suspect may be lying. Verify statements with another Suspect.
- Assistant Detectives have a maximum of 45 minutes to solve the mystery but the first team to turn in the correct answer wins. Inspector La Rue will mark down the time that each team finishes. After a team has turned in the form to Inspector La Rue, it may return to the meeting room.

WHO DID IT?

Each team fills out this sheet as they solve the mystery.

Team Name: _____

Finishing Time: _____

Criminal: _____

Motive (Why they did it): _____

_____

_____

_____

The team that turns in this form with the correct answer in the fastest time wins the prize!

Inspector La Rue: Rhoda Bordtuteers, would you say you've had a few problems at your dig site?

Rhoda Bordtuteers: Yes, and people are starting to blame me.

Inspector La Rue: I understand that you have friends in Peru on a successful dig, and that they have invited you to join them.

Rhoda Bordtuteers: Yes.

Inspector La Rue: So, why don't you?

Rhoda Bordtuteers: As tempting as that is, I promised Sir Edward that I would supervise this dig and I can't go back on my promise.

Inspector La Rue: Perhaps if you sabotaged the site, Sir Edward would fire you, and then you would be free to leave.

Rhoda Bordtuteers: That is a bizarre line of reasoning. (Inspector La Rue shrugs.)

Inspector La Rue: Miss Highbrow, is it true that you are madly in love with Professor Linton?

Athena Highbrow: Yes, I'm desperately in love with him, and he won't give me the time of day!

Inspector La Rue: Now I want the truth from you, young lady, because I understand that you are spreading some rumors of your own. Have you been guilty of criminal activities to try to make Professor Linton fall in love with you?

Athena Highbrow: (after much hesitation) I told Peter I did it, but I really am not guilty.

Inspector La Rue: Linda Lonsuffrin, tell us what Sir Edward told you when you wanted to break your governess contract and leave the Middle East.

Linda Lonsuffrin: He refused and told me I would have to serve the last 12 months—in this horrible place! I miss my little cottage and my garden.

Inspector La Rue: Perhaps in your anger at his answer, you decided to get some revenge.

Linda Lonsuffrin: Of course not! I agreed to the contract. Just because he hasn't got a kind bone in his body, doesn't mean that I should reciprocate.

Inspector La Rue: Dan Ahman, tell me what you think of Westerners and foreigners in general.

The Highbrow Curse Mystery | The Highbrow Curse Mystery | The Highbrow Curse Mystery | The Highbrow Curse Mystery

Lord Highbrow's archaeological site is said to be cursed. Is the site really cursed or is it a matter of sabotage? Whodunit? Sign up now to help solve this exotic mystery. Prizes will be awarded to the winning team. Refreshments served.

LIBRARY NAME
ADDRESS
DATE, TIME
REGISTRATION
INFORMATION
AGE LIMITATIONS

Lord Highbrow's archaeological site is said to be cursed. Is the site really cursed or is it a matter of sabotage? Whodunit? Sign up now to help solve this exotic mystery. Prizes will be awarded to the winning team. Refreshments served.

LIBRARY NAME
ADDRESS
DATE, TIME
REGISTRATION
INFORMATION
AGE LIMITATIONS

Lord Highbrow's archaeological site is said to be cursed. Is the site really cursed or is it a matter of sabotage? Whodunit? Sign up now to help solve this exotic mystery. Prizes will be awarded to the winning team. Refreshments served.

LIBRARY NAME
ADDRESS
DATE, TIME
REGISTRATION
INFORMATION
AGE LIMITATIONS

Lord Highbrow's archaeological site is said to be cursed. Is the site really cursed or is it a matter of sabotage? Whodunit? Sign up now to help solve this exotic mystery. Prizes will be awarded to the winning team. Refreshments served.

LIBRARY NAME
ADDRESS
DATE, TIME
REGISTRATION
INFORMATION
AGE LIMITATIONS

Dan Ahman: At first I did not mind foreigners. However, I have observed that many steal all of the goodness from the land and put nothing back. It is time for all of them to leave this land.

Inspector La Rue: Did you sabotage the dig to get rid of Sir Edward?

Dan Ahman: What would be the point? Someone else, like Linton, would just replace him.

Inspector La Rue: Shawn Steele, your secretive actions around the dig site have caused some suspicion.

Shawn Steele: I don't know why.

Inspector La Rue: I think you do know why. You're really a member of Interpol, are you not?

Shawn Steele: I don't know how you found out, but now that you've blown my cover, I'll tell you why I'm here. Interpol has heard that different Nazi spies are working undercover on archaeological sites. Hitler is looking for specific information from

 Professor Peter Linton

 Rhoda Bordtuteers

 Athena Highbrow

 Linda Lonsuffrin

 Dan Ahman

 Shawn Steele

 Rebecca Eberhardt

 Jackie Gruj

 Bethany Holiday

 Inspector LaRue

 Sir Edward Highbrow

ancient manuscripts. (At this point, Rebecca Eberhardt slowly stands up and begins to walk toward the door.) Inspector—perhaps you should stop the Nazi spy? (Shawn points to Rebecca, who is trying to make a getaway. Inspector La Rue stops her before she leaves and brings her back to the front of the room.)

Inspector La Rue: Rebecca Eberhardt, do you deny being a Nazi spy? (She says nothing.) Do you deny sabotaging the dig?

Rebecca Eberhardt: I had nothing to do with the sabotage business. Why would anyone want to destroy ancient manuscripts?

Inspector La Rue: Mr. Steele, I release Miss Eberhardt to your custody. (Shawn Steele takes Rebecca Eberhardt aside and cuffs her.)

Inspector La Rue: Jackie Gruj, when did you first meet Sir Edward?

Jackie Gruj: I met him about 50 years ago.

Inspector La Rue: What did he agree to do in exchange for one of your kisses?

Jackie Gruj: He said he would marry me.

Inspector La Rue: And what happened after he kissed you?

Jackie Gruj: He took off, and I didn't see him again until I brought Miss Highbrow and her governess out here.

Inspector La Rue: Did you try to destroy his site because of your 50-year grudge?

Jackie Gruj: That's a good thought, but I'm too old and frail to think of such things.

Inspector La Rue: Bethany Holiday, I understand that you look at Rhoda Bordtuteers as a role model.

Bethany Holiday: Yes, I do. She's a great inspiration to young archaeology students. (Other suspects murmur dissent to Bethany's obvious lie.)

Inspector La Rue: Are you prepared to work as an assistant for many years before you are in a prominent role like hers?

Bethany Holiday: I suppose. It is somewhat discouraging, though. I do feel just as capable as a seasoned archaeologist.

Inspector La Rue: Maybe you would like to advance in the field without a lot of effort?

Bethany Holiday: Well, that would be nice.

Inspector La Rue: Do you know anything about the site being cursed?

Bethany Holiday: No.

Inspector La Rue: I heard that you were spreading that rumor.

Bethany Holiday: It's going around.

Inspector La Rue: I find it interesting that you are the only suspect who knows how to operate this newfangled photographic equipment. The only problem is that it never works when it's needed. (Silence.) In addition, I understand that your bedsheet is missing. Is this it? (The chief inspector pulls out the sheet slicked with oil from her backpack. Bethany shrugs.) Perhaps you know where all the missing tools have gone. (The chief inspector pulls Bethany's backpack from her feet and empties it. All the missing tools fall out. Other suspects gasp and exclaim over the missing tools.)

Bethany Holiday: All right! I did it. It isn't fair that I should have to work like a slave—for her [points to Bordtuteers]—for years and years when I am just as smart or smarter than she is! I wanted her job, so I tried to make it look like she was cursed.

Inspector La Rue: Sir Edward, you will be glad to know that Miss Bordtuteers was not cursed or incompetent, but a victim of Bethany Holiday, who hoped you would give up on Bordtuteers and hire her instead. (Bethany is taken away.)

After Bethany Holiday is revealed as the criminal, Inspector La Rue will announce the winning team. While he is giving out prizes, the rest of the cast will stand in a row (or two rows), wait for Inspector La Rue to join them, and then bow in unison one time. The cast leaves the room or the curtain closes.

OPTIONAL CLUES AND PROPS
- Oilcan lid
- Backpack with archaeological "tools" in it
- Bedsheet with oil slick on it. Any vegetable or olive oil could be used on an old sheet.
- A camera
- Cuffs for Rebecca Eberhardt

COSTUMES
Look at 1930s fashions for ideas. Most of the characters could get away with wearing brown and white khakis. Characters like Athena Highbrow who don't do any work might want to dress impractically in a ball gown.

DECORATIONS

Think *Indiana Jones* for this script. You could have an elaborate Casablanca club setting or create a camp look with white sheets set up around the room like tents.

FOOD

Falafel, fruit, pastries, and coffee.

GRAPHICS AND PUBLICITY

A reproducible recruitment form, publicity poster, publicity bookmarks, Assistant Detective Worksheets, and name tags are included in this chapter.

TO-DO LIST

• Recruit suspects, chief inspector, and other non-suspects
• Assign places to stand or sit during Parts I–III

  ○ Parts I and III: Suspects should be seated in a long row at the front of the room as follows: Linda Lonsuffrin, Athena Highbrow, Professor Peter Linton, Dan Ahman, Rhoda Bordtuteers, Bethany Holiday, Jackie Gruj, Shawn Steele, Rebecca Eberhardt. Place Rebecca Eberhardt closest to the exit.

    ○ Part II: Arrange the suspects in a large circle around the room starting with Rhoda Bordtuteers, Linda Lonsuffrin, Athena Highbrow, Jackie Gruj, Bethany Holiday, Professor Peter Linton, Dan Ahman, Shawn Steele, Rebecca Eberhardt, and back to Rhoda Bordtuteers.

- Purchase refreshments
- Purchase prizes
- Take pictures, if desired
- Write thank-you notes and/or buy small gifts

BOOK TIE-INS

Set up a display with fiction and nonfiction books on archaeology, spies, and/or the history of the Middle East. To add more interest, include action adventure movies like the Indiana Jones trilogy or the Lara Croft movies.

PRODUCTION NOTES

Each character should attempt to pull off the accent of their character. Rebecca Eberhardt does not necessarily need to have a German accent since she is supposed to be a spy.

Shivermetimbers!
A Pirate Mystery

PLACE:

DATE:

TIME:

Captain Shivermetimbers
Carlos the Cook
George (Georgina), Cabin Boy
Madeleina Fransisco, Captive
Barnacle Bill, Quartermaster
Mummy Shivermetimbers
Bruno Diggory, Helmsman
Captain Padilla, Prisoner
Gustav the Great, Musician

SCRIPT COVER

- Name of Mystery: Shivermetimbers! A Pirate Mystery
- Date of Program: _____
- Time of Program: _____
- Location of Program: _____
- Names of Suspects

Captain Shivermetimbers, played by _____
Carlos, cook, played by _____
George (Georgina), cabin boy, played by _____
Madeleina Fransisco, daughter of Spanish governor, played by _____
Barnacle Bill, quartermaster, played by _____
Mummy Shivermetimbers, mother of the captain, played by _____
Bruno Diggory, helmsman, played by _____
Captain Padilla, prisoner, played by _____
Gustav the Great, musician, played by _____

PURPOSE

The purpose of *Shivermetimbers! A Pirate Mystery* is entertainment. It could conceivably be tied into a history study as well.

SETTING

Set in the 1500s, this mystery takes place aboard a pirate ship in the Caribbean.

CRIME

Right after the weekly poetry recitation aboard ship, the coveted treasure map went missing.

TIMELINE

- Very early today, while most of the crew was sleeping or dozing on duty, Captain Shivermetimbers and Madeleina Fransisco opened the treasure chest with the captain's key, and removed the map.
- At the start of the mystery theater program, as is his usual practice, Captain Shivermetimbers will torture his crew with his weekly poetry recitation. Since no one else ever volunteers to contribute, it will be a one-man show.
- After the recitation, as is their usual practice, all of the pirates will gather round the treasure chest to view the booty that will be divided up when they reach their next port of call. (Gambling is forbidden on the ship, so there is no reason for anyone to need their share before they reach another port of call.) Strangely, when Captain Shivermetimbers reaches for the key around his neck, it appears to be missing. The captain begins to get suspicious at this point and insists that the

lock on the treasure chest be broken. When the chest is finally opened, all of the treasure is there, but the treasure map is gone!

SUSPECT BIOGRAPHIES

NAME: CAPTAIN SHIVERMETIMBERS

Description of Character: The captain takes on the role of chief inspector even though he is one of the two guilty crewmembers. He is in love with his prisoner, Madeleina Fransisco (secretly his wife). The two of them have stolen the treasure map. The captain has promised Madeleina that when they recover the treasure, he and she will retire happily to a life of ease. The captain, though tough at times, is a romantic at heart, spouting poetry to his crew every week at a mandatory meeting. When the pirate ship last raided the Spanish port, Captain Shivermetimbers and Madeleina chanced to meet, instantly fell in love, and were married. Madeleina was not thrilled with the idea of living the rest of her life aboard a pirate ship, so Captain Shivermetimbers agreed to steal the map from the treasure chest (which is inspected weekly after the poetry reading by all crewmembers) and retire at a ripe young age with Madeleina to a carefree life off the ship.

> Would you learn the secret of the sea? Only those who brave its dangers, comprehend its mystery!
>
> *Henry Wadsworth Longfellow*

Motivation: Captain Shivermetimbers stole the map in order to keep all of the treasure for himself and his love, Madeleina.

Alibi: Captain Shivermetimbers and Madeleina are the only ones with alibis (each other). No one else has an alibi that matches. The captain will continue to state that Madeleina is his alibi. He will say he was torturing her in his stateroom. The captain is the only crew member with a key to the chest, but shockingly that key is missing.

Discredit Carlos, the Cook: Carlos is addicted to gambling. Captain Shivermetimbers will say that Carlos is probably the criminal. The captain has told Carlos many, many times that if he does not stop trying to coerce the other crew members into gambling with him—an activity strictly forbidden among the crew because of their proclivity toward violence—he will throw him overboard. The only thing that stops Carlos most of the time is that he has nothing to gamble with. If Carlos had the treasure map, perhaps he would have plenty of money to follow his impulses on land, at least.

NAME: CARLOS, THE SHIP'S COOK

Description of Character: Carlos is addicted to gambling. Gambling is expressly forbidden aboard the ship because too many pirates have killed each other over gambling-related arguments. Anyone caught gambling will walk the plank, but the gambling addiction is too strong for Carlos to resist at times. He sometimes feels it is worth taking the risk with other pirates, even though it may cost him his life.

Motivation: If Carlos had possession of the map, he might be able to get off the ship and go to a town where he would be able to gamble to his heart's content.

Alibi: Carlos has no alibi. He was in the kitchen area.

Discredit Bruno Diggory: Not everyone on board knows this, but Bruno Diggory is a runaway slave. Bruno has told Carlos that he is slowly saving his share of their pirated booty so that he can eventually get away from the world of greed and avarice and settle somewhere in his own little hut. Perhaps he stole the treasure map to speed up the process.

Name: George (Georgina), Cabin Boy

Description of Character: In actuality, "George" is Georgina, a girl in disguise aboard the ship. Normally, girls are considered bad luck aboard pirate ships, so Georgina had to pass herself off as a boy. Georgina is a reckless sort of tomboy in search of high adventure, and she thought it a great lark to work aboard a pirate ship, especially with no one knowing her secret except for the prisoner Captain Padilla, to whom she was bragging the other day when she brought him a hard lump of bread. She isn't worried that the prisoner would tell anyone. Who would believe him if he did blab?

Motivation: Georgina is a daredevil and loves to live dangerously. To fend off boredom in between raids, she may have stolen the treasure map.

Alibi: Georgina has no alibi. She was swabbing the deck.

Discredit Captain Padilla: Georgina knows how bad Captain Padilla feels about losing his cargo and ship. If he ever gets back to Spain, a new boat filled with treasure would go a long way toward restoring him to his superiors' good graces.

Name: Madeleina Fransisco, Daughter of the Spanish Governor

Description of Character: Madeleina is the Spanish governor's daughter, and everyone thinks she is being held captive aboard the ship. When Madeleina and Captain Shivermetimbers first met on one of his raiding trips to the Spanish port, he and she fell instantly in love and were married in secret. Perhaps part of Madeleina's instant love for the captain was to get out of an arranged marriage to an old coot. Madeleina is a little spoiled and not used to the swarthy, swashbuckling life, and so, before she agreed to marry Captain Shivermetimbers and live aboard the pirate ship, she made Captain Shivermetimbers promise that they would settle down somewhere soon with a fantastic treasure. To keep their marriage a secret, the captain and Madeleina made up a story about how she is his prisoner.

Motivation: Secretly in love with Captain Shivermetimbers, who rescued her from an unwelcome arranged marriage, Madeleina is in cahoots with the captain to soon enjoy a life of ease away from the stinky pirate ship.

Alibi: Madeleina will say that she was being tortured by Captain Shivermetimbers in his stateroom.

Discredit Mummy Shivermetimbers: Mummy is a terrible mother to Captain Shivermetimbers. She continually ridicules her son, saying how wimpy he is and how if she were the captain, she would get rid of the poetry readings and do some "manly" activities. If power-hungry Mummy Shivermetimbers had the treasure, she could bribe the crew to elect her the captain instead of her son.

Shivermetimbers!
A Pirate Mystery

NEEDED!

A swarthy crew of library staff members and high school teens to come on board for a Mystery Theatre program for teens. The coveted treasure map has just been discovered missing from Captain Shivermetimbers' pirate ship. Whodunit? We are now looking for volunteers to play the following roles:

Captain Shivermetimbers
Carlos the Cook
George (Georgina), Cabin Boy
Madeleina Fransisco, Captive
Barnacle Bill, Quartermaster

Mummy Shivermetimbers
Bruno Diggory, Helmsman
Captain Padilla, Prisoner
Gustav the Great, Musician

Be a part of the fun! If you sign up, you are responsible for your own costume and props, but I will provide assistance if necessary.

Rehearsal Date:

Performance Date: _____ Time: _____ Place: _____

Please return form to _____ by _____ .

Name: _____

_____ Yes, I would love to help.

_____ My first choice of character is _____ . My second choice is _____ .

_____ I need help with my costume!

_____ I will help only if you are absolutely desperate.

Shivermetimbers!
A Pirate Mystery

All Aboard!

Someone has stolen Captain Shivermetimbers' treasure map, and it is up to you to decide who should walk the plank! Sign up now to help solve this piratical Mystery. The winning team will be awarded prizes. Refreshments will be served.

Library
Name
Address
Phone

Date, Time
Registration
Information
Age Limitations

Name: Barnacle Bill, Quartermaster

Description of Character: As quartermaster of the ship, Barnacle Bill is as tough as nails. He is a hard man who goes nowhere without his cat-o'-nine-tails. Most of the crew lives in fear of his harsh words and violent tendencies. Barnacle Bill wasn't always so tough. As a young man, Bill ran away from his family, who thought he would amount to nothing. He ended up living the rough and wild life of a pirate. He rapidly grew from a soft youth to the grizzled man he is today. A part of him still longs for his family and he would like to return home and prove to them that he is successful, but he knows he can't go back with his meager share of the treasure from their raids.

Motivation: If Barnacle Bill had the wealth from the treasure promised in the treasure map, he would be able to go back to his family and prove to them that he has succeeded in life.

Alibi: Barnacle Bill was at the stern of the ship and has no alibi.

Discredit Gustav the Great: Gustav is a sorry excuse for a sailor and a pirate. He's useless on raids and can play the _____ [insert an instrument] only passably. He's always looking for attention among the crew, but no one seems to pay him any mind. Perhaps if Gustav had riches, he could buy their love.

Name: Mummy Shivermetimbers, the Captain's Mother

Description of Character: Mummy is the mother of Captain Shivermetimbers. The captain has a soft spot for his mummy and brings her everywhere. Mummy is a rather hard-boiled egg, however, often tougher than her sometimes-philosophical son. She thinks he is a wimp because of his silly poetry and sentimentality. She would like to get rid of him and run the ship herself, but she doesn't have the influence or power—yet.

Motivation: Mummy may have stolen the map to get the treasure, with which she would bribe the crew to elect her the new captain in place of her weak son.

Alibi: Mummy was resting and has no alibi.

Discredit Madeleina Fransisco: Mummy Shivermetimbers does not like the prisoner, Madeleina Fransisco. She cannot fathom why her son has seemed to take a fancy to Madeleina, giving her regular food instead of prisoner food filled with maggots (like they give the other prisoner, Captain Padilla). She has never been able to understand her son. He even lets Madeleina read all the books in his stateroom. Read, read, read! That's all she does all day long! No one else can be bothered to read. Well, no one else knows how to read, not even the captain. Mummy just knows that Madeleina is up to something. She just can't figure out what that something is, but she will.

Name: Bruno Diggory, the Helmsman

Description of Character: Helmsman of the ship, Bruno is a runaway slave. Working aboard a pirate ship is sometimes no better than being a slave, so Bruno's goal is to get out of it all and live happily in a little hut somewhere, with the nest egg he has been building up.

Motivation: If Bruno could find a treasure, he'd be closer to his dream of living the life of ease.

Alibi: Bruno was steering the ship. He has no particular alibi.

Discredit Captain Shivermetimbers: The captain is the only person who has ever had access to the treasure chest key. He has always guarded it like a hawk, and the key has never been missing before. The map has been there every week, too. No one knows exactly what is going on, but Captain Shivermetimbers has been acting very strange ever since Madeleina Fransisco came on board. Captain Shivermetimbers and Madeleina seem to have a close relationship, given the fact that she is his prisoner.

Name: Captain Padilla

Description of Character: The former captain of a Spanish galleon filled with treasure that Captain Shivermetimbers and his crew of pirates took, Captain Padilla is slowly being starved to death aboard the ship. Over the years, he has achieved greatness in his career in the Spanish Armada. He had gained much prestige as the only captain to cross the Atlantic Ocean unhindered by pirates. Now his record and fame have been besmirched by Captain Shivermetimbers.

Motivation: If Captain Padilla had a treasure map and could manage to get away somehow, the treasure gathered might atone for the lost cargo he previously carried. It also might help him to get back into his superiors' good graces.

Alibi: Captain Padilla has no alibi other than that he was down below with the rats.

Discredit George/Georgina: George/Georgina has bragged to Captain Padilla that she is a girl pretending to be a boy. The girl obviously loves dangerous situations. Captain Padilla thinks that Georgina may have stolen the treasure map just to get a rise out of everyone right now because she's a little bored.

Name: Gustav the Great

Description of Character: Self-named, Gustav "the Great" has issues of low self-esteem. He does his best to live up to his name, but in actuality, everyone always makes sport of Gustav. He has tried to master the _____ [instrument of your choice], but plays only passably.

Motivation: Gustav is tired of being ridiculed by his fellow pirates. If he had wealth and riches, they would have to respect him.

Alibi: Gustav was busy trying to perfect the _____ [insert an instrument] and has no alibi.

Discredit Barnacle Bill: Gustav is a light sleeper. Many times Barnacle Bill has had restless dreams where he has called out for his family. Barnacle Bill is not the type of person to confide in the rest of the crew, so Gustav doesn't know the details, but Barnacle Bill seems torn up about his past. Gustav has a feeling that there is more to Barnacle Bill than meets the eye.

Shivermetimbers!
A Pirate Mystery
Assistant Detective Worksheet

Suspects:

Captain Shivermetimbers

Carlos, cook

George (Georgina), cabin boy

Madeleina Fransisco, daughter
to Spanish Governor

Barnacle Bill, quartermaster

Mummy Shivermetimbers,
mother to the Captain

Bruno Diggory, helmsman

Captain Padilla, prisoner

Gustav the Great, musician

Ask the Suspects:

What were you doing before the poetry reading took place?

Can anyone confirm your whereabouts?

Is there any reason you would want to have possession of the treasure map?

Do you think any of the other Suspects had a reason to steal the treasure map? Why?

Guidelines:

- Each Suspect will wear a nametag.
- Only one team is allowed to ask questions of a Suspect at a time.
- Assistant Detectives should not necessarily believe any of the Suspects right away when they are told something. The Suspect may be lying. Verify statements with another Suspect.
- Assistant Detectives have a maximum of 45 minutes to solve the mystery but the first team to turn in the correct answer wins. Captain Shivermetimbers will mark down the time that each team finishes.
- After a team has turned in the form to Captain Shivermetimbers, it may return to the meeting room.

Shivermetimbers!
A Pirate Mystery
Who Did It?

Each team fills out this sheet as they solve the mystery.

Team Name: _____

Finishing Time: _____

Criminal: _____

Motive (Why they did it): _____

_____

_____

_____

The team that turns in this form with the correct answer in the fastest time wins the prize!

SUMMARY

Name	Alibi	Discredit
Captain Shivermetimbers	Madeleina	Carlos
Carlos	No alibi	Bruno Diggory
George/Georgina	No alibi	Captain Padilla
Madeleina Fransisco	Captain Shivermetimbers	Mummy Shivermetimbers
Barnacle Bill	No alibi	Gustav the Great
Mummy Shivermetimbers	No alibi	Madeleina Fransisco
Bruno Diggory	No alibi	Captain Shivermetimbers
Captain Padilla	No alibi	George/Georgina
Gustav the Great	No alibi	Barnacle Bill

OTHERS ON THE SCENE WHO ARE NOT SUSPECTS

There is no need for any non-suspects in this script. A staff member to organize attendees into teams will be necessary, however.

PROGRAM SCHEDULE

PART 1 (15 MINUTES): INFORMATION FOR CAPTAIN SHIVERMETIMBERS AND THE SUSPECTS

A non-cast staff member should greet participants at the door and assign them to a team starting 15 minutes before the program begins. This staff member should explain the Assistant Detective Worksheet to each team individually, since Captain Shivermetimbers may not explain it in as much detail as a normal chief inspector would. The information to pass on includes:

- Each suspect will wear a name tag.
- Only one team is allowed to ask questions of a suspect at a time.
- Assistant detectives should not necessarily believe any of the suspects right away when they are told something. The suspect may be lying. Verify statements with another suspect.
- Assistant detectives have a maximum of 45 minutes to solve the mystery, but the first team to identify both criminals wins. Captain Shivermetimbers will mark down the time that each team finishes.
- After a team has turned in its form, it may return to the meeting room.

You can begin this mystery theater program in a couple of ways. The cast can walk into the room and commence with Captain Shivermetimbers's comments, or you could open the curtain and then have the action begin as follows.

Captain Shivermetimbers: And so, mateys, to conclude our weekly poetry reading, I will recite one more poem:

> There once was a sailor from Spain,
> Who thought he could live without pain,
> He met up with us,
> He began to cuss,
> And was never seen from again.

(The rest of the cast will laugh somewhat forcedly.)

Captain Shivermetimbers: And now, as is our custom, we will all view the treasure in this chest. Gather round!

The captain reaches around his neck for the key, but suddenly realizes that it's not there. He makes a big fuss about the key being gone. Everyone denies knowledge of the location of the key. Captain Shivermetimbers then asks Barnacle Bill to crack open the chest. He bangs the lid with his head (assign someone to be in charge of a sound effect), and the chest pops open. Everyone oohs and aahs over the jewels and gold. Suddenly Mummy Shivermetimbers shouts, "Where is the treasure map? It's not here! Someone must have it!" Everyone denies having seen it. Captain Shivermetimbers starts telling everyone that there must be an investigation to find out who stole the treasure map—and who better to conduct it than the people in the audience? Barnacle Bill suggests that the captain might be just as guilty as any one of them, and that any investigation has to include him as a suspect. The captain reluctantly agrees to this suggestion. He tells the other suspects to wait for questioning in the other room. He explains the rules and details on the worksheets to the assistant detectives. At this point, the non-cast staff member will interject the information that there are two criminals and that the first team to correctly identify both criminals wins the prize.

Part II (45 minutes): Information for Captain Shivermetimbers and the Suspects

In another room, suspects will stand in their assigned places and answer questions from the assistant detectives. Suspects should be prepared to answer the following questions:

- "What were you doing before the poetry reading took place?"
- "Can anyone confirm your whereabouts?"

- "Is there any reason you would want to have possession of the treasure map?"
- "Do you think any of the other suspects had a reason to steal the treasure map? Why?"

When the assistant detectives have written down the names of the suspects they believe are guilty and have given the worksheets to Captain Shivermetimbers (who writes the finishing time and order of completion on each form), they may return to the original room and wait for the suspects to return.

Part III (15 minutes): Information for Captain Shivermetimbers and the Suspects

During the third portion of the program, the suspects will return to the original room for the final interrogation. Captain Shivermetimbers will ask questions of each suspect, one by one. Although there are suggested questions and answers, both the suspects and Captain Shivermetimbers should be prepared to ad-lib. In the end, shock of shocks, Captain Shivermetimbers will not come up with any definitive results.

Final Interrogation Questions

Captain Shivermetimbers: Carlos, admit once and for all that you are addicted to gambling!

Carlos: Well . . . yes, I *am* addicted to gambling. I've tried to quit, but I can't stop, even though you and your rules prohibiting gambling make it impossible to have any fun around here.

Captain Shivermetimbers: Did you take the map so that you could get off this ship and have the ability to gamble to your heart's content?

Carlos: Good idea, but, no, I didn't steal the map.

Captain Shivermetimbers: George, I've heard you've been finding life on board the ship a little boring lately.

George/Georgina: Yeah, I guess so.

Captain Shivermetimbers: Now isn't that just too bad. It's kind of ironic that you came on board for a life of excitement and aren't having any fun. It's even more ironic that you have broken my cardinal rule that no women are to be part of the crew. You've disguised yourself as a boy, haven't you?

Georgina: I . . . I . . .

Captain Shivermetimbers: Did you steal the map to make life more exciting aboard the ship?

Georgina: No. I may be guilty of pretending to be a boy, but I didn't steal the map. Are you going to make me leave the ship now?

Someone has stolen Captain Shivermetimbers' treasure map, and it is up to you to decide who should walk the plank! Sign up now to help solve this piratical Mystery. The winning team will be awarded prizes. Refreshments will be served.

Someone has stolen Captain Shivermetimbers' treasure map, and it is up to you to decide who should walk the plank! Sign up now to help solve this piratical Mystery. The winning team will be awarded prizes. Refreshments will be served.

Someone has stolen Captain Shivermetimbers' treasure map, and it is up to you to decide who should walk the plank! Sign up now to help solve this piratical Mystery. The winning team will be awarded prizes. Refreshments will be served.

Someone has stolen Captain Shivermetimbers' treasure map, and it is up to you to decide who should walk the plank! Sign up now to help solve this piratical Mystery. The winning team will be awarded prizes. Refreshments will be served.

Library Name, Address
Phone, Date, Time
Registration Information
Age Limitations

Library Name, Address
Phone, Date, Time
Registration Information
Age Limitations

Library Name, Address
Phone, Date, Time
Registration Information
Age Limitations

Library Name, Address
Phone, Date, Time
Registration Information
Age Limitations

Captain Shivermetimbers: We'll see.

Captain Shivermetimbers: Madeleina Fransisco, how are you finding your life aboard this ship? Not too boring, I hope?

Madeleina: It's not boring. It's actually better than I expected.

Captain Shivermetimbers: Thank you. That's all for now. You may sit down.

Captain Shivermetimbers: Barnacle Bill, tell us about your childhood.

Barnacle Bill: There's not much to tell. My family thought I was good for nothing, so I ran away.

Captain Shivermetimbers: Is there a part of you that would like to prove them wrong?

 **Captain Shivermetimbers**

 Carlos, Cook

 **George, Cabin Boy**

 Madeleina Fransisco

 Barnacle Bill

 **Mummy Shivermetimbers**

 Bruno Diggory

 Captain Padilla

 **Gustav the Great, Musician**

Barnacle Bill: Yes, I would like to return someday and show them that I am a success in life.

Captain Shivermetimbers: If you had treasure, it would be easy to prove you've made something of your life.

Barnacle Bill: Yes, but I believe in doing things honestly. Someday I'll return on my own merit. I didn't steal the treasure map.

Captain Shivermetimbers: Mummy dearest, let's cut to the chase. You want my job.

Mummy Shivermetimbers: You're a poor excuse for the captain of a pirate ship with your silly poetry readings. Sentimental bosh! You'd be better off letting me run the ship.

Captain Shivermetimbers: I must say I'm shocked, Mummy. Shocked and saddened by your attitude. Did you steal the map in order to bribe the crew to make you captain?

Mummy Shivermetimbers: That's a nice thought, but I didn't do it.

Captain Shivermetimbers: Bruno Diggory, what did you do before you came on board my ship?

Bruno Diggory: I was a slave.

Captain Shivermetimbers: Have you enjoyed working aboard my ship?

Bruno Diggory: Yes and no. No disrespect meant. I do my work, but I dream of going somewhere peaceful and quiet. It's hardly calm on board a pirate ship.

Captain Shivermetimbers: If you had a treasure, your dream of living on an island with your own hut would come true. (Bruno shrugs.)

Captain Shivermetimbers: Captain Padilla, did you take the map so you could get back into your superiors' good graces?

Captain Padilla: How do you think I got out of that hole you put me in—with the rats—to steal the map?

Captain Shivermetimbers: Answer the question.

Captain Padilla: It would have been impossible for me to steal the map.

Captain Shivermetimbers: Gustav, everyone knows that you don't play your instrument or do anything very well. Did you steal the map so that you could impress everyone with all of your wealth and riches?

Gustav the Great: Why are you yelling at me? Why is everyone so mean to me? Why can't anyone be nice for once?

Captain Shivermetimbers: Quit your whining. Did you steal the map?

Gustav the Great: No.

Captain Shivermetimbers: Well, it seems obvious that we'll never get to the bottom of this. We might as well call it a day and go on with our business. (To audience:) Thank you all for coming and trying to figure out all of this, but I guess we'll never know. (Captain Shivermetimbers turns to leave.)

Barnacle Bill: Now, wait just one minute. Someone here has to be the guilty party.

Bruno Diggory and Mummy Shivermetimbers (together): And I think I know who it is!

Mummy Shivermetimbers: I think it's Madeleina. She's the only one on board who knows how to read. Who else would be able to find the treasure with the map? (There is a lot of agreement among the crew.)

Bruno Diggory: I think it was the captain. He was the only one with the key. The treasure chest wasn't broken into last week when we saw the map, so it had to be him.

Mummy Shivermetimbers: Or maybe it was both of them!

Captain Shivermetimbers: This is ridiculous.

Barnacle Bill: Silly or not, tell us about your relationship with Madeleina Fransisco.

Captain Shivermetimbers: All right. I'll admit the truth but then you have to stop all this accusing going on. The secret we've been trying to hide is that she's my wife. We fell in love and were married. However, because of my no-women-on-board rule—Mummy doesn't count as a girl—we had to pretend that she was my captive. And that's all there is to it.

Madeleina Fransisco: That's right. We just wanted to be together.

Barnacle Bill: I think there is a little bit more. I think Madeleina wanted to leave pirate life behind and retire luxuriously. Unfortunately, you hardly had the ability to do that since you never saved any of your treasure. But, there was the treasure map with its untold treasure, wasn't there?

Captain Shivermetimbers: Now wait just a minute. I don't like what you are suggesting.

Barnacle Bill: I'm suggesting that with your key to the treasure chest and Madeleina's ability to read the map, you two planned to steal the treasure for yourselves.

Madeleina Fransisco: (angrily and incautiously) And what is so wrong with that? We have to be happy. After all that Shiverme has done for this crew, he deserves a little reward. (Madeleina will clap a hand over her mouth. The crew is in an uproar.)

Captain Shivermetimbers: Come on, Madeleina. To the dinghy!

He will grab her hand and they will try to run out of the room, but will be stopped by members of the crew. The key and treasure map will fall out of Captain Shivermetimbers's coat. Barnacle Bill will take the rope or chains off of Captain Padilla and tie up Captain Shivermetimbers and Madeleina. Barnacle Bill will thank everyone for coming, read the names of the winning team, and give out prizes. The entire cast will line up and bow in unison one time. The cast will leave the room or the curtain will close.

OPTIONAL CLUES AND PROPS
- A treasure map
- Large skeleton key
- Treasure chest filled with "gold" and "jewels" (foil-wrapped candy, chocolate money, and costume jewelry)
- Cat-o'-nine-tails
- Musical instrument for Gustav the Great
- Rope to tie up Captain Padilla

COSTUMES

Once again, look at books for ideas. Madeleina is the only female who needs to be in a dress. She could wear pretty shoes with an elegant and frilly gown, perhaps a make-over from a resale shop. Mummy Shivermetimbers could wear a frumpy dress and mobcap or dress like the rest of the pirates. The captain should be dressed in slightly

finer clothing than the rest of the crew. Below are some general ideas for pirates, but adapt costumes from whatever you have on hand or find at resale shops.

- **Shoes.** Black/brown leather shoe with slight heel. Make buckles from cardboard, cover with silver foil or paint silver or gold, tie on a wide floppy ribbon in a bow, and attach with book tape. Crew members could also go barefoot.
- **Stockings.** White nylons or tights.
- **Pants.** Cut bottoms off pants in a jagged fashion around shins. Finish with a fray-blocking substance from a fabric store.
- **Shirt.** Remove buttons from a regular, loose-fitting men's hip-length button-up shirt. Stitch front closed most of the way, but leave the collar open at the top. You could also attach grommets at the top and put a ribbon through.
- **Belt or sash.** Purchase at resale shop.
- **Headgear.** Purchase a tricornered hat and add feathers and flounce, or fold a bandanna in half, cover most of the forehead, and tie it in the back.
- **Accessories.** Pretend swords, daggers, or pistols; lace tucked in a pocket.

DECORATIONS

Make the stage area or meeting room look like a ship. Use fishnet, ropes, and an anchor for accents. Borrow or make a treasure chest and fill with costume jewelry and gold foil candy for the assistant detectives to help themselves to at the end of the program.

FOOD

A possible menu consists of stew, biscuits, and "ale" (ginger ale or apple cider). If you just wanted to serve snacks, you could serve crackers, cheese, and "ale."

GRAPHICS AND PUBLICITY

A reproducible recruitment form, a publicity poster, publicity bookmarks, Assistant Detective Worksheets, and name tags are included in this chapter.

TO-DO LIST

- Recruit suspects
- Assign places to stand or sit during Parts I–III

  - Parts I and III: Shivermetimbers will lead the conversation in Parts I and III. Other suspects will sit in a long row: Bruno Diggory, Carlos, Gustav the Great, Barnacle Bill, George/Georgina, Captain Padilla, Mummy Shivermetimbers, and Madeleina Fransisco.
  - Parts II: Suspects should form a large circle around the room as follows: Captain Shivermetimbers, Bruno Diggory, Carlos, Gustav the Great, Barnacle Bill, George/Georgina, Captain Padilla, Mummy Shivermetimbers, Madeleina Fransisco, and back to Captain Shivermetimbers.

- Purchase refreshments
- Purchase prizes
- Take pictures, if desired
- Write thank-you notes and/or buy small gifts

> **SHORT NEWS RELEASE**
>
> Someone has stolen Captain Shivermetimbers' treasure map! Whodunit? Everyone has a motive, from the cabin boy to the cook. Come to the _____ _____ Library on _____ and interrogate the suspects being held for questioning. It's up to you and your friends to solve the mystery and decide who should walk the plank. Form a team or we will assign you to one. Open to students in grades __ to __. Prizes will be awarded to the winning team. Spaces are limited, so sign up now! Call _____ for details.

BOOK TIE-INS

A set of swashbuckling adventure fiction novels would make a fabulous display. Add informational books on pirates.

PRODUCTION NOTES

This mystery theater script is more advanced in its production than most of the scripts in this book, and so I recommend that you not attempt this mystery until you have a confident cast that can handle the extra work entailed. The person who plays Captain Shivermetimbers will have to remember specific lines in Part I. In Part III, Bruno Diggory, Mummy Shivermetimbers, and Barnacle Bill will have to do a little bit of extra rehearsing to get the timing just right so the ending will be dramatic.

Assistant detectives will need to figure out that one criminal is able to read (so that they will understand the treasure map). This criminal will be Madeleina. The second criminal (Captain Shivermetimbers) is the owner of the key. The key and treasure map will fall out of the captain's pocket during the final interrogation.

10

The Fairground Fiasco

THE FAIRGROUND FIASCO

PLACE:

TIME:

DATE:

SUSPECTS:

Adam Smith, Farmer
Benjie Smith, teenager
Karina Smith, teenager
Suzie Kane, teenager
Julia Crenshaw

Antonia Anxious
Doctor Sarah Scalpel
Lucas Lemone, Postal Worker
Emily Easel, Art Teacher

NON~SUSPECTS:

Officer Sharyn Shadow
Helen Smith, Blueberry Pie Maker

SCRIPT COVER

- Name of Mystery: The Fairground Fiasco
- Date of Program: _____
- Time of Program: _____
- Location of Program: _____
- Names of Suspects

  Adam Smith, farmer, played by _____
  Benjie Smith, teenage son, played by _____
  Suzie Kane, teenage science whiz, played by _____
  Karina Smith, teenage daughter, played by _____
  Julia Crenshaw, professional pie contest entrant, played by _____
  Antonia Anxious, sister to Julia Crenshaw, played by _____
  Doctor Sarah Scalpel, general practitioner, played by _____
  Lucas Lemone, postal worker, played by _____
  Emily Easel, high school art teacher, played by _____

- Others on the Scene but Not Suspects, Including the Chief Inspector and the Victim

  Officer Sharyn Shadow, played by _____
  Helen Smith, blueberry pie maker, played by _____

PURPOSE

The purpose of this script is primarily to entertain.

SETTING

This mystery is set in your town during the annual summer fair.

CRIME

[Town name]'s annual fair is taking place this week. Every year townsfolk vie for the championship ribbon in animal, craft, baking, and cooking competitions. There has traditionally been a fierce competition in the blueberry pie category between several contenders, including Helen Smith. The pie contest was scheduled for 2:00 p.m. Unfortunately, Helen's famous blueberry pie completely disappeared at 1:30 p.m.

TIMELINE

Dreamy Emily Easel arrived at the fairground around noon. By 1:15 p.m., Emily had seen enough, and she was ready to leave. It was then that she spotted Helen Smith's beautiful blueberry pie. Transfixed, she observed it for a time in wonder. Eventually she realized she had to have the pie to paint in her studio. No one noticed her take the pie and put it in her car. At about 1:30 p.m., Emily was about to drive away when she heard a big commotion in the baked goods tent. Out of curiosity, she returned to the scene of the crime. All of the other suspects heard the hubbub as well and gathered near the crime scene. At that point, Officer Sharyn Shadow gathered all of the suspects together for the investigation.

SUSPECT BIOGRAPHIES

> A finger in every pie.
>
> *Miguel de Cervantes*

NAME: ADAM SMITH, FARMER

Description of Character: Adam is Helen Smith's husband. He is a hardworking farmer who always enters the fair's contests with his livestock, but he doesn't enjoy the same success as Helen. His favorite pig received a second place ribbon and he is feeling rather blue about the whole affair.

Motivation: A little jealous of Helen's success every year, Adam may have removed her pie so that she wouldn't get yet another first place finish and make him look bad in comparison.

Alibi: In the barn area, Adam was telling his daughter, Karina, about how he wished, just for once, he could have won first place.

Discredit Julia Crenshaw: Julia probably did it. She has always been envious of Helen's success in the blueberry pie contest. Adam doesn't know why Julia is getting upset. After all, she wins all of the other pie contests. Let Helen have her success.

NAME: BENJIE SMITH, TEENAGE SON OF ADAM AND HELEN SMITH

Description of Character: Adam and Helen's teenage son, Benjie, has an insatiable appetite. A growing teenager, he is always hungry. His favorite food is blueberry pie.

Motivation: In their rush to get to the fair today, the Smith family did not have the opportunity to eat a meal. Benjie complained of being very hungry. He may have eaten the pie even though he knows how hard his mother worked to make it.

Alibi: Benjie was riding the Ferris wheel with his girlfriend, Suzie Kane, at 1:30 p.m. She was prattling on about the velocity of the Ferris wheel.

Discredit Lucas Lemone: Lucas thinks he has a right to Helen's pies every week after his mail delivery is done. This week Helen was too busy with her pie preparations for the fair to offer any pie to Lucas as was her custom, and Lucas got in a big snit. Maybe he stole the pie so he wouldn't miss out completely.

NAME: SUZIE KANE, TEENAGE SCIENCE WHIZ

Description of Character: Suzie is a teenage girl with a very curious and scientific mind. She loves to experiment and even has her own laboratory in her parents' basement. She knows her boyfriend, Benjie Smith, loves his mother's blueberry pie, and she would love to make it for him herself. This last week, Suzie took Helen's discarded pies and worked them up in her lab in an attempt to find out in a scientific manner the exact ingredients and process Helen uses to make her famous pies. Asking for the recipe would be the easy way out, and Suzie loves a good problem.

Motivation: Suzie wasn't quite finished observing and experimenting with Helen's pies, so it is possible that Suzie stole Helen's pie from the fairground to complete her experiment.

Alibi: Suzie was riding on the Ferris wheel with her boyfriend, Benjie Smith. He kept talking about how hungry he was since he had missed lunch.

Discredit Doctor Sarah Scalpel: Doctor Scalpel does not believe in eating sweets. She feels that people eat too much sugar in general, and it is her job as the town doctor to promote healthy eating habits. Perhaps she took the pie to drive home her lesson.

Name: Karina Smith, Teenage Daughter of Adam and Helen Smith

Description of Character: Karina is the teenage daughter of Adam and Helen Smith. Karina is very sensitive and takes things to heart. Right now she is worried about fruits and vegetables that are picked before their prime and do not have the chance to "die a natural death." She feels that she must be a strong voice to get the message across that fruits and vegetables should not continue to be murdered. Each time someone eats a blueberry that did not fall off the branch of its own volition, a crime is being committed.

Motivation: Karina may have stolen her mother's pie to make a statement to protest the murder of innocent fruits.

Alibi: Karina was in the barn area with her father, Adam Smith, discussing the need to stop the murder of fruits and other innocent organisms.

Discredit Antonia Anxious: Antonia is trying to get everyone in town to sign a petition to stop the baking contests. She is trying to look out for her sister, Julia Crenshaw, who always gets extremely angry when Helen Smith's blueberry pie wins out over her own. Karina signed the petition because it might help stop the murder of blueberries. Antonia may have stolen the pie so that Julia's feelings wouldn't be hurt when Helen's pie inevitably won again.

Name: Julia Crenshaw, Professional Pie Contest Entrant

Description of Character: Julia Crenshaw is a sophisticated widow who has won all of the berry pie competitions at the fair every summer—with the exception of the blueberry pie competition. This has enraged her to no end.

Motivation: Wanting to be completely undefeated in all of the berry pie competitions, Julia may have gotten rid of Helen's blueberry pie to remove her competition.

Alibi: Julia and her sister, Antonia Anxious, were eating a late lunch several tents away from the baked goods tent area.

Discredit Adam Smith: Adam acts supportive of his wife's success, but you know he must be feeling hurt and disappointed each year when she gets the first place ribbon and he goes home with second or third. Maybe he has finally gotten sick and tired of playing second fiddle.

THE FAIRGROUND FIASCO

NEEDED!

A team of library staff members and high school teens to help with a Mystery Theatre program for teens. Helen Smith's blueberry pie has been stolen from the fairground! Whodunit? We are now looking for volunteers to play the following roles:

SUSPECTS:

Adam Smith, Farmer

Benjie Smith, teenager

Karina Smith, teenager

Suzie Kane, teenage science whiz

Julia Crenshaw

Antonia Anxious

Sarah Scalpel, Doctor

Lucas Lemone, Postal Worker

Emily Easel, High School Art Teacher

NON~SUSPECTS:

Officer Sharyn Shadow

Helen Smith, Blueberry Pie Maker

Be a part of the fun! If you sign up, you are responsible for your own costume and props, but I will provide assistance as necessary.

Rehearsal Date:

Performance Date: Time: Place:

Please return form to _____ by _____.

Name: _____

___ Yes, I would love to help.

___ My first choice of character is _____.

    My second choice is _____.

___ I need help with my costume!

___ I will help only if you are absolutely desperate.

THE FAIRGROUND FIASCO

Someone has stolen Helen Smith's blueberry pie from the fairground! Whodunit? Sign up now to help solve this tasty mystery.

The winning team will be awarded prizes. Refreshments will be served.

LIBRARY NAME
ADDRESS, PHONE
DATE, TIME
REGISTRATION
INFORMATION
AGE LIMITATIONS

NAME: ANTONIA ANXIOUS, SISTER TO JULIA CRENSHAW

Description of Character: Antonia is very anxious about how all of the people in her town become caught up in the fair contests every year. Feelings get hurt and people become upset. In the blueberry pie category, particularly, someone inevitably walks away with a broken heart after the ribbons are handed out (namely, her sister Julia). Antonia has started a petition to end the competitions once and for all, but so far, no one has seemed too interested except that nut, Karina Smith.

Motivation: In order to prevent her sister from being hurt again when she loses the grand championship ribbon to Helen Smith, Antonia may have gotten rid of Helen's blueberry pie.

Alibi: Antonia and Julia Crenshaw were eating a late lunch several tents away from the baked goods tent area.

Discredit Karina Smith: Karina is a bizarre sort of teenager. She is obsessed with preserving fruits and veggies. She will go on for hours about the "murder" of innocent fruits and vegetables if you let her. She probably stole the pie as a form of protest.

NAME: DOCTOR SARAH SCALPEL, GENERAL PRACTITIONER

Description of Character: As the town doctor, she is very concerned about the health of her patients. All of this pie eating is unhealthy and needs to stop.

Motivation: Doctor Scalpel may have taken Helen's pie to teach a lesson to the community about the evils of pie eating.

Alibi: Doctor Scalpel and Lucas Lemone were taking a brisk walk around the perimeter of the fairgrounds. She was counseling him that he should discontinue eating sweets and should have a more balanced diet. He needs to stop eating pie at the Smith home all the time.

Discredit Emily Easel: Emily is one of Doctor Scalpel's patients. She knows Emily to be a bit of a dreamer. Emily is fascinated by perfection in everyday objects. During one visit, Emily sat and observed a tongue depressor in Doctor Scalpel's office for at least 10 minutes, and then she asked if she could take it home to paint it in all of its glory. Something similar could conceivably have happened with Helen Smith's pie.

NAME: LUCAS LEMONE, POSTAL WORKER

Description of Character: Lucas Lemone is the town postal worker. After he delivers the mail, Lucas Lemone stops by Helen Smith's for a piece of blueberry pie. This week, in her flurry of preparations to make the perfect blueberry pie yet again, Helen told Lucas Lemone that he would have to come back another time.

Motivation: Angry and sour at being denied his customary blueberry pie this last week, Lucas Lemone may have stolen Helen's pie at the fair.

Alibi: Lucas was taking a brisk walk around the fairgrounds with Doctor Sarah Scalpel. It certainly wasn't his idea. He would rather have been milling around the baked goods tent, but she took it into her head to give him a lecture on the evils of sugar at that particular time.

Discredit Benjie Smith: Benjie loves to eat. Lucas is lucky on most days after his rounds if there is any pie left for him to eat, since Benjie usually eats it all. He heard Benjie complaining earlier today that he hadn't had any lunch. Lucas wouldn't be surprised if Benjie ate the missing pie himself.

Name: Emily Easel, High School Art Teacher

Description of Character: Emily is a dreamer and an art teacher who was casually walking around at the fair. She had no particular interest in the blueberry pie contest.

Motivation: When Emily saw Helen's pie, she was amazed at how beautiful it was as an art form. Without even quite realizing it, Emily found herself taking the pie home to study in all of its simplistic perfection.

Alibi: Emily has no alibi. She will state that she was walking around the fairgrounds.

Discredit Suzie Kane: Suzie is a student at the high school where Emily teaches. Suzie is very scientifically minded. This last week, Suzie was telling Emily about how she has been analyzing the makeup of Helen Smith's pies to be able to replicate them to perfection for her boyfriend (Benjie Smith), but was so far having difficulty identifying all of the ingredients. Maybe Suzie took the pie to try to replicate it once again.

Summary

Name	Alibi	Discredit
Adam Smith	Karina Smith	Julia Crenshaw
Benjie Smith	Suzie Kane	Lucas Lemone
Suzie Kane	Benjie Smith	Doctor Sarah Scalpel
Karina Smith	Adam Smith	Antonia Anxious
Julia Crenshaw	Antonia Anxious	Adam Smith
Antonia Anxious	Julia Crenshaw	Karina Smith
Doctor Sarah Scalpel	Lucas Lemone	Emily Easel
Lucas Lemone	Doctor Sarah Scalpel	Benjie Smith
Emily Easel	No alibi	Suzie Kane

Others on the Scene Who Are Not Suspects, Including the Chief Inspector and the Victim

Name: Officer Sharyn Shadow

Description of Character: The local law enforcement officer on duty, Officer Shadow is determined to get to the bottom of the mystery and find the pie thief.

Name: Helen Smith, Blueberry Pie Maker

Description of Character: Helen is famous all over the farm community for her delicious blueberry pies. She practices all year long in anticipation of the moment when the judge tastes her pie, and inevitably chooses her pie as the winner of the grand prize.

FAIRGROUND FIASCO

Assistant Detective Worksheet

SUSPECTS: Adam Smith, Benjie Smith, Karina Smith, Suzie Kane, Julia Crenshaw, Antonia Anxious, Doctor Sarah Scalpel, Lucas Lemone, Emily Easel

NON~SUSPECTS: Officer Sharyn Shadow, Helen Smith

ASK THE SUSPECTS:

Where were you at 1:30 p.m. today when Helen Smith's pie was stolen?
Can anyone confirm your whereabouts?
What were you talking about?
Did you have any reason to want to steal the pie?
Do you think any of the other Suspects had a reason to steal the pie? Why?

GUIDELINES:

- Each Suspect will wear a nametag.
- Only one team is allowed to ask questions of a Suspect at a time.
- Assistant Detectives should not necessarily believe any of the Suspects right away when they are told something. The Suspect may be lying. Verify statements with another Suspect.
- Assistant Detectives have a maximum of 45 minutes to solve the mystery but the first team to turn in the correct answer wins. Officer Shadow will mark down the time that each team finishes.
- After a team has turned in the form to Officer Shadow, it may return to the meeting room.

FAIRGROUND FIASCO

Who Did It?

Each team fills out this sheet as they solve the mystery.

Team Name: _____

Finishing Time: _____

Criminal: _____

Motive (Why they did it): _____

_____

_____

_____

The team that turns in this form with the correct answer in the fastest time wins the prize!

PROGRAM SCHEDULE

PART I (15 MINUTES): INFORMATION FOR OFFICER SHADOW AND THE SUSPECTS

Fifteen minutes before the program begins, all cast members except Officer Shadow are in their places. Officer Shadow will wait for the participants at the room entrance and assign them to a team.

Officer Shadow will introduce the suspects, hand out a worksheet to each team, and explain how it is to be filled out. Officer Shadow will also enlighten assistant detectives as to their role throughout the investigation.

Officer Shadow will talk about the crime that has occurred: "Our annual fair is taking place this week. Unfortunately, Helen's famous blueberry pie disappeared at 1:30 p.m. Assistant detectives need to solve the mystery and right the wrong!"

Officer Shadow will then tell the suspects to leave the scene of the crime and to wait for questions in the main room. The officer will then explain the rules to the assistant detectives:

- Each suspect will wear a name tag.
- Only one team is allowed to ask questions of a suspect at a time.
- Assistant detectives should not necessarily believe any of the suspects right away when they are told something. The suspect may be lying. Verify statements with another suspect.
- Assistant detectives have a maximum of 45 minutes to solve the mystery, but the first team to turn in the correct answer wins. Officer Shadow will mark down the time that each team finishes.
- After a team has turned in the form to Officer Shadow, it may return to the meeting room.

PART II (45 MINUTES): INFORMATION FOR OFFICER SHADOW AND THE SUSPECTS

In another room, suspects will stand in their assigned places and answer questions from the assistant detectives. Suspects should be prepared to answer the following questions:

- "Where were you at 1:30 p.m. today when Helen Smith's pie was stolen?"
- "Can anyone confirm your whereabouts?"
- "What were you talking about?"
- "Did you have any reason to want to steal the pie?"
- "Do you think any of the other suspects had a reason to steal the pie? Why?"

When assistant detectives have written down the name of the suspect they believe is guilty and have given their worksheet to Officer Shadow (who writes the finishing time and order of completion on each form), they may return to the original room and wait for the suspects to return.

THE FAIRGROUND FIASCO

Someone has stolen Helen Smith's blueberry pie from the fairground! Whodunit? Sign up now to help solve this tasty mystery. Prizes will be awarded to the winning team! Refreshments served.

LIBRARY NAME
ADDRESS, PHONE
DATE, TIME
REGISTRATION
INFORMATION
AGE LIMITATIONS

THE FAIRGROUND FIASCO

Someone has stolen Helen Smith's blueberry pie from the fairground! Whodunit? Sign up now to help solve this tasty mystery. Prizes will be awarded to the winning team! Refreshments served.

LIBRARY NAME
ADDRESS, PHONE
DATE, TIME
REGISTRATION
INFORMATION
AGE LIMITATIONS

THE FAIRGROUND FIASCO

Someone has stolen Helen Smith's blueberry pie from the fairground! Whodunit? Sign up now to help solve this tasty mystery. Prizes will be awarded to the winning team! Refreshments served.

LIBRARY NAME
ADDRESS, PHONE
DATE, TIME
REGISTRATION
INFORMATION
AGE LIMITATIONS

THE FAIRGROUND FIASCO

Someone has stolen Helen Smith's blueberry pie from the fairground! Whodunit? Sign up now to help solve this tasty mystery. Prizes will be awarded to the winning team! Refreshments served.

LIBRARY NAME
ADDRESS, PHONE
DATE, TIME
REGISTRATION
INFORMATION
AGE LIMITATIONS

PART III (15 minutes): Information for Officer Shadow and the Suspects

During the third portion of the program, the suspects will return to the original room for the final interrogation. Officer Shadow will ask questions of each suspect, one by one. Although there are suggested questions and answers, both the suspects and Officer Shadow should be prepared to ad-lib. When Emily Easel is questioned, a dramatic finish is in order.

Final Interrogation Questions

Officer Shadow: Benjie Smith, did you have breakfast this morning?

Benjie Smith: No, my mom was too busy with her pie to fix it.

Officer Shadow: Did you eat lunch?

 Adam Smith

 Benjie Smith

 Karina Smith

 Suzie Kane

 Julia Crenshaw

 Antonia Anxious

 Dr. Sarah Scalpel

 Lucas Lemone

 Emily Easel

 Officer Sharyn Shadow

 Helen Smith

Benjie Smith: No. We didn't have time to get anything in the rush to get here for the pie contest. I'm starving.

Officer Shadow: In your hunger, did you eat your mother's pie?

Benjie Smith: Are you kidding? She'd kill me if I touched her prize pie.

Officer Shadow: Suzie Kane, what is your favorite subject at school?

Suzie Kane: Science, definitely! I love to figure out how things work.

Officer Shadow: I hear you've been trying to determine the exact chemical makeup of Helen Smith's pie and the exact ingredients of the pie without using the recipe.

Suzie Kane: Yes, I want to make Mrs. Smith's pie for my boyfriend, Benjie.

Officer Shadow: Wouldn't it be easier just to ask for the recipe?

Suzie Kane: I suppose so, but it wouldn't be nearly as much fun.

Officer Shadow: Suzie, did you steal Helen Smith's pie in order to analyze it?

Suzie Kane: Of course not. In fact, I believe I've already figured out her secret!

Officer Shadow: Julia Crenshaw, you enter all of the pie contests, and you win first place all the time.

Julia Crenshaw: I win all of the pie contests—except for the blueberry pie contest. Someday I will win.

Officer Shadow: Perhaps you thought you would win this year by removing Helen Smith's pie?

Julia Crenshaw: Don't be ridiculous. I want to win fair and square. Really, what is all the fuss about over a mere *blueberry* pie?

Officer Shadow: Antonia Anxious, everyone knows about your petition to stop the annual competitions at the fair. What, exactly, is your point?

Antonia Anxious: Why, I just know that every year the losers feel hurt and—

Julia Crenshaw: I am not a loser!

Antonia Anxious: Of course not. I just mean that sometimes people take these things too seriously and get very upset for no good reason.

Officer Shadow: Did you take the pie to protest the contest and save your sister from getting hurt?

Antonia Anxious: No, no. I had nothing to do with it. I would feel bad for Helen if she lost because of me.

Officer Shadow: Karina Smith, I understand that you believe that blueberries have feelings.

Karina Smith: That is true. Someone has to stand up for innocent fruit. It's time that we stopped the assassination of these poor fruits for these competitions once and for all.

Officer Shadow: Did you try to stop the blueberry pie contest by stealing your mother's pie?

Karina Smith: No. I am confident that the right will prevail eventually.

Officer Shadow: Doctor Scalpel, as the town doctor, how far do you go to improve your patients' health?

Doctor Scalpel: It is very important to get everyone to understand that they need to watch what they eat. I'm afraid that all of this pie eating will just lead to bigger problems.

Officer Shadow: Is that why you took Helen Smith's pie?

Doctor Scalpel: I did no such thing. As a doctor, I can only advise.

Officer Shadow: Lucas Lemone, what is your usual habit after delivering the mail each week?

Lucas Lemone: I usually stop by the Smith home where Helen gives me a piece of pie.

Officer Shadow: And was this the case on your last delivery day?

Lucas Lemone: I'm afraid Helen was just too busy making her blueberry pie to let me in and give me some pie.

Officer Shadow: In revenge for not getting your pie, did you steal Helen Smith's pie?

Lucas Lemone: I deny everything.

Officer Shadow: Adam Smith, how did your pig fare this year?

Adam Smith: My Bessie received a second place ribbon . . . as usual.

Officer Shadow: How does it make you feel that you never win first place in your category and your wife achieves first place every year?

Adam Smith: I do feel sad at times. Nevertheless, I am very proud and supportive of my dear wife in whatever she does, no matter how bad it makes me feel.

Officer Shadow: So you didn't take your wife's pie so that she wouldn't make you look bad in comparison?

Adam Smith: No. I love my wife dearly and would never do anything to hurt her. I know how much this contest means to her.

Officer Shadow: Emily Easel, you teach at the local high school, correct?

Emily Easel: Yes, I teach art.

Officer Shadow: I've heard that you love to paint.

Emily Easel: Yes, I adore finding new subjects to analyze and paint.

Officer Shadow: Emily, earlier today when you were walking around the fair, did you stop by the baking tent?

Emily Easel: Yes, I think I did.

Officer Shadow: Do you remember stopping by the pie booth, oh, about a half hour ago?

Emily Easel: Oh, yes. Now I remember! I was so enraptured by this vision of a pastry concoction—I think it was a blueberry pie . . .

Officer Shadow: Could it be Helen Smith's missing blueberry pie?

Emily Easel: You mean that I wasn't supposed to take the pie? (Everyone reacts with shock.) I thought—I mean, I—

Officer Shadow: Emily—those pies were being judged for the blueberry pie contest.

Emily Easel: I'm so sorry if I caused any inconvenience. I just thought it was the perfect specimen. I haven't come across such artistry in some time. The pie is in my car. I'll just go and get it. (Emily goes out and returns with the pie, much to the delight of everyone except Julia Crenshaw.)

After Emily Easel has been revealed as the true criminal, Officer Shadow will announce the winning team. While he is giving out prizes, the rest of the cast will stand in a row (or two rows), wait for Officer Shadow to join them, and then bow in unison one time. The cast leaves the room or the curtain closes.

OPTIONAL CLUE
- Blueberry pie

COSTUMES
Doctor Sarah Scalpel should wear a white doctor's coat over her clothes. She could walk around with a stethoscope or other medical paraphernalia. Emily Easel should

dress in an artsy manner, perhaps with a long skirt and flowing blouse or a romantic-looking dress. Lucas Lemone needs a postal uniform or reasonable facsimile of one. Adam Smith should dress in overalls or jeans, work shirt, and cap. Julia Crenshaw should be a little more glamorous than her peers. Everyone else should put themselves in the place of their character in a small town setting when deciding what to wear.

DECORATIONS

Picture a country fair with a big tent, bright colors, and a sense of festivity all around. You could set up a table with different pies and put first, second, and third prize ribbons on some of the winning pies. Create an obvious space for Helen's missing pie. Put a sign above the table that says, "Blueberry Pie Judging, 2:00 p.m." If funds permit, purchase a couple of straw bales.

FOOD

In addition to the pies mentioned above, you could serve some of the following: hot dogs, cotton candy, popcorn, Italian ice, candy apples, and soft drinks.

GRAPHICS AND PUBLICITY

A reproducible recruitment form, a publicity poster, publicity bookmarks, Assistant Detective Worksheets, and name tags are included in this chapter.

TO-DO LIST

- Recruit suspects, chief inspector, and other non-suspects
- Assign places to stand or sit during Parts I–III

  ○ Parts I and III: Suspects should sit in a row as follows: Adam Smith, Julia Crenshaw, Benjie Smith, Lucas Lemone, Emily Easel, Suzie Kane, Doctor Sarah Scalpel, Karina Smith, and Antonia Anxious.
  ○ Part II: Suspects should form a large circle, starting with Adam Smith, Julia Crenshaw, Benjie Smith, Lucas Lemone, Emily Easel, Suzie Kane, Doctor Sarah Scalpel, Karina Smith, Antonia Anxious, and back to Adam Smith.

- Purchase refreshments
- Purchase prizes
- Take pictures, if desired
- Write thank-you notes and/or buy small gifts

> **SHORT NEWS RELEASE**
>
> Someone has stolen Helen Smith's famous blueberry pie from the fairground! Whodunit? Everyone has a motive, from Helen's husband to the postman! Come to the _____ Library on _____ and interrogate the suspects being held for questioning. It's up to you and your friends to find the criminal and solve the mystery. Form a team or we will assign you to one. Open to students in grades __ to __. Prizes will be awarded to the winning team. Spaces are limited, so sign up now! Call _____ for details.

BOOK TIE-INS

Set up a "The Suspects Recommend . . ." display table. Create a bookmark that states, "This book was recommended by _____" [fill in appropriate suspect's name]. Subject areas that could be covered are agricultural and gardening topics (Adam

Smith), cookery (Julia Crenshaw), art (Emily Easel), and science experiments (Suzie Kane). It would also be appropriate to include a general mixture of mystery fiction.

PRODUCTION NOTES

Alter the time of the crime to occur one-half hour before your teens are scheduled to arrive. The blueberry pie judging would have begun at the time the program begins.

THE CASE OF THE MISSING BASEBALL

Location:

Date:

Time:

SUSPECTS:

Prunella Persnickety

Suzie Souffle

Homerun Hank

Nellie News

Big Al

Mortimer Mopp

Rae Lynn Ryder

Poppie Chase

NON-SUSPECTS:

Chief Inspector

Mickey Mantle

SCRIPT COVER

- Name of Mystery: The Case of the Missing Baseball
- Date of Program: _____
- Time of Program: _____
- Location of Program: _____
- Names of Suspects

  Prunella Persnickety, curator, played by _____
  Big Al, head coach of the Yankees, played by _____
  Suzie Soufflé, caterer, played by _____
  Mortimer Mopp, custodian, played by _____
  Homerun Hank, hotshot baseball player, played by _____
  Rae Lynn Ryder, Hank's girlfriend and aspiring country singer, played by

  _____

  Nellie News, reporter, played by _____
  Poppie Chase, groupie, played by _____

- Others on the Scene but Not Suspects, Including the Chief Inspector

  Chief inspector, played by _____
  Mickey Mantle, baseball player, played by _____

PURPOSE

I wrote this script for a friend for his 30th birthday party, since he was a big Mickey Mantle fan. You could adapt this script to use for any sport or player just by changing a few statements here and there. All you would have to do is choose another famous sports figure and event, and then tie in a stolen item. It would work well for either a school or public library program.

SETTING

This mystery takes place in the Hall of Fame Gallery at the Baseball Hall of Fame in Cooperstown, New York. The year is 1974.

CRIME

Mickey Mantle is being inducted into the Baseball Hall of Fame. Friends, fans, and foes have gathered for the spectacle. Unfortunately, partway into the evening, the baseball that Mickey Mantle had hit his first homerun with—valued at $1.2 million—is stolen!

TIMELINE

- In this mystery, suspects-to-be mingle with participants in the National Baseball Hall of Fame Gallery. Everyone is excited about the induction of Mickey Mantle into the Hall of Fame. Mickey Mantle's baseball, valued at $1.2 million, is displayed prominently at one end of the room.

- In a speech at the other end of the Hall of Fame Gallery, Big Al officially inducts Mickey Mantle into the Baseball Hall of Fame. While he is talking, Nellie News steals the baseball and stows it in a dusty cabinet. Poppie Chase has recorded the entire ceremony on her camcorder. She doesn't realize that purely by accident she has also taped Nellie News stealing the baseball. (In reality, you will have already recorded Nellie News stealing the ball for the "instant replay" at the end of the evening.)

SUSPECT BIOGRAPHIES

All suspects will state that they were watching the induction ceremony just like everyone else.

> Where secrecy or mystery begins, vice or roguery is not far off.
> *Samuel Johnson*

NAME: PRUNELLA PERSNICKETY, MUSEUM CURATOR

Description of Character: Prunella is sick and tired of keeping the museum in meticulous order. She has dreams of traveling around the world, but this is impossible with her low curator's salary.

Motivation: Prunella might have stolen the baseball so that she could have money to travel the world.

Discredit: Mortimer Mopp drives Prunella crazy. He always tries to find out her personal information (such as how much money she makes) and information about her job that she is not permitted to relinquish. Mortimer should mind his own business. He has also talked about how he wants to retire soon but he has said that he doesn't have enough money to do so. Perhaps he stole the baseball for that reason.

NAME: BIG AL, HEAD COACH OF THE YANKEES

Description of Character: Big Al is resentful that he had to give up the game after a knee injury. He dislikes dealing with baseball players like Mickey and Hank, who he feels cater only to their fans and act snooty. He can't believe that he is the one who has to officially induct Mickey Mantle into the Baseball Hall of Fame.

Motivation: He would love to start up a fresh new team in the minor leagues but lacks the cash.

Discredit: Rae Lynn Ryder is just one example of the problems with major league baseball. The girl is just interested in fame, money, and connections. There doesn't seem to be any heart in the sport anymore. Instead of contributing to the sport, Rae Lynn is merely a distraction to the players.

NAME: SUZIE SOUFFLÉ, CATERER FOR THE EVENING

Description of Character: Suzie dreams of opening her own restaurant someday. She has saved almost enough money to put a down payment on the fabulous downtown building that she wants, but she doesn't quite have the required amount.

Motivation: Time is of the essence. Another bidder is trying to get her dream building.

THE CASE OF THE MISSING BASEBALL

NEEDED!

A team of library staff members and high school teens to help with a Mystery Theatre program for teens. Mickey Mantle's baseball has been stolen! Whodunit? We are now looking for volunteers to play the following roles:

SUSPECTS: Prunella Persnickety, Big Al, Suzie Souffle, Mortimer Mopp, Homerun Hank, Rae Lynn Ryder, Nellie News, Poppie Chase

NON-SUSPECTS: Chief Inspector, Mickey Mantle

Be a part of the fun! If you sign up, you are responsible for your own costume and props, but I will provide assistance as necessary.

Rehearsal Date:

Performance Date: Time: Place:

Please return form to _____ by _____.

Name:_____

_____ Yes, I would love to help.

_____ My first choice of character is _____. My second choice is _____.

_____ I need help with my costume!

_____ I will help only if you are absolutely desperate.

Discredit: It seems that Prunella Persnickety—who has told Suzie of her dreams of world travel—would do anything for a change of scenery. She has seen Prunella's office—it's dingy and a horrible place to work, except for the tattered travel posters that Prunella has put up.

Name: Mortimer Mopp, Custodian

Description of Character: Mortimer had hoped to retire early but can't because he has never earned or saved much money. Mortimer is a big snoop who always has his nose in other people's business.

Motivation: Mortimer can't retire because he doesn't have enough money put aside.

Discredit: Well-known for his snoopy behavior, Mortimer knows a lot of dirt about the baseball world. Merely by chance, Mortimer found a letter that fell out of Homerun Hank's pocket. The letter was from Hank's creditors demanding that they be paid.

THE CASE OF THE MISSING BASEBALL

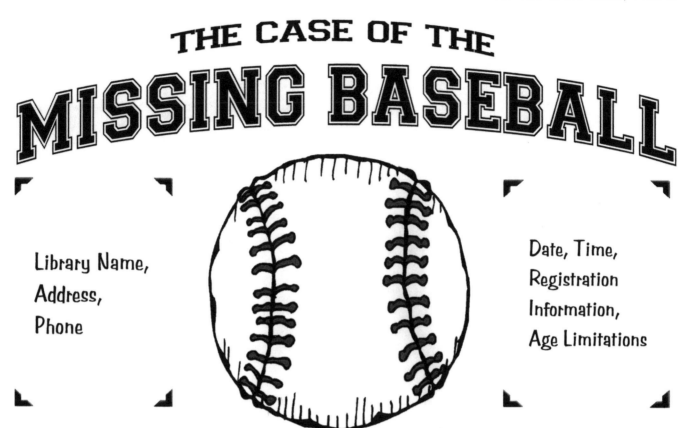

Library Name,
Address,
Phone

Date, Time,
Registration
Information,
Age Limitations

MICKEY MANTLE'S BASEBALL HAS BEEN STOLEN! SOLVE THE MYSTERY AND WIN THE PRIZE!

NAME: HOMERUN HANK, HOTSHOT BASEBALL PLAYER AND MICKEY'S BEST FRIEND

Description of Character: Hank enjoys baseball, but right now he has other things on his mind. He invested all of his money in a freezer company in Alaska that went under. Having a reputation to uphold, he doesn't want anyone to find out about his financial problems. He knows he will have to do something about paying his creditors soon. He had kept his secret until Mortimer Mopp found out.

Motivation: If Homerun Hank doesn't pay his creditors soon, his reputation will be ruined.

Discredit: Big Al is useless as a coach. His heart obviously isn't in the game. He has often said that he would prefer to give up on the Yankees and start a minor league team. Unfortunately for everyone, Big Al doesn't have enough money to fund the idea.

NAME: RAE LYNN RYDER, HANK'S GIRLFRIEND

Description of Character: Hailing from Nashville, Tennessee, Rae Lynn absolutely adores country music. She just knows that she could make it big in the country music industry if she had either money or connections. She likes Hank mainly for the influence she hopes he will have on her career. He's not really her type.

Motivation: Rae Lynn could buy her way into the country music industry if she had the money a signed Mickey Mantle baseball would provide.

Discredit: Poppie Chase is an incredibly annoying groupie who follows the team around. She gets in everyone's way. She probably stole the ball just to have something else with Mickey Mantle's signature on it.

Name: Nellie News, Reporter

Description of Character: Community stories have been really dry lately. Nellie desperately needs something spectacular to write about. Her job is on the line, and her boss has given her one last chance to bring in the goods before she is canned.

Motivation: Thinking that the evening is going along pretty slowly and that her job is lost for sure, Nellie News steals Mickey Mantle's baseball, believing that a good story will be the result.

Discredit: While hanging out in the kitchen earlier, Nellie found out that Suzie is in desperate need of quick cash to make a down payment on the restaurant of her dreams.

Name: Poppie Chase, Groupie

Description of Character: As Mickey Mantle's biggest fan, Poppie collects everything she can about Mickey Mantle and follows the team around as they tour.

Motivation: Mickey is Poppie's all-time favorite player. It would be wonderful just to touch Mickey's baseball.

Discredit: Poppie keeps an eye on everything that might affect "her" Mickey—good or bad. Something tells her that Nellie News is bad news, but Poppie doesn't exactly know why. Nellie was acting awfully jumpy earlier. Poppie just happened to look at Nellie's notebook and saw a note from Nellie's boss saying, "This is your last chance. Get some good dirt or you're out of a job!"

Summary:

Name	Discredit
Prunella Persnickety	Mortimer Mopp
Big Al	Rae Lynn Ryder
Suzie Soufflé	Prunella Persnickety
Mortimer Mopp	Homerun Hank
Homerun Hank	Big Al
Rae Lynn Ryder	Poppie Chase
Nellie News	Suzie Soufflé
Poppie Chase	Nellie News

THE CASE OF THE MISSING BASEBALL

Assistant Detective Worksheet

SUSPECTS:

Prunella Persnickety

Big Al

Suzie Souffle

Mortimer Mopp

Homerun Hank

Rae Lynn Ryder

Nellie News

Poppie Chase

NON-SUSPECTS:

Chief Inspector

Mickey Mantle

ASK THE SUSPECTS:

Where were you during the induction ceremony?

Can anyone confirm your whereabouts?

Would you benefit in any way by stealing the baseball?

Do you think any of the other Suspects had a reason to steal the baseball? Why?

GUIDELINES:

- Each Suspect will wear a nametag.
- Only one team is allowed to ask questions of a Suspect at a time.
- Assistant Detectives should not necessarily believe any of the Suspects right away when they are told something. The Suspect may be lying. Verify statements with another Suspect.
- Assistant Detectives have a maximum of 45 minutes to solve the mystery but the first team to turn in the correct answer wins. The Chief Inspector will mark down the time that each team finishes.

THE CASE OF THE MISSING BASEBALL

Who Did It?

Each team fills out this sheet as they solve the mystery.

Team Name: _____

Finishing Time: _____

Criminal: _____

Motive (Why they did it): _____

_____

_____

_____

The team that turns in this form with the correct answer in the fastest time wins the prize!

OTHERS ON THE SCENE WHO ARE NOT SUSPECTS, INCLUDING THE CHIEF INSPECTOR AND THE VICTIM

NAME: CHIEF INSPECTOR

Description of Character: Businesslike and to the point, the chief inspector lives only for his or her work and to get to the crux of every mystery.

NAME: MICKEY MANTLE

Description of Character: This character is the famous baseball player, who is being inducted into the Baseball Hall of Fame.

PROGRAM SCHEDULE

PART I (15 MINUTES): INFORMATION FOR THE CHIEF INSPECTOR AND THE SUSPECTS

Fifteen minutes before the program begins, all cast members except the chief inspector are in their places. The chief inspector will wait for the participants at the room entrance and assign them to a team.

After everyone realizes that a crime has occurred, the chief inspector will step forward and state that a crime has been committed. "Mickey Mantle's first homerun baseball, valued at $1.2 million, was stolen here tonight. The baseball was last seen on this shelf one-half hour ago [adapt to your time frame], right before the induction ceremony for Mr. Mantle."

At this point, the chief inspector will introduce the suspects, hand out a worksheet to each team, and explain how it is to be filled out. He or she will tell the suspects to leave the scene of the crime and to wait for questions in the main room. The chief inspector will also enlighten assistant detectives as to their role throughout the investigation. He or she will then explain the rules to the detectives:

- Each suspect will wear a name tag.
- Only one team is allowed to ask questions of a suspect at a time.
- Assistant detectives should not necessarily believe any of the suspects right away when they are told something. The suspect may be lying. Verify statements with another suspect.
- Assistant detectives have a maximum of 45 minutes to solve the mystery, but the first team to turn in the correct answer wins. The chief inspector will mark down the time that each team finishes.
- After a team has turned in the form to the chief inspector, it may return to the meeting room.

Part II (45 minutes): Information for the Chief Inspector and the Suspects

In another room, suspects will stand in their assigned places and answer questions from the assistant detectives. Suspects should be prepared to answer the following questions:

- "Where were you during the induction ceremony?"
- "Can anyone confirm your whereabouts?"
- "Would you benefit in any way by stealing the baseball?"
- "Do you think any of the other suspects had a reason to steal the baseball? Why?"

When assistant detectives have written down the name of the suspect they believe is guilty and have given their worksheets to the chief inspector (who writes the finishing time and order of completion on each form), they may return to the original room and wait for the suspects to return.

Part III (15 minutes): Information for the Chief Inspector and the Suspects

During the third portion of the program, the suspects will return to the original room for the final interrogation. The chief inspector will ask questions of each suspect, one by one. Although there are suggested questions and answers, both the suspects and the chief inspector should be prepared to ad-lib. When the criminal is questioned (usually last), a dramatic finish is in order.

Final Interrogation Questions

Chief Inspector: Prunella, do you like your job?

Prunella Persnickety: Not really. I need a change. I'd love to travel around the world.

Chief Inspector: So why don't you?

Prunella Persnickety: (laughs) Do you have any idea how poorly curators are paid?

Chief Inspector: So you would obviously benefit from selling Mickey's baseball.

Prunella Persnickety: Yes. But I am not a thief.

Chief Inspector: What are your future career plans, Mortimer?

Mortimer Mopp: Well, I work here at the museum. May be thinkin' of retiring soon.

Chief Inspector: Is that really possible, considering the meager savings you have accumulated?

Mortimer Mopp: Probably not.

Chief Inspector: Imagine how you could retire on $1.2 million. (Mortimer just makes a face.)

Chief Inspector: Since we're talking about work, Nellie, tell me how your boss feels about your work.

Nellie News: She's not too happy right now. She said I have to get a good story soon, or I'll be fired.

Chief Inspector: It looks as if you'll have plenty of interesting things to write about today.

Nellie News: Yes, I think she'll be happy for once.

Chief Inspector: I hear that you would love to open up your own restaurant some day, Suzie.

Suzie Soufflé: Yes, that is my dream.

Chief Inspector: I have also learned that the perfect restaurant you want to purchase requires a down payment that you do not have.

Suzie Soufflé: Yes.

Chief Inspector: Perhaps you are now cooking up a different scheme to obtain the needed cash?

Suzie Soufflé: Absolutely not! I was brought up to earn my money honestly.

Chief Inspector: What are your feelings about major league baseball today, Big Al?

Big Al: Players are overpaid, spoiled, and don't appreciate their fans.

Chief Inspector: It seems strange that with your attitude toward the sport, you choose to work as the head coach for the Yankees.

Big Al: A man has to work. I don't have too many other options financially. I would love to start a team in the minor leagues, but that is impossible right now.

Chief Inspector: Because you don't have the money.

Big Al: Correct.

Chief Inspector: Perhaps you stole Mickey's ball so you'd have some ready cash?

Big Al: I'd never do that. It would go against my code of ethics.

Chief Inspector: Homerun Hank, you've made some interesting investments. Tell us about the Alaskan Freezer Company you invested all of your money in.

THE CASE OF THE MISSING BASEBALL

Mickey Mantle's baseball has been stolen! Whodunit? Everyone has a motive, from the head coach to the fans. Sign up to solve this puzzling mystery. Prizes will be given to the winning team. Refreshments will be served.

LIBRARY NAME
ADDRESS, PHONE
DATE, TIME
REGISTRATION
INFORMATION
AGE LIMITATIONS

THE CASE OF THE MISSING BASEBALL

Mickey Mantle's baseball has been stolen! Whodunit? Everyone has a motive, from the head coach to the fans. Sign up to solve this puzzling mystery. Prizes will be given to the winning team. Refreshments will be served.

LIBRARY NAME
ADDRESS, PHONE
DATE, TIME
REGISTRATION
INFORMATION
AGE LIMITATIONS

THE CASE OF THE MISSING BASEBALL

Mickey Mantle's baseball has been stolen! Whodunit? Everyone has a motive, from the head coach to the fans. Sign up to solve this puzzling mystery. Prizes will be given to the winning team. Refreshments will be served.

LIBRARY NAME
ADDRESS, PHONE
DATE, TIME
REGISTRATION
INFORMATION
AGE LIMITATIONS

THE CASE OF THE MISSING BASEBALL

Mickey Mantle's baseball has been stolen! Whodunit? Everyone has a motive, from the head coach to the fans. Sign up to solve this puzzling mystery. Prizes will be given to the winning team. Refreshments will be served.

LIBRARY NAME
ADDRESS, PHONE
DATE, TIME
REGISTRATION
INFORMATION
AGE LIMITATIONS

Homerun Hank: Well, sad to say, the company just froze up and I've lost all of my money.

Chief Inspector: How do you plan to maintain your current lifestyle?

Homerun Hank: Just hit a few more homeruns, I guess.

Chief Inspector: You didn't steal Mickey Mantle's baseball to pay off your debt?

Homerun Hank: No sir.

Chief Inspector: Rae Lynn Ryder, you're hoping to make it big in the country music industry, are you not?

Rae Lynn Ryder: Yes, I am! Fame and fortune, here I come!

Chief Inspector: That is your goal in life?

Rae Lynn Ryder: Yes, I want to be happy with all of the money I make.

Chief Inspector: Are you starting early . . . by stealing the Mantle baseball?

Rae Lynn Ryder: Of course not—tempting though an easy $1.2 million would be!

Chief Inspector: Poppie Chase, we all know you are Mickey's biggest fan. Did you steal his baseball so that you would have something else with his signature on it?

Poppie Chase: No! (truly shocked) That baseball belongs in this museum. I would never desecrate its value by taking it from its rightful home. I try to memorialize everything about Mickey, not destroy it. That's why I taped the induction ceremony earlier today. Someday my documentaries will be put in this museum as well.

Chief Inspector: You say you taped the induction ceremony?

Poppie Chase: Yes, it's right here. (She pulls the tape out of her bag.)

Chief Inspector: Perhaps we should watch the tape. We might gain some interesting clues about the true criminal. (The chief inspector puts in the tape and everyone watches as Nellie News sneaks away from the group during the ceremony, takes the baseball, and stows it away on a dusty shelf.)

Chief Inspector: Ladies and gentlemen! Our criminal is Nellie News! I hope you're happy, Nellie. You'll get your story now. Except now you will be on the cover of your newspaper . . . as the criminal.

The chief inspector takes Nellie News away and comes back into the room. He or she then announces the winning team. While prizes are given out, the rest of the cast will stand in a row (or two rows), wait for the chief inspector to join them, and then bow in unison one time. The cast leaves the room, or the curtain closes.

OPTIONAL CLUES AND PROPS
- A notebook for Nellie News with a note handwritten on a sheet of paper: "This is your last chance. Get some good dirt or you're out of a job!"
- A letter from a creditor addressed to Homerun Hank, telling him to pay up or else
- A videotaped scenario of the theft, to be played during Part III (have the cast meet earlier than usual to create this scenario)
- A bag or a backpack for Poppie Chase
- A few travel guides to exotic places for Prunella to carry around

COSTUMES
Baseball players need to obtain uniforms. Prunella should dress somewhat dowdily. Mortimer should dress as a janitor, perhaps in jeans and a grungy T-shirt. Suzie will wear a chef's hat and apron. Rae Lynn Ryder would look glamorous in an evening gown. Poppie should look like an older teen wearing lots of baseball paraphernalia.

DECORATIONS
Since the program is set in a museum, go for a serious look. Keep in mind, however, that it is set in a baseball museum, so you might use bats, mitts, and pennants for some of your decorations even though it's not a perfect replica of the real room. Look online at the real Baseball Hall of Fame website for ideas (www.baseballhalloffame.org).

FOOD
Serve snacks and soft drinks. You might go with a baseball park lineup of food: hot dogs, popcorn, and so on.

GRAPHICS AND PUBLICITY

A reproducible recruitment form, a publicity poster, publicity bookmarks, Assistant Detective Worksheets, and name tags are included in this chapter.

TO-DO LIST

- Recruit suspects, chief inspector, and other non-suspects
- Assign places to stand or sit during Parts I–III

  - Parts I and III: Seat suspects in a long row, left to right: Prunella Persnickety, Mortimer Mopp, Nellie News, Suzie Soufflé, Big Al, Homerun Hank, Rae Lynn Ryder, Poppie Chase. Mickey Mantle can be seated at the side of the room.
  - Part II: Arrange suspects in this order in a large circle: Prunella Persnickety, Mortimer Mopp, Homerun Hank, Big Al, Rae Lynn Ryder, Poppie Chase, Nellie News, Suzie Soufflé, and back to Prunella Persnickety.

- Purchase refreshments
- Purchase prizes
- Take pictures, if desired
- Write thank-you notes and/or buy small gifts

SHORT NEWS RELEASE

Mickey Mantle's baseball has been stolen! Whodunit? Everyone has a motive, from the head coach to the fans. Come to the _____ Library on _____ and interrogate the suspects being held for questioning. It's up to you and your friends to find the criminal and solve the mystery. Form a team or we will assign you to one. Open to students in grades __ to __. Prizes will be awarded to the winning team. Spaces are limited, so sign up now! Call _____ for details.

Chapter II

BOOK TIE-INS

Pull out just baseball or a variety of sports books—both fiction and nonfiction. Create a display with the colors of the team of the player you are honoring. Hang a jersey above the display to focus attention on the display.

PRODUCTION NOTES

Although real people are named, this mystery script is purely fictitious in its entirety. Record the entire cast viewing Mickey's ceremony. In the background, Nellie News must be seen stealing the baseball.

12

Who Will Survive Teen Mystery Night?
Heather Blicher

The Virginia Beach
Public Library

presents

*Teen Mystery Night 20__
Who Will Survive?*

July 26, 20__
7 PM

The *Who Will Survive Teen Mystery Night?* mystery theater program was written by Heather Blicher. This is a wonderful program with a lot of drama and excitement and includes a research element that some librarians may wish to incorporate in their school library media center or public library.

The creaking voices of rainforest frogs resonate throughout the dark as you enter the Virginia Beach Central Library's Teen Mystery Night. A murder has taken place and the suspects have gathered to account for their movements over the past twenty-four hours. Isolated in an unidentified location of South America, the suspects have been competing in a *Survivor*-like competition to win an exorbitant amount of prize money. There are many possible motives for the killing, but who would commit murder, how, and why? Who will survive Teen Mystery Night?

It is July 26th and the library is abuzz with the activity of last-minute preparations for the event that has been planned and organized for months. As we watch from the Information desk, cardboard palm trees, potted ferns, and tiki masks roll past on carts headed toward the auditorium. The script is finally finished, the characters have been cast, and now we are allowed to feel the relief that an opening night brings. No, this is not a Broadway production, but it is one of Central Library's most popular annual events, the pre-registration for the program totaling fifty participants aged thirteen to eighteen.

Just before 7:00 p.m., the young adults arrive and eagerly clutch the clue packets each received upon signing in and rifle through them frantically. Staff members advise, "Pay attention to the surroundings. Everything is a clue." And indeed everything *is* a clue, right down to the sound effects and the injuries of certain suspects.

Within the packets, teens find character profiles providing in-depth peeks into each suspect's background and personality quirks, the medical examiner's report details how the victim died, but the item that causes the most excitement is the brightly colored bandanna tucked inside. Divided into groups of five, each participant is assigned to a team named after an existing South American tribe. Each of the ten tribes is set apart by their bandannas.

As the mystery night begins, the house lights dim and the host steps forward to address the audience. Bandanna-covered heads lean forward expectantly. "You have been asked here tonight to serve as witness and judge to the proceedings that will begin shortly. Goldie is dead!" Screams of disbelief and outrage erupt from the suspects. "Suspects? Who is she calling a suspect?" Everyone has a reason to hate Goldie, but who would kill her? Could it be Muriel, an anthropology professor whose field experience as a doctoral student led to her expertise in making poisonous blow darts? Could it be Sookie, a former librarian who is desperate to win the prize money to salvage her bankrupt book-printing business? Or Myra, an underpaid pharmacologist with a specialty in frog toxins? Or could it be Jay, a software operator whose fetish for exotic amphibian pets is just plain creepy?

The suspects are lined up to defend themselves and to tell who *they* think killed Goldie. Every suspect's version of the truth is questionable, and so the tribes are given time to mingle with the suspected murderers to pry the details out into the

The Cast:

Survivor Host: *Mary Lovell Swetnam*

Jay Grints *Beth Carlton*

Myra O'Brien *Sarah Bell*

Muriel Demon *Tanya Harris*

Sookie Smith *Alice Peach*

Goldie Jones *Patricia Cook*

Coroner *Diane Buckley*

Producers *Sean O'Connell, Karen McFatridge*

Cameraperson *Susan Paddock*

Sheriff's Deputies *Jill Duarte, Valerie Whaley*

Original Script By:

Heather Blicher

Schedule of Events

6:45 PM - 7:00 PM   Registration

7:05 PM   Welcome and Introductions

7:10-7:20 The Mystery Unfolds

7:20 The Search for Clues

8:00 The Murderer is Revealed

8:15 Special Guest **Rudy Boesch** *of*

Survivor Presents Door Prizes

8:30 Refreshments and Fun!

open. Following the interrogations, the tribes are led into the library by tribal leaders (staff members who have been well informed of the clues and their relationship to the crime). Each clue-station is designated for one clue, whether it is found on a print, non-print, or electronic resource, including microfiche, reference sources, *EBSCO-host*, *InfoTrac*, and *SIRS Discoverer*, among others. The tribal leaders are ready to focus the teens' attention toward specific questions and facts (which have been organized ahead of time) that a source reveals. Ultimately, the question becomes: which tribe can out-research the others?

Once the research is completed, everyone gathers again in the auditorium rainforest. The tribe members cluster in corners where clips of heated discussion can be heard. One by one, a spokesperson from each tribe stands to offer their solution to the who, the how, and the why. Every tribe is a winner with their introduction (and for some the re-introduction) to the library's resources!

As police carted off the murderer, both teens and staff were rewarded by a visit of Virginia Beach's own survivor, Rudy Boesch. Rudy, a participant in the first season of CBS's famed reality program *Survivor: Pulau Tiga* (2000), arrived to award door prizes, sign countless autographs, and regale the crowd with recollections from his experiences on the island. The night approached an end as the crowd moved across the hall for refreshments, music, and a raucous round of limbo.

SUSPECT PROFILES

NAME: JAY GRINTS

Occupation: Software Operator

  Hometown: Creepy, New Mexico

  Luxury Item: Pet frog "Sparky"

  Quote: "No one touches Sparky."

If Jay Wins: He will create a full-functioning, indoor ecosystem to house his amphibian friends and to showcase this unique set-up by charging admission to visitors.

  Description of Character: Jay has an odd personality. He prides himself on his collection of amphibians, both the rare and the common. He cares for them lovingly and shows a great possessiveness toward them. In fact, as his one luxury item, Jay chose to bring—not a toothbrush, not a camera and film—but his pet frog "Sparky," which he keeps confined in a jar-shaped plastic container hanging from his neck (the better to protect him). Sparky is hardly ever away from his human, always calmly residing in his miniature habitat (and since Sparky is an uncommonly small breed of frog—*phyllobates terribilis* [½ to 2 inches only]—he doesn't mind it much). On the rare occasion that Sparky and Jay are separated, it is only because it is Jay's turn to cook the tribe's dinner. Hanging near the flames of the campfire is a bit too stressful for Sparky.

NAME: MYRA O'BRIEN

Occupation: Pharmacologist

  Hometown: Lion, California

  Luxury Item: First-aid kit

  Quote: "Anyone can be a victim of heart disease."

If Myra Wins: She will buy a cottage by the sea in Ireland where she will never have to work with amphibians again and she will spend the rest of her life happily serving drinks in a pub, married to a stable-boy named Ian.

  Description of Character: Myra is an unappreciated, underpaid researcher of pharmacology [the science dealing with the preparation, uses, and especially the effects of drugs] in a highly respected institute that specializes in heart issues. For the past couple of years, Myra has been part of a team that has focused solely on creating new drugs for cardiac patients using the toxins of specific frog skins—*phyllobates terribilis.* She is well spoken, polite, and liked by the other survivors. She is a straight-to-the-point, no-nonsense individual who plays the *Survivor* game well, making alliances, breaking alliances, and still appearing to be a genuinely good person. She is there to win and win she shall.

NAME: MURIEL DEMON

Occupation: Professor of Anthropology

Hometown: Sleepytime, Idaho

Luxury Item: Picture of her deceased husband

Quote: "You must protect what you love."

If Muriel Wins: She hasn't thought about the money; she is participating for the experience of it.

Description of Character: Muriel is a professor of anthropology at a small college in her hometown. She has an enormous amount of knowledge to share and is often the survivor entertaining the others around the campfire. She is very laid back and is surrounded by a sense of constant calm that rubs off on those around her. She enjoys gardening and growing her own vegetables. Her daily life is a calm one, undoubtedly making up for her overwhelming past. While earning her Ph.D., she studied and lived somewhere in South America. What was meant to be a one-year study turned into two, two turned into five, until almost ten years had passed. As an honorary member of the Choco Indian tribe, the culture she had planned to *only* study, Muriel lived her life from a completely different cultural perspective. This perspective included the traditional use of blow darts dipped in frog toxins—from *phyllobates terribilis*—to hunt for small game. Content and at peace, Muriel married and enjoyed her life in the rainforest. But as is the nature of our world, commerce and industry arrived to cut down what it could and in the process murdered her husband. Grief stricken, she immediately went home (to America), sold her journals of the past years as a manuscript in a lucrative publishing deal, and settled comfortably in the next phase of her life . . . or so it would seem.

NAME: SOOKIE SMITH

Occupation: Entrepreneur

Hometown: Lolly, Maine

Luxury Item: Her checkbook

Quote: "I've got to win or my company will go bankrupt."

If Sookie Wins: She will pay off her debts, loans, and completely avoid the embarrassing notion of having to beg her relatives for money.

Description of Character: Sookie is a former librarian who recently got her bookprinting company started. She is likable and humorous, not devious at all. She desperately wants to win the money so that she won't go bankrupt, but she is completely up front about it and doesn't play the usual *Survivor* games, no alliances here, folks. In her spare time she writes mystery fiction and hopes to be published one day.

NAME: GOLDIE JONES

Occupation: Field Supervisor for major gasoline conglomerate

Hometown: Gagging, Minnesota

Luxury Item: Razor

Quote: "I'd rather die than lose this one."

If Goldie Wins: She will move to some far-off country with very few taxes and spend frivolously until Steven Spielberg calls her to star in his next film.

Description of Character: Goldie is one of those people you should avoid, if only to preserve what little mental health you possess. She is mean, not even attempting to hide the viciousness in her voice. She preys on people's insecurities and enjoys the fact that she gets a whole lot more on-camera time than the other survivors (only because she is always stirring up trouble). An aspiring actress, Goldie is currently one of the top field supervisors of the largest gasoline supplier of the United States. She is in charge of finding the most suitable foreign locations, negotiating with the local citizens, and ultimately supervising the construction of pipelines. You don't have to have a real good reason to hate Goldie, although some of the survivors do.

SURVIVOR SCRIPT

OUT-THINK, OUT-RESEARCH, OUT-LAST

[Audience enters auditorium from the back stairs; frogs and tropical sounds clearly in background; all seated; stage lighting—dim, audience lighting—high]

CAMERAPERSON: *[camera on shoulder, wearing baseball cap; circulates the stage filming events taking place]*

HOST: *[steps forward; tired, grim-faced, serious, worn-out, dirty]*

[Frogs fade to soft background noise; audience lights dim, SPOTLIGHT on HOST]

You have been asked here tonight to serve as witness and judge to the proceedings that will begin shortly. It is your responsibility to listen *[pause]*, observe *[pause]*, and ultimately decide who among the remaining survivors has committed the crime. You must use your observations, your *[shake fist]* gut instincts, and the evidence that the producers of this show have discovered.

PRODUCERS: *[step forward from a corner in the background; arms crossed in front of chest, well dressed]*

[HOST and PRODUCERS step back as stage lights dim; SURVIVORS file in and take their seats]

HOST: *[to SURVIVORS]* You have been asked to this tribal council meeting to account for your movements of the last 24 hours. *[Matter-of-factly, flat tone, no emotion]* Goldie is dead.

SURVIVORS: *[all in unison (except SOOKIE who screams) as lights on stage turned up]* GASP! *[Followed by frantic discussion]*

HOST: *[loud, angry]* There will be no discussions among the suspects!

SURVIVORS: *[variations of, "Suspects!? Who is she calling a suspect!?"]*

HOST: *[LOUD]* SILENCE!

[SURVIVORS completely silent]

HOST: One of you is responsible for the murder. We have snapshots taken from the film footage that shows all of you, except for Sookie, had reason to dislike Goldie. This is your only chance to defend yourselves before formal charges are filed, to convince those present that you are innocent. . . . Be truthful, be frank, *[low, menacing tone]* it will be better for you in the end; however *[pause]* the choice *[pause for dramatic effect, tone more intense, expression on face flares]* is yours.

[SPOTLIGHT on voting booth, lights on stage dim]

[Turn to completely face direction of audience; looking off into space] You will approach the voting booth where the other survivors will not hear you. Describe the last 24 hours. Tell us who *you* think murdered Goldie and why.

[HOST steps back; JAY approaches voting booth; picture of Goldie taunting Jay—projected]

JAY: *[menacing; constantly clutching and handling Sparky's container; scrapes on face]*

["Well first of all, I hate these people"; goes on to say that he believes Muriel (the professor) killed Goldie. He has no reasonable reason to believe this, except that he especially hates this person because she tried to touch Sparky while he was distracted with cooking last night. He can't believe that after he has made it so clear that no one is to even go near Sparky that she would have the gall to attempt it.]

[Excited, flustered] She tried to touch Sparky! *[Still clutching jar, turns around to look at survivors, turns back to face audience, LOW, clear, mean voice]* Nobody touches Sparky.

[Pause to write down vote; holds up to audience; paper reads "Muriel"]

I vote for Muriel.

[JAY returns to seat; HOST steps forward]

HOST: This Sparky business is pretty suspicious. . . . I think you need to look into it further.

[HOST steps back; MYRA approaches voting booth; hand bandaged, tired, dirty, but still very crowd pleasing; picture of Goldie celebrating a win over Myra who is looking a bit mean and frustrated—projected]

MYRA: The last 24 hours, all I've been thinking about is taking a vacation from my life. First I get this nasty rash on my hand and then Goldie starts acting strange, saying she's having chest pains and can't breathe well and has to be taken to the hospital, what next? *[Talks about how she is so upset that Goldie died . . . how she had been hoping and praying that Goldie would pull through. Goldie was an opinionated and strong person; some of the other survivors had issues with Goldie because of that reason. She and Goldie were in an alliance from the beginning. . . . "We were like sisters . . . even though Goldie was always beating me in the challenges, she respected me." Believes that Jay killed Goldie because Goldie would constantly taunt him about his frog. He never took the taunting lightly, he would get really angry, scream, stomp off . . . he has a lot of anger issues.]*

[Pause to write vote down; holds up to audience; paper reads "Jay"]

I vote for Jay.

[MYRA returns to seat; HOST steps forward]

HOST: An alliance doesn't always mean you can trust someone; I think we need to research Myra's occupation a little more . . . and what's the deal with that rash?

[HOST steps back; MURIEL approaches voting booth; serenely calm; speech is understandable, but she drifts from topic to topic with no explanation; dirty, arm is broken in a sling; picture of Goldie surveying land and Muriel angry, clenching fists—projected]

MURIEL: Goldie was a pleasant person mostly; I didn't get to know her very well and after I found out she worked as a field supervisor for a gasoline company and basically is the one who decides where to construct pipelines—I didn't really want to get to know her *[talks about how yesterday, Jay got upset with her ("Which he had every right to be, by the way; he had made it very clear that he was protective of Sparky and I had no right to disrespect his wishes") when he found her holding Sparky's container with the lid off, etc. He broke her arm by slamming it into a palm tree, it hurts a lot, but the swelling has gone down significantly since last night. MURIEL is not fazed that her arm was just broken, still very calm. She doesn't like to name names with no evidence, but since she is required to make a choice, her choice is MYRA; the reason behind it—killed Goldie so that she could ensure that she won, because she really wanted the money.]*

[Pause to write down vote; holds up to audience; paper reads "Myra"]

I vote for Myra.

[MURIEL returns to seat; HOST steps forward]

HOST: By the way, this *[holding up the blow-dart tube]* was found among Muriel's belongings. What is its use, what the heck is it? I think you need to look into Muriel's past to figure this one out.

MEDICAL EXAMINER'S REPORT

Name of Deceased: Goldie Jones
Date of Death: 20 July 2002
Estimated Time of Death: 6:40 PM

Observations:

-Lower right calf - what appears to be a roughly made dart of some sort embedded 2 inches into flesh, 5 inches remaining protruded

- bruises, scrapes consistent with rugged camp life throughout body

Results:

Autopsy confirms that Ms. Jones suffered irregular and traumatic heart contractions which caused irreversible damage within a short time, ultimately causing her death

Blood tests confirm the presence of compounds known as pumiliotoxins A + B

Notes:

- Dart appears to have been carved from a local wood
- Tests confirm that the tip - which penetrated the skin - has residue which is amphibian-like, but unidentifiable at this time

Medical Examiner _Georgia Fishbahn_ 7/26/02
Laboratory Technician _Qiner Anwozi_ 7-26-02

[HOST *steps back;* SOOKIE *approaches voting booth with a sheepish,* "Just my luck, I can't believe this is happening to me" *kind of look, head covered in layers of bandages, blood seeping through one side.*]

SOOKIE: [*Believes that Muriel killed Goldie because she was always flaunting her experience living near here and how she knows* all *about plants—what is safe to eat, what is poisonous . . .* "I mean, who knows what she is capable of?" *If anyone could have found a way to kill Goldie, it would have been Muriel. ALSO, when we were out gathering wood for the fire, she accidentally whacked me in the head with a tree branch.* "What if I get a blood clot . . . I DON'T HAVE HEALTH INSURANCE!"]

[*Pause to write down vote; holds up to audience; paper reads* "Muriel"]

I vote for Muriel.

[SOOKIE *returns to seat;* HOST *steps forward*]

HOST: Would money be a good enough reason to kill for Sookie, or could there be something more?

[HOST *gives any final instructions she thinks are necessary; interrupted by* MEDICAL EXAMINER *running into room*]

MEDICAL EXAMINER: [*out-of-breath; to the host*] I finished the autopsy, I hope this will help!

[*As the audience leaves, the medical examiner's report is distributed at the exit; audience disperses to pursue clues*]

SURVIVAL TIPS
(Clues used by tribal leaders [staff members] to guide teens)

Tip #1
Is it possible that Sparky is poisonous?
  Check out May 1995 *National Geographic* article on microfiche for a clue.

Tip #2
What is significant about poison dart frogs that are bred in captivity? If a human simply holds a poison dart frog, how can its toxin penetrate the skin?
  Help in locating the answers to these questions can be found using the Google search engine. In the search engine, type "p. terribilis dart frog" and then look at the Poison Frogs site from allaboutfrogs.org.

Tip #3
How does the dart frog's poison cause death?

For the answer, go to *SIRS Discoverer* on the library's list of electronic resources. Search by using the keywords "poison dart frog" and read the first article on the list.

Tip #4

Sparky is a pet. Most pets can be touched. How did Jay get Sparky into that jar? Can Sparky be touched? Has Jay ever handled Sparky? With his bare hands? BETTER ASK JAY!

For more information on whether or not dart frogs can be touched, check the reference book *Encyclopedia of Reptiles and Amphibians*, call number _____. Look for Sparky in the index under his scientific name.

Tip #5

Find out more about the poison from poison dart frogs. The poison that this frog secretes is one of the most toxic poisons known. What chemicals are found in this poison?

Go to *InfoTrac's General Reference Center Gold* on the library's list of electronic resources. Do a subject guide search for "poison dart frogs" and "chemicals." Read the first two paragraphs of the article to find the name of the chemicals in the poison.

RETURN TO SCRIPT

[Later the same evening . . . upon return of the audience, all characters in their original positions with the addition of POLICE *in the opposite corner from* PRODUCERS]

HOST: *[steps forward; says that it is now time to reveal who you think killed Goldie]* We need the who, the how, and the why.

*[*HOST *asks each team's representative to stand up and give the team's findings]*

*[*POLICE *step forward and take* MURIEL *(who has covered her face with her hands and is very upset) and* MYRA *(silently angry) into custody]*

HOST: *[thanks audience for their services; directs the handing out of prizes, the introduction of* SPECIAL GUEST, *and directs audience and others to the refreshments—in whichever order is decided].*

NOTE

Who Will Survive Teen Mystery Night? reprinted with permission of Heather Blicher, Virginia Beach Central Library, 2002.

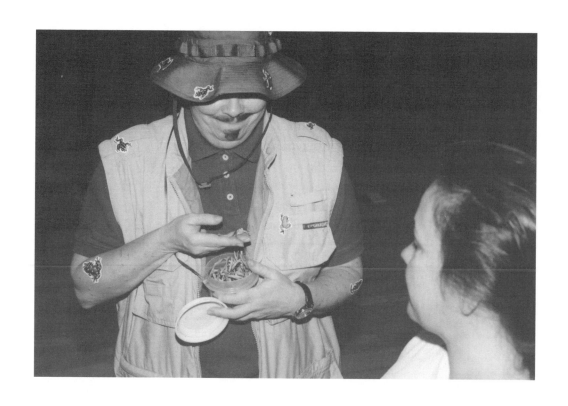

13 Mystery Theater Program Album

There are many, many other ideas out there for mystery theater programs that can be created using the basic formula provided in this book. The photographs in this segment show adult and teen actors in some popular culture mystery theater programs: *The Simpsons: Who Shot Sideshow Bob? Star Wars*, *Lord of the Rings*, and a Superhero mystery. As the photos illustrate, you can take an idea from whatever is popular with the teens in your community, and create a mystery theater program around it to use in your own library or school library media center.

APPENDIX: SCRIPTS, PARTY GAMES, AND KITS AVAILABLE FOR PURCHASE

Note: Please use these sources at your own discretion.

From www.amazon.com

These boxed kits are advertised as teen appropriate:

- Alphabet Mystery Jigsaw Puzzle Games
- Clue Suspects
- Gamewright Three of a Crime
- Harry Potter Mystery at Hogwarts Game
- How to Host a Murder: Roman Ruins
- How to Host a Murder: The Chicago Caper
- How to Host a Teen Mystery: Barbecue with the Vampire
- Mona Lisa Mysteries
- Murder Mystery Party Games: Panic at the Prom for Teens
- 30-Second Mysteries Board Game

Anyone's Guess Mystery Kits

Created by Janet Dickey, are available from Highsmith, Inc., www.highsmith.com (accessed August 18, 2009). These Mystery Program kits are designed to assist those serving teenagers in grades 6–9. Available kits include: Death Gets a Red Card, The Disappearance of Angela Day, Rock 'n' Roll Over Dead, and The Pharaoh's Curse.

Host a Murder Mystery Party

Available at mystery.host-party.com/default.asp. Included are customized murder mystery games. Most of the teen mysteries are for fewer than 20 guests, but there are some designed for a larger crowd.

Murder Mystery Games and Companies

www.darkshire.net/jhkim/rpg/murder/othergames.html#freeform (accessed August 18, 2009). Recommendations for commercially available murder mystery games. The companies included are:

- Bepuzzled Brand
- Decipher, Inc.
- Dinner and a Murder Mystery Games
- Freeform Games LLP
- Haley Productions
- Merrymurder.com
- Murder in a Box
- Murder on Us
- Murder Party Game.com
- Murder Mystery Games Limited
- MurderToMeasure
- My Dark Secret
- The Original Murder Company
- Pentalpha Game Corporation
- Playmurdermystery.com
- Tailor-Made Mysteries
- Youdunit Productions, Inc.

Mystery Games and Puzzles

www.mysterynet.com/mystery/games (accessed August 18, 2009). Information and descriptions of several mystery games are detailed on this site.

BIBLIOGRAPHY AND RESOURCE LIST

Alessio, Amy J., and Kimberly A. Patton. *A Year of Programs for Teens*. Chicago: American Library Association, 2006. This title includes information on how to put on a murder mystery, including all programming details.

Barack, Lauren. "Libraries Catch On to '39 Clues.'" *School Library Journal*, May 2009. Libraries attract students with the use of mystery programs.

Borchardt, Bob. "Cops Team Up with Teens to Figure Out 'Who Done It' in Cedaredge." *Delta County Independent*, July 2009. The Cedaredge Public Library in Colorado involved the police in a unique mystery program.

Charles, John, and Joanna Morrison. "Clueless? Adult Mysteries with Young Adult Appeal." *Voice of Youth Advocates*. This column is published each December in *Voice of Youth Advocates*.

Conklin, Tom, ed. *Mystery Plays: Eight Plays for the Classroom Based on Stories by Famous Writers*. New York: Scholastic Professional Books, 1997.

Dickey, Janet. "Mystery Planning Tips." www.dbldog.com/jdpage.htm (accessed August 18, 2009).

Edwards, Kirsten. *Teen Library Events: A Month-by-Month Guide*. Westport, Conn.: Greenwood Press, 2002. A complete mystery script is included in the November chapter of this book.

Goldsmith, Francisca. "Murder, We Wrote . . . and Played." *Voice of Youth Advocates* 20 (1998): 367–69.

Gray, Che-Mai. "Everyone Loves a Mystery: A Genre Study." www.readwritethink.org/lessons/lesson_view.asp?id=796 (accessed August 18, 2009). Students examine story elements and vocabulary associated with mystery stories, complete Internet activities designed to increase exposure to and appreciation of the mystery genre, write their own original mystery stories, and publish them online.

Greene, Grace W. *Solve the Mystery: Read! Program Guide*. Chicago: American Library Association, 1994.

Honnold, RoseMary. *101+ Teen Programs That Work*. New York: Neal-Schuman, 2003. This book shares ideas for all sorts of teen programs, including the author's creation called "Live Clue," based on the *Clue* board game.

Karle, Elizabeth M. *Hosting a Library Mystery: A Programming Guide*. Chicago: American Library Association, 2009. Five original mystery scripts are included.

Kellicker, Patricia. "Mission Possible: Read! Teens Produce Their Own Summer Reading Game." *Voice of Youth Advocates* 21 (1998): 16–18, 23.

Kids Love a Mystery. www.kidsloveamystery.com/ (accessed August 18, 2009). This site is geared to kids and the promotion of mysteries.

MysteryNet and Newfront Productions, Inc. "The Edgar Awards." www.mysterynet.com/edgars/ (accessed August 18, 2009). The Mystery Writers of America bestow the Edgar Allan Poe Awards in the mystery field each April.

Mystery Readers International. www.mysteryreaders.org/ (accessed August 18, 2009). This site is the world's largest fan/mystery organization. The Macavity Award is voted on by its members each year.

Mystery Writers of America. www.mysterywriters.org (accessed August 18, 2009). Mystery and crime writers will enjoy this site.

Ownes, Dodie. "Teen Advisory Board Responsible for Murder of a Homecoming Queen." *School Library Journal*, November 2008. Mystery program performed at the Albright Memorial Library in Scranton, Pennsylvania.

Purdy, Susan. *Costumes for You to Make*. Philadelphia: Lippincott, 1971. You will find great basic information in this book on how to make simple costumes from scratch.

Rogers, Barb. *Instant Period Costumes: How to Make Classic Costumes from Cast-Off Clothing*. Colorado Springs, Colo.: Meriwether, 2001. This is an excellent book to show you the techniques of altering resale clothing.

Shader, Robin. "The Butler Did It." *School Library Journal*, June 2002, 37. Information is provided about how to start a mystery book club.

Karen Siwak is the media specialist at Christa McAuliffe Elementary School in Tinley Park, Illinois. She obtained her master's degree in library and information science from Dominican University (River Forest, Illinois). Since then, she has worked as a librarian in both public libraries and schools. In addition to creating scripts for mystery programs, Karen has directed several plays with the Tinley Park Public Library's amateur teen theater group, including *The Wizard of Oz*, *The Princess Bride*, and *Robin Hood*.